Better Rags

A Police Officer's Story

By Lt. William L. Aumiller
Retired, Denver Police Department

BETTER RAGS

Copyright © 2012 by William L. Aumiller
Reprint 2018*

This is a true story. The dates and places are as accurate as I can remember, and no names have been changed to protect the innocent—it's been years since any of the people I've written about were innocent.

ISBN 978-0-9852982-3-4

Cover design by Abby Hoke: AEB Graphics, Denver, Colorado

Available through:
Amazon Books
betterrags.com
william.aumiller@comcast.net

From Pauper to Policeman —
From Rags to Better Rags

~ A Friend is Born ~

My special thanks to Dr. Gordon Farley, M.D., Psychiatry, Child Psychiatry, Denver, Colorado, for his honest, unbiased, and gracious review of my book.

"Since my partial retirement several years ago, I have read on the average of one or two books a week, and have decided that I will not spend my relatively brief remaining time on this earth reading anything that doesn't meet my high standard of inter-esting—even captivating writing early in the book. In other words, if I don't like it right away, I put it down and go on to something I do enjoy. Your book caught my interest immed-iately and held it throughout its entire length. I read it in about three days involving two late nights and found it highly pleasurable from beginning to end.

Your picture of farm life on the plains is authentic, touching, humorous and at the same time uplifting and optimistic. I also enjoyed your setting family events in your book in the context of current events of the time. Your organization guides the reader, is easy to follow and shows great attention to the read-er's sensibilities and comfort. Writers talk about "finding one's literary voice" and it seems to me that you have found yours on your first attempt.

There are too many fine features of your book to mention them all, but I will note that the photographs you included enriched the text immeasurably, and your attention to the detail of re-minding the reader exactly who the person you are writing about at any given point is, and how they are related to you and others, is very helpful to the reader and markedly in-creases the reader's comfort and pleasure. Your first-hand, behind the scenes, unvarnished view of the inner workings of a large city police department with its flaws and strengths gave me particular pleasure and is an important and authen-tic literary contribution. There is a genuineness to your writing that carries the reader along effortlessly and maintains the reader's interest from beginning to end. Your Forward and Table of Contents are both well thought out and instructive as a guide to readers. Your parents truly would have enjoyed your book and are honored by your writing. This book certainly deserves wide circulation and I hope that you pursue this and also future writing efforts."

A letter of praise from such a well-respected psychiatrist and distinguished published author confirmed (at least in my mind) that the countless hours I'd spent huddled over my keyboard weren't spent in vain. It was gratifying to learn my efforts to write a literarily competent and entertaining story had been so well received by a man of his esteemed academic and professional credentials . . . an equal review from Tom Brokaw couldn't have been more flattering!

Before Gordon read my book, he was an acquaintance at best; a friend of a friend I'd only see at occasional luncheons that were hosted by our good friends, retired Denver Police Sergeant Phil Gotlin, and his older brother, Dr. Ronald Gotlin, MD. But our relationship changed the very day he finished my book. He'd always been cordial and quite pleasant, and was quick to welcome me into his circle of friends, but to be honest, I've always been a little afraid of men who were trained to analyze my mind, and when I asked him to read and critique my work, I was more than a little apprehensive in baring my soul to the intimidating mind of a psychiatrist (with all of the crazy things I'd done in my life, a loony bin could have been my next new home). But when he stroked my needy little ego with his accolades and kind words of praise, he became one of my most appreciated friends. I think you can understand why.

CONTENTS

To Mom and Dad ~

I think you would have enjoyed this

FORWARD

Dad was my hero.

He was the product of the Greatest Generation, and in my mind, everything a real man was supposed to be. He'd grown up during the worst economic period of America's history . . . honorably served his country in Germany at the end of World War II, and spent nearly twenty-six years of his life as a Denver Fireman before retiring in 1973. He was a strong man . . . a tough man . . . a man I always looked up to.

As a child I was mesmerized by his stories of his poverty-stricken childhood on the farmlands of northwest Kansas; marveled over his stories of the lean early years of his marriage, and was thrilled even more by his exciting war stories from the fire department. Even as an adult, I still loved to sit at his table, sip from a hot cup of coffee and enjoy a smoke or two while I listened to his fabulous stories. And it didn't matter that I'd already heard most of them a hundred times before . . . *they never lost their appeal!* But when he died on Friday, May 14th, 1993, I suddenly realized I'd never hear them again, and knew if I didn't commit my favorite stories to writing, they'd be lost forever. So shortly after he died, I sat down with Mom at her kitchen table and we thumbed through her old pictures and talked about their past. I video recorded her as she described the who's, what's, and where's of each priceless image, and thought I'd someday either make a narrated Ken Burns video from these pictures or write a book about their fifty-four years together . . . someday. But I never seemed to have time to get started on this project, and the videotapes were relegated to a cardboard box in my basement for the next twelve years.

But that all changed in 2005 when I saw John Travolta on Leno's The Tonight Show. Responding to Jay's questions, he couldn't help but brag about his nearly completed autobiography, but quickly added that it wasn't just about his fame and fortune, but rather a record of his family's history that could be passed down from one generation to the next. He thought it was one of the most important things he'd ever done, and strongly suggested that someone in every family, famous or ordinary, should write their own family's story, even if it was never published. And I thought to myself, *"What a great idea! It's time to get busy."*

The next day, I dug out the archived videos and started taking notes. There was a wealth of information on these tapes, but because they lacked the kind of in-depth details and personal nuances I wanted for this book, I turned to Mom for help. Over the next several weeks, we'd sit and talk, and with pen in hand, I'd question her about our family's history. We talked about things that happened over a period of more than eighty years, and even though her memories were still quite vivid about most of the important events in her life, she had a little trouble remembering when certain others occurred. When this happened, she'd give me her best guess of the general dates, and in most cases, I was able to confirm them through personal documents or other family records.

My original intention in writing this book was to pass these great stories along to everyone who's ever known and loved my parents, and to briefly put into perspective just how our clan actually began. But as the book slowly progressed, I realized this was also my chance to tell my family and friends about the people who've impacted my life more than anyone else, and share some of the most cherished and exciting moments of my life as well. (I've always claimed my life was an open book, and this was my chance to prove it).

I took great care to be as honest and straightforward as I could (and probably revealed far more than I should have), but if I've offended anyone with what I've written (or failed to write), it's only a reflection of my inability to say what I really meant, and not a deliberate attempt to make them feel uncomfortable. This was an absolute labor of love for *everyone* who's ever been near and dear to me, and there was absolutely no malice or ill will in my heart toward any one of them . . . ex-wives included.

I spent weeks organizing my notes . . . thumbing through boxes of old pictures, funeral notices, personal receipts and letters, but to my deepest regret, Mom died before I'd finished even a simple draft of my story, and never saw a single page I'd written. I hated that I'd waited too long for her to see any of my work, but took solace in knowing how pleased she was that our family's story would be told.

By late October 2006, a full six months after her death, I finally sat down at my desk, wiped the dust from my computer, and began writing what I hoped would be a readable and hopefully enjoyable story about two of the greatest ordinary people on earth: my mom and dad . . . and of course, their three *wonderful* children.

Because this is probably the only book that will ever be written about my family, I wanted it to be as complete and accurate as it could possibly be, and to help in assuring this goal, I've only written about those events that could be confirmed through detailed conversations with Mom (and our shared memories of Dad's stories), from conversations with my Aunt Rainie and Aunt Annie (Dad's sisters) and Opal (Dad's Stepmother), from my cousin Merna (Oldson) Johnson (the unofficial historian of the Oldson family), from Uncle Bill Oldson (Mom's brother), from my sisters, June and Darlene, from old family records and Internet queries, and from my own personal memories and perspectives.

I've also included information about certain dramatic events in America's history that help give a feel for the troubled times during Mom and Dad's early years, and I've described in detail many of the places that were so important to me throughout my life. Many of these places are gone now, and while they may not be of interest to anyone outside of my immediate family, they were an essential part of our family history that can only be revisited through the narrative of this book. And that holds true for those boring who begat who details at the beginning of Chapters One and Two. These are details only my family will appreciate, so, please, skim through them if you need to. The story gets better . . . I promise.

In an effort to make this a more enjoyable read, I admit to taking a certain amount of creative license in retelling those wonderful stories from my parents' past, and perhaps even enhancing some of the stories with my attempt at humor. But the final story is a true and reasonably accurate representation of the chronology and events of our lives, with all the blemishes, goodness, love, excitement, laughter, and soul wrenching sadness.

Since this is my writing debut, I feel obligated to warn you this story may lack the finesse and structure a real author can offer, and may be rife with punctuation, grammar, and syntax errors (whatever a syntax is)—but please remember—I'm just an ordinary boy doing my best to record my family's history. My only experience with writing has been with the investigative reports and departmental procedures I'd written during my nearly thirty-six years with the Colorado Springs and Denver Police Departments, and while they certainly appreciated accuracy, sentence structure, and a modicum of legibility, they highly discouraged any form of creative writing. So let me apologize in advance if my writing has too many "Just the facts, Ma'am" police characteristics, and bear with me as I relate the details of our family's humble past.

I'm hopeful that despite my personal and literary flaws, my family will pass this book on from generation to generation . . . and the stories that would have almost certainly died with my ultimate passing will live on forever.

CHAPTER 1

"The Aumillers"

The name Aumiller, and its variants Aumüller, Aufmiller and Aufmüller, are relatively common names in Germany, and were probably derived from the occupations of our earliest family members. Loosely translated, this means we were named after one who owned a mill. That sounds good enough, but in reality, our ancestors were far more likely to have been simple farmers or farm laborers than actual mill owners; serfs in old-world Europe.

I've always known our name was rare here in Colorado, but never realized how few of us there were until I read a brief genealogy report Mom and Dad received in 1970. With a population of 203,302,031, there were only 775 Aumillers living throughout the entire country, which made our family a very rare breed in America, and, with few exceptions, still members of a very modest working class community.

●

The earliest Aumillers I'm aware of were my dad's paternal grandparents. They were a hardworking, humble, salt of the earth kind of people, who spent their entire lives tilling the fertile farmlands of northwest Kansas.

My Great-Grandfather Ulysses Grant Aumiller was born on March 2nd, 1864 and his future wife Cora Sophia Buell was born on September 29th, 1870. He died at the age of seventy-five on July 23rd, 1939, and she died at the age of ninety on July 30th, 1961; both in Selden, Kansas. They were married in the early 1890s and had the following nine children: Renie, Claude, Truman LaVate, Fern, Nola, Warren, Winslow, and twins Glenn and Oca. Truman LaVate Aumiller, who'd later become my Granddad Aumiller, was born on May 9th, 1897 in Phillipsburg, Kansas.

My Great-Grandparents on Dad's mother's side of the family were John Murray, who was born on May 18th, 1856 (and moved to the United States from Ireland when he was seventeen), and his future wife Maud Moore, who was born on May 17th, 1870. He died at the age of ninety-one on February 8th, 1948, and she died at the age of sixty-one on February 26th, 1932; both in Selden, Kansas.

They were married in the late 1890s and had three children: Annie Virginia, Ruth and Inza. Annie Virginia Murray, who'd later become my Grandma Annie (Dad's mother), was born on February 23rd, 1899 in Hoxie, Kansas.

•

In 1914, the horrendous war in Europe began following the June 28th assassination of Austrian Archduke Franz Ferdinand in Sarajevo by a Serbian rebel. In the next few weeks, Austria declared war on Serbia, Germany declared war on both Russia and France, and England declared war on Germany, setting in motion "The War To End All Wars." America chose to stay out of the conflict as long as possible, but on Friday, April 6th, 1917, President Woodrow Wilson declared war against Germany, and America entered the arena of a very costly and devastating world war.

As the deadly shadow of war spread across America, eligible young men from even the smallest of communities were drawn into the Armed Forces, and by early 1918, the Draft finally reached the tiny little farm town of Selden, Kansas. The timing couldn't have been worse for my Granddad "Vate" Aumiller, since he'd just married Sheridan Elementary School's prettiest young teacher; his nineteen-year-old sweetheart, Annie Virginia Murray, on Thursday, May 9th, 1918 . . . his twenty-first birthday. There was little time to celebrate their new union before he was whisked away to boot camp, and by November, he was on his way to Europe to fight the ferocious German army.

On the 11th hour of the 11th day of the 11th month of 1918, while Granddad was halfway across the Atlantic Ocean, Germany surrendered. After nearly four and a half years of war (with America's involvement during the last nineteen months), World War I was over, but at a cost of 16 million dead, including over 126,000 brave American soldiers.

None of the soldiers on his ship were told the war had ended, and when the ship made a wide turn and headed back to America, the change in direction went unnoticed by most everyone on board. When the ship finally approached New York's Upper Bay Harbor, a statue that bore a striking resemblance to the Statue of Liberty and a long row of majestic city skyscrapers were clearly visible along the horizon, and Granddad was shocked to see that "Europe" looked just like New York City!! *Did I mention Granddad was an innocent young farm boy from Kansas?*

After being honorably discharged from the army, he returned to his home in Selden. He'd survived the probable death sentence the war had to offer, but soon after his arrival, he became deathly ill . . . probably suffering from the effects of the Spanish Flu pandemic of 1918-1919. He and Grandma Annie went to Denver for treatment, where by the grace of God and the best medical care of the times, he was able to survive the worst pandemic in history, even surpassing the devastating Black Plague that consumed Europe during the late 1340s.

The catastrophic Spanish Flu was first observed in Fort Riley, Kansas on Monday, March 11th, 1918, and in just over eighteen months (according to some accounts), a staggering 50 to 100 million people worldwide died from this strain, including 800,000 Americans. Indeed, he was very lucky to be alive.

The newlyweds were now living on a small farm just five miles south of Selden, and stayed in a house directly across the road from Granddad's parents' home.

There were no conveniences on the farm . . . no electricity, radio, telephone, natural or propane gas, and no indoor plumbing. Kerosene lanterns and candles provided light in the evenings, and coal-burning stoves were used for heat and cooking. A rugged outhouse sat at the rear of the house, complete with a half-moon cutout on the door and a dog-eared Montgomery Ward catalog sitting next to the splintery old toilet seat.

A milk house sat near the main house and provided the only form of refrigeration for their food. A small rustic shack, it housed a milk separator, a large barrel for their salted pork, and a cooling barrel that was used to cool their milk and eggs. It drew cold water directly from the windmill, and the overflow drained into a large tank outside the shack, which was then used to water the livestock. There were no modern tractors or other types of motorized farming implements to help with their farming chores, and the fields were cultivated with horse drawn plows, just as they'd been done a hundred years before.

On Wednesday, February 12th, 1919, they were blessed with the birth of their first child, but after two very short days, the excitement turned to tragedy when their infant son Stanley Adrain suddenly and inexplicably died. It was a very difficult time for them, but over the next twelve months their wounds slowly healed as they prepared for the birth of their second son.

By 1920, America was well on its way toward a full recovery from the war and flu epidemic and was aggressively moving forward to a brighter and more rewarding future. This was a year of both enlightenment and censure in America, when women were finally given the right to vote, and (on Friday, January 16th), prohibition became the accepted, yet equally despised law of the land. In major cities across the nation, decadent late night speakeasies began to flourish as crowds were drawn to defiantly celebrate the night life in their own special way, and the lawlessness of organized crime soon gained momentum as the decade was just beginning to live up to its reputation as The Roaring Twenties.

4

But on Friday, February 13th, 1920, in the dimly lit farmhouse on the hushed plains of Middle America, the nightlife for twenty-two-year-old Truman LaVate and twenty-year-old Annie Virginia Aumiller was the 11pm birth of my dad, Kennedy Murray Aumiller. He was a very healthy baby, and judging from his early pictures, was very well fed!

Granddad continued to work the fields of his father's farm until after Aunt Lorraine Anna Laura (Rainie) was born on Saturday, April 16th, 1921, and by 1922 the family moved to a little house on the west end of Selden, on the north side of U. S. Highway 83 (where Granddad's brother Uncle Glenn and Aunt Margie would later live). They owned a restaurant for a short time, but because their business was so slow, they closed up shop and Granddad found work managing the town's pool hall. Over the next six years, they had four more children: Aunt Beulah Oleva, who was born on Wednesday, May 17th, 1922, Uncle LaVate Lyle on Monday, December 17th, 1923, Aunt Annavate on Monday, December 6th, 1926, and Aunt Ruth Marie on Thursday, April 19th, 1928.

●

The sleepy little farm town of Selden rests silently along U.S. Highway 83, about 75 miles east of Colorado and 40 miles south of Nebraska. It was founded in 1888, and in its heyday, was inhabited by about 400 residents, many of whom worked for the newly completed railroad. The city limits ran seven blocks long from west to east; four blocks long from north to south on the west end of town, and seven blocks long north to south on the east end of town. What's now U.S. Highway 83 was the town's northern boundary, and ran diagonally upward from the west end of town to its east city limit.

In the 1920s, Selden was still home to about 400 people and was filled with rustic wood framed and brick homes, and a business district of one and two-story stone, brick, and wood framed buildings. Indoor plumbing hadn't reached this rural community yet, and every home and most of the businesses had their own outhouses modestly stationed on the backside of their property. Water was drawn from outdoor wells, and even though some of the people may have had hand pumps inside their homes, this was not a luxury enjoyed by any of the Aumillers.

During the summer months, the fields surrounding Selden were alive and vibrant with lush crops of wheat and corn, and the town itself blossomed into a grid of colorful shrubs and broad-leafed trees. But by early winter the colors would quickly fade. As summer trees were reduced to mere skeletons of gnarled and naked branches, the bleakness of the town's time weathered homes and withered yards was unceremoniously revealed.

There were no paved roads in Selden and the broad dirt streets they had were designed to accommodate horse drawn wagons and carriages. The production of the popular and affordable Model T Ford between 1908 and 1927 meant more sophisticated paved roadways were needed in the more congested areas of America, but in the early 1920s, very few motorized vehicles were driving through the mud and snow on the streets of Selden.

Today, the town is a picturesque community of modest homes, with a smattering of much older and somewhat neglected homes mingled in with the new. The business district runs south on Kansas Avenue from U.S. Highway 83, and those ancient buildings that survived the devastating hailstorm on Wednesday, June 3rd, 1959, still stand alongside most of its newer businesses. It's home to Karl's Cash Store, the Southwind Steakhouse & Saloon, The Bank, a Post Office, the Selden Lumber Company, Koerperich Bookbinders, the Midway Bar & Grill, and the three-unit Midway Motel. It also has a small community funded fitness center in the back of the library that was once the town's old "Mayberry" style jail. There are two churches in town; the Sacred Heart Catholic Church and the United Methodist Church, and I can only imagine that they're filled to capacity on Sunday mornings.

Mayor Darrel Bruggeman, a lifelong resident of this town of 248 people and friend of the local Aumiller family for over sixty years, is a proud advocate of the town's charm and independence, and serves as an ambassador of good will for anyone passing through.

•

As a small boy, Dad was already a handful for his parents, and his energy and imagination seemed to get him into far more than his fair share of trouble. When he was only about three-years-old, he'd infuriate his mother when he'd rip his clothes off and run naked through the streets of downtown Selden, screaming wildly while shaking his little tallywacker at everyone in his path. Grandma Annie would chase him down, swoop him up and rush his naked little butt back to their home, but her lectures and spankings were never quite enough to stop his irreverent behavior. When he finally pushed the limit one too many times, she snatched him by the nape of his neck, marched him back home and held him under the spigot of their water pump as she nearly drowned him with each deliberate pump of the handle. He may have been a slow learner, but this finally put an end to his childhood streaking.

By the time he was five-years-old, he found a new and much more creative way to exasperate his parents, and this time it nearly cost him his life. As the cars and trucks sped past his home on the old country highway, he'd run into the road like his neighborhood dogs; yipping and howling as he chased away every car that dared to violate his domain. With each new victory he grew more brazen and confident until he foolishly stepped into the path of an oncoming truck. Black smoke poured from the screeching tires of the enormous feed truck as the driver frantically slammed on his brakes and brought it to a shuddering stop . . . just inches from crashing into the body of this scraggly little boy. The driver jumped from his truck; shaking his fists and screaming obscenities as he watched the fastest little boy he'd ever seen scamper fearfully away. Unfortunately for Dad, the truck driver knew who he was and wasted no time in going to the pool hall to tell Granddad about his maniacal little son. Within minutes, Dad found his butt getting kicked every other step on his way back to his home as Grand-dad yelled, *"I'll teach you to bark at cars."* Dad said he never chased another car.

●

Doctors and dentists are taken for granted today, but in the 1920s and 30s, they were a luxury the Aumiller family could rarely afford. When someone got sick or injured in those days, they usually treated the ailment with home remedies and just toughed it out the best they could. But on Wednesday, August 13th, 1929, Dad's mother Annie became the tragic exception to that rule. She'd been suffering for several days with a terrible toothache, and nothing she did could relieve the pain. When she finally couldn't stand the agony any longer, she went to see a dentist in the nearby town of Norton.

The dentist pulled the impacted tooth, but she developed ser-ious complications during the next two days that led to blood poisoning and even greater pain. Granddad Aumiller drove her and her parents back to Norton on Friday, August 15th, but her terminal condition was well beyond the capacity of this small town dentist, and there was nothing he could even suggest that would help. While Granddad was driving her back to Selden, she suddenly started gagging and gasping for air. He stopped the car just long enough to crawl in the back seat with his wife, while Grandpa Murray jumped behind the wheel and continued driving toward Selden. When they were just a few blocks from home, Grandpa Murray looked over his shoulder and watched in horror as his daughter literally fought for her life. In the panic of watching his baby's life quickly slipping away, he ran off the right side of the road and rolled the car onto its side in the steep roadside ditch. They all climbed into the back seat and frantically worked to revive her, but within seconds, my thirty-year-old Grandma Annie was dead.

Granddad walked back to his home and saw his tiny little children waiting on the front steps of their house. He walked up to them and quietly said, *"She didn't make it."* Four little words . . . four terrifying words . . . words no child should ever have to hear. Cries of anguish and despair rang out as they tried to understand why their mother was gone, but nothing could calm their grief, and in the darkness of that singularly tragic moment, they learned that life isn't always fair.

In later years, Dad would talk about the horror he felt when he ran to the scene of that crash and helplessly watched as his mother laid dead in the back seat of the car. It was the most horrible moment of his life, and one that remained vivid in his mind for the remainder of his years.

It would be impossible for Granddad to still work his job and raise six little children by himself, so he sent his two-and-a-half year-old daughter Annavate and his fifteen-month-old daughter Ruthie to live with their Grandma Maude Murray (Grandma Annie's mother), then sent the rest of his kids back to live at his parents' farm while he stayed in town and continued to run the pool hall.

Allowing his two youngest daughters to move in with their maternal grandparents was probably the only viable option Granddad really had, but no matter how much this real-life Little Orphan Annie and her baby sister were loved by their new family, it didn't make it any easier for them to be away from their brothers and sisters.

When the remaining kids were moved to the farm, Granddad sat them all down for a family meeting and told them there were new rules and responsibilities for each of them to bear. He told them my nine-year-old dad was now their boss, and they were to do everything he said . . . my eight-year-old Aunt Rainie would prepare all the meals (and if anyone complained about her cooking, they'd have to assume her duties), and my seven-year-old Aunt Beulah and five-year-old Uncle Lyle were given the task of keeping the house clean. These were non-negotiable duties and everyone understood there would be serious consequences if they didn't comply.

There were no vacuum cleaners to help sweep the floors; laundry had to be hand washed on scrub boards and hung out to dry, cooking was done on coal or wood burning stoves, and water had to be hauled into the house and heated in order to wash their dishes. Taking care of the house was not an easy task for these little urchins, but it was one they all accepted without question.

After a month or two Granddad quit his job in Selden and moved back to the farm with the rest of his family. The Great Depression had just begun and the Aumillers were soon demoted from the ranks of the poor to the depths of absolute poverty. And this was a level of poverty few Americans today understand. There were no food stamps or food banks to fill their pantry when it was empty, and because being poor (in those days) meant you were skinny, there wasn't a fat little kid to be found. Granddad didn't even own a car to help him get around town, and certainly didn't have anything frivolous that would be remotely comparable to the cell phones, I-Pods, or big screen television sets and DVD players most "poor" people seem to have today. There were no Goodwill Stores or charitable donors to provide them with decent clothing . . . no government subsidized housing or free public health care, and every little bit that they owned was *earned* by honest and dedicated hard work.

Granddad continued to work the fields of his father's farm from early spring until harvest time in the fall, then trapped badgers in the winter. But there was very little money to be made, and just feeding his kids became a desperate struggle.

Chicken, pinto beans, potatoes and corn were the most common meals in the Aumiller household, with beef or pork as a rare family treat, and fried bread as a welcomed dessert. Aunt

Rainie did her very best at her chores, but as an eight-year-old child with very few groceries to choose from (and even fewer cooking lessons to guide her), she was pretty limited in what she could prepare. And her lack of experience was never more evident than on the night she proudly served her "special" beans and onions for dinner. After taking a single bite from his plate, Granddad openly grimaced and said, *"Damn, these onions are hot!"* He looked at the questioning stares from every child at the table, then quickly smiled as he said, *"But just the way I like them."* He was no fool . . . he knew the rules of the house and wasn't about to become the next new cook.

By early 1932, Aunt Annavate and Aunt Ruthie had lived in relative comfort with their grandparents for the past two and a half years, but when Grandma Murray died on Friday, February 26th, 1932, a sad but equally excited five-year-old Aunt Annavate was sent back to live with her real family. Because my three-year-old Aunt Ruthie was so attached to her surrogate family, she was allowed to continue living with Grandma Murray's daughter Ruth until she reached early adulthood.

Aunt Annavate was so happy to be back where she belonged, but it wasn't without its consequences. She didn't get the same special attention she'd received from her doting grandparents, and because she always thought she was such an ugly little duckling, she was far less secure than any of her siblings. That's hard to imagine since she's always been such a beautiful and stunning woman, but if she looked anything like the freckle faced, stringy red-haired scrawny little moppet she claims to have been, she just may have been right.

There was a period of adjustment for her when she returned to her home, and she soon learned her father wasn't nearly as tolerant as her grandparents had been. While the family was gathered around the table for dinner one afternoon, she started fussing about one thing or another, when Granddad suddenly reached over and slapped her face with the back of his hand. The slap didn't hurt her, but she'd never been more crushed in her life! She quickly finished her meal and crawled down from the tall wooden chair; tears still evident on her freckled little cheeks as she walked out the back door. Once again her little heart had been broken, and as she walked away in sorrow, she woefully sang, *"Nobody likes me! Everybody hates me!! I'm gonna eat worms . . . big fat wooly ones, little short squiggly ones, and then I'll die. And then everybody will see they were sorry they picked on me."* Because that was just about as cute and pitiful as it sounds, that may well have been the very day she became her father's favorite daughter.

●

Since Dad was forced into adulthood at such an uncomfortably young age, he learned very early about the rigors of hard work. Daily and sometimes grueling chores were the rule rather than the exception, but he and his brother still found time to play Cowboys and Indians in the fields around the farm. Dime store novels were still glamorizing wild-west adventures, so there was never a lack of images to feed their impressionable young minds.

The flat plains of Kansas didn't provide the ideal backdrop for a traditional childhood western fantasy, but there were several deep forged gullies running along the creek beds that were fitting substitutes for the great Rocky Mountains that helped to enhance their cowboy illusion. Riding imaginary horses and shooting guns they'd whittled from scraps of wood, they continued to defeat the already beleaguered Native American Indians . . . and not surprisingly, Dad preferred to be the cowboy.

●

Dad often spoke of having to walk ten miles to school each day . . . in the snow . . . and uphill both ways. My sisters and I knew this was just a joke, but it was clear to us that his childhood was very harsh, and even though we never showed it, we were truly sympathetic.

In the spring and summer months Dad and Uncle Lyle worked the fields alongside their dad, and in the fall, they'd help harvest the crops. Even going to school didn't relieve them of these chores. They'd hoe a row of crops each morning on a portion of their one-mile walk to school, and complete another on their way back home.

But hard work didn't guarantee wealth and they were still a family of poor farmers. Since money was scarce, new clothes were rare, and the Aumiller kids were forced to wear their old clothes until they were beyond repair. As the oldest boy, Dad was the first to wear any new clothes and Uncle Lyle got all his hand-me-downs, and probably never had a new set of clothes his entire childhood. It was probably even harder for his sisters, though, since their clothes had to be passed down through each of the girls.

The kids never complained about their lack of suitable clothing, but having to wear tattered and sole bare shoes to school each day was a real source of embarrassment for them all. Stuffing cropped newspapers inside their shoes easily added another fifty miles of life for each pair, but this slipshod solution to their obvious need for new shoes only confirmed in their own minds just how poor they really were.

In 1933, Granddad and the kids left the farm and moved back into their little house alongside the highway inside the city limits of Selden. They'd survived the first four years of the depression, and by now, were accustomed to living without even the barest of necessities.

They each compensated for their poverty in their own way. The girls and Uncle Lyle channeled their energy into excelling in school, while Dad apparently chose to embrace the dark side and continually got into trouble whenever he could.

School was always difficult for Dad. When he started in the fall of 1925 (four years before his mother died), Aunt Rainie was upset because she couldn't go to school with him, and was jealous that he started before her. She secretly wished she was ahead of him, and by 1927, her wish was nearly granted when he flunked the third grade and had to repeat it in 1928. This may have made her feel a little better, but it certainly didn't do anything to help his self-esteem.

When he was in the seventh grade, he and another boy were sent to pump water for the rest of the kids in their class and thought it would be a great prank to pee in the water pail. They chuckled to themselves as each of their classmates lined up to ladle a cup of the tainted water, but soon learned it was a pretty bad idea when they got thirsty themselves. To keep from being detected and suffering the inevitable wrath from their teacher, they were forced to drink from the same pail, and with each nauseating sip, vowed to one another . . . *"Never Again!"*

He didn't get caught for this latest stunt, but it was a clear indication of just how ornery he was, and his level of mischief didn't go unnoticed by his tyrannical schoolmarm teacher. By the end of the school year she decided he was too immature to be in the seventh grade and moved him back to the sixth grade, putting him in the same class as Aunt Beulah. And if that wasn't insulting enough, she arbitrarily flunked every sixth grader in his class that year, even though Aunt Beulah was an outstanding student. When the school year began in 1934, Dad was still in the sixth grade and Aunt Rainie was in the ninth grade . . . her dream come true!

●

Winters were very harsh in northwest Kansas, and fighting the bitter cold was a full time job. A railroad ran past the north edge of town, and in its haste, would inadvertently provide some relief for the poor people along its route. As the firemen shoveled coal from bins into the billowing furnaces of their steam engines, fragments would fall below to the railroad beds, and became welcomed treasures for the neediest of families.

Bracing against the wind and cold arctic chill, Dad and Uncle Lyle walked side by side, filling their metal coal bin as they trudged along the warped wooden ties. If they were lucky, the train would come through while they were there and the firemen would reward them by scooping a shovelful of coal to the ground. When the bin was filled to the capacity they could still carry, they'd shuffle their way home to feed their antique cast iron stoves and assure another night's comfort.

As the years passed and Dad became comfortable with his role in the family, things drastically changed. On Thursday, September 12th, 1935 (six years after his mother died), our thirty-nine-year-old Granddad Aumiller married fifteen-year-old Opal May Smith, who lived in the neighboring town of Hoxie, Kansas.

Opal was born to Edward Mac Smith and Nora Bailey on Tuesday, November 11th, 1919 in Luray, Kansas. Edward was born in St. George, Kansas on May 2nd, 1875 and died at the age of sixty on Wednesday, July 17th, 1935 in Hoxie, Kansas. I have no information about Nora's roots, but know she already had two children from two previous relationships when she married Edward: Clinton (who was exactly four years older than Opal), and a younger sister, Chrysie. Opal was the only child Edward and Nora had together.

When she was just four or five years old, her mother ran off with another man and abandoned her three small children. Because Nora was declared to be an unfit mother, the courts placed Clinton and Chrysie in an orphanage, and awarded custody of Opal to her father. Opal wouldn't see her mother again for another twenty-two years, and only then when Clinton brought her to Denver for a visit.

In later years she and her father moved to Hoxie, Kansas, where they continued to live a stark and impoverished life. They lived in a tiny two-room shanty along the riverbed, with its unframed rear bedroom tunneled into the side of a steep dirt hill, and its crudely framed living room exposed at the front. There were no frills in Opal's life and even regular meals were considered to be an absolute luxury. This was a level of poverty even the Aumillers weren't accustomed to.

Opal became a frequent visitor with her neighbor Fern Spillman (Granddad's sister), and soon became acquainted with Granddad and the rest of his family. When her father died she was forced to stay with an uncle for a short while, but it didn't take long for her to realize this wasn't the way she wanted to live. She was still very young, but old enough to know she wanted a man who would take care of her for the rest of her life, and convinced Granddad that he was that man. They were married fifty-seven days after her father died, and spent the better part of the next forty-eight years together.

She took her marriage very seriously and considered it to be her job to raise six children who were young enough to be her own brothers and sisters. The five youngest kids willingly accepted her into the family, but Dad wasn't ready to relinquish his authority to a new mother his own age, and there were severe battles between the two of them. After one particularly physical encounter (I remember hearing about bullwhips and knives), Dad told Granddad, *"You've got to get rid of that girl before she kills us all!"* Of course, Granddad didn't get rid of her, and his siding with Opal probably fostered even more resentment from Dad.

Dad was a stubborn and aggressively chauvinistic young man who was heavily influenced by the men in his family. He was raised around a pretty rowdy group of hard working, hard fighting (and after the repeal of prohibition on Tuesday, December 5th, 1933), hard drinking men.

He once told me his dad and uncles would get drunk and race their horse drawn wagon through the streets of Selden, shooting those tiny green glass resisters from telephone poles with their rifles . . . just like a gang of rustlers terrorizing the innocent townsfolk in all of those old cowboy movies you saw as a child. And if other tough guys came to town looking for trouble, the two fisted Aumiller boys were called out to take care of them. They were not the kind of men you wanted to cross. Clearly Dad learned well from them, because he was one of the toughest men his size I'd ever known, and until he got old, loved a good fight.

In late 1938, Grandpa Grant became ill and knew he was dying. He didn't want Grandma Cora living alone on their remote farm, so he sold the farm and bought a little house inside Selden, just across the highway from Dad's home. When he died at the age of seventy-five on Sunday, July 23rd, 1939, Grandma Cora continued to live in this house, and cared for her thirty-six-year-old handicapped daughter Oca for the next twenty-two years.

Opal's half-brother Clinton would eventually marry Aunt Beulah (her stepdaughter), and they'd have five children together: Rodney, Tina, Melody, Lisa and Chris Kennedy. (I'm not quite sure how that branch on the family tree should look).

Ulysses Grant &
Cora Aumiller

John & Maud Murray

Truman LaVate Aumiller

Annie Virginia Aumiller

LaVate & Annie Aumiller
On their Wedding Day

Annie, Ruth & Inza Murray

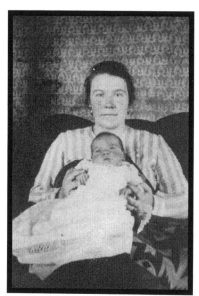

Grandma Annie & Dad

Our Dad
Kennedy Murray Aumiller

Dad & his sister Lorraine

Grandpa Murray & Dad

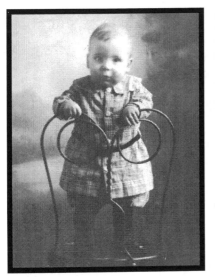

Dad - At one year
and one day old

Beulah, Lorraine, Lyle, Dad
& Juanita—In front of the
milk house on the farm

FOUR GENERATIONS
Great-Great Grandpa Buell, Great Grandma Cora, Granddad
LaVate, & Dad - On the Aumiller farm outside Selden, Kansas

Dad's home inside Selden, Kansas

Juanita, Dad, Lorraine, Lyle, Beulah, Connard, Wanda, Cora Fern, Loy, Buell, Clive, Orris and Norman

Unknown man on the left; Great Grandma Cora; unknown little girl; Uncle Warren, and Granddad Aumiller in front of Grandma's house in Selden

Great Grandma Aumiller at her home in Selden --
Late 1940s

Granddad & Opal
At the beginning of their
48 year marriage

Granddad & Opal in Selden

CHAPTER 2

"The Oldsons"

My Great-Great-Great-Grandfather Samuel Oldson was the earliest member of the Oldson family Mom knew about, and documents from 1821 revealed he was a member of the Masonic Lodge in West Union, Ohio. He was also the father of James Russell Oldson.

My Great-Great-Grandfather James Russell Oldson was born on May 18th, 1822 in West Union, Ohio, and went on to become a captain in the Union Army during the American Civil War of 1861-1865. He married Margaret Lafferty, who was born on May 12th, 1824 in West Union, Ohio. He died at the age of seventy-five on September 25th, 1897 in Downs, Kansas, and she died at the age of ninety on November 24th, 1914, also in Downs, Kansas. They were the parents of George Randolph Oldson.

My Great-Grandfather George Randolph Oldson was born on June 23rd, 1850 in West Union, Ohio, and his future wife Elizabeth Ann Pitt was born on April 10th, 1858 in South Port, Illinois. He died at the age of seventy-seven on February 17th, 1928, and she died at the age of seventy-seven on March 30th, 1936; both in Downs, Kansas.

Elizabeth was the daughter of Sidney Pitt, who was born in 1830 in either Nottinghamshire or Devonshire, England, and Sarah Else, who was born in 1837 in Nottinghamshire, England. They were married in 1855, and were together until he died in Cawker City, Kansas at the age of forty-three in 1873. She died at the age of eighty-six in 1923.

Sidney came to America around 1847, and family legend has it that he was descended from William Pitt (The Younger), who, in 1783, at the incredibly young age of twenty-four, became

England's youngest Prime Minister. I like to imagine this lineage makes Brad Pitt, and by extension, Angelina Jolie, distant cousins of mine . . . which is probably the only reason Angelina and I have never been romantically involved. Yeah, *that's* the reason.

Anyway, my Great-Grandparents George Randolph Oldson and Elizabeth Ann Pitt were married in Osborne, Kansas on May 30th, 1876, and had the following eight children: Nell (Ella), Sadie, Elizabeth (Lizzie), William Russell, Carlotta (Lottie), Clara, George and John. William Russell Oldson, who'd later become my Grandpa Oldson, was born on March 3rd, 1885 in Downs, Kansas.

My Great-Grandfather James Valentine Boggs was born in North Carolina on October 7th, 1855, and his future wife Sarah Luella Mount was born on September 18, 1858 in Mount Vernon, Illinois. He died at the age of ninety on August 1st, 1946 in Cawker City, Kansas, and she died at the age of seventy-five on April 1st, 1934.

They were married in Mount Vernon, Illinois on March 19th, 1878 and had the following nine children: Daisy, Lora Edith, Fern, Nina, Stella, Iva, Walter, Earl and Orbin. Lora Edith Boggs, who'd later become my Grandma Oldson, was born on June 6th, 1887 in St. Francis, Kansas.

And finally, on Thursday, March 21st, 1907, my twenty-two year-old Grandpa William Russell Oldson married his nineteen year-old sweetheart Lora Edith Boggs, who fifteen years later gave birth to the greatest woman on earth . . . my mother, little Margie.

●

Not to be outdone by the Pitts, the Boggs family claimed to have a bloodline with Dr. David Livingstone, the Scottish explorer and missionary who went missing in Africa in 1864 while searching for the source of the Nile River.

Seven years after his disappearance, Mr. George Bennett, the publisher of the New York Herald, commissioned adventurer/reporter Henry Stanley to find the missing doctor, and on March 21st, 1871, he led his expeditionary force of 200 men on this grueling quest. On November 10th, after searching for nearly eight months and losing two-thirds of his porters through desertion or death, he found Dr. Livingstone in the small village of Uijiji on the shore of Lake Tanganyika in present day Tanzania. Elated by his discovery, he described their meeting:

"I pushed back the crowds, and, passing from the rear, walked down a living avenue of people until I came in front of the semicircle of Arabs, in the front of which stood the white man with the gray beard. As I advanced slowly toward him I noticed he was pale, looked wearied, had a gray beard, wore a bluish cap with a faded gold band round it, had on a red-sleeved waistcoat and a pair of gray tweed trousers. I would have run to him, only I was a coward in the presence of such a mob—would have embraced him only, he being an Englishman, I did not know how he would receive me; so I did what cowardice and false pride suggested was the best thing—walked deliberately to him, took off my hat, and said, "Dr. Livingstone, I presume?"

I've never seen documented evidence to prove the Prime Minister and famous explorer were actually related to the Pitt or Boggs families, but I can't imagine why anyone would allege those particular family connections unless they were true. In any event, the stories were passed down in good faith to my mother, and if she believed they were true, that's good enough for me.

•

On Saturday, November 4th, 1922, one of the most exciting archeological finds of modern times occurred when English Egyptologist Howard Carter discovered the outer tomb of the 3,000 year old Tutankhamen "King Tut" in the Egyptian

Valley of the Kings. After a seven-year search he was within weeks of finally entering the inner tomb, and on Friday, February 16th, 1923, he and his benefactor, Lord Carnarvon, scraped away the seal to the tomb and found the King *"encased in a coffin of pure gold, lying in the blackest darkness, surrounded by unfathomable silence."* The splendor of the moment was almost too much to bear.

But for my family the discovery of the outer tomb was paled by an even greater event that occurred just twenty-three days earlier, when on Thursday, October 12th, 1922 at 3pm, my mother Edith Marguerite Oldson was born to thirty-seven year-old William Russell and thirty-five-year-old Lora Edith Oldson in Flagler, Colorado. It was in all the newspapers.

She was the youngest of six children, preceded by Aunt Verne (no middle name), who was born on Sunday, January 12th, 1908, Uncle Voyde DeWitte on Tuesday, August 24th, 1909, Uncle Dan (no middle name) on Wednesday, August 16th, 1911, Uncle Duane Russell on Tuesday, March 18th, 1913, and Uncle William Earl (Bill) on Monday, March 14th, 1921.

Flagler was a typical farm town of about 500 people on the eastern plains of Colorado, about 110 miles southeast of Denver. Mom lived on a farm inside Flagler until she was two-years-old, then, in 1924, the family moved twenty-five miles east to another farm, just north of the town of Stratton. By this time, Grandpa was firmly established as a master carpenter, and had little trouble finding work to support his large family.

In her earliest memory from 1926 when she was four-years-old, Mom recalled being at a family Christmas party at their home. By this time, her older sister Verne was already an old married woman of eighteen, her brother Voyde was seventeen, Dan fifteen, Duane thirteen, and Bill just five.

Fresh snow had fallen during the day and a white blanket of powder coated the landscape of their home. Grandma was wearing her finest dress and brightly colored holiday apron, and was busy finishing the evening's meal. The room was warm and bright, and the aroma of turkey roasting in the oven and strong scent of percolating coffee filled the room. Freshly baked cookies were stacked on a plate from their finest dinnerware, just waiting for the appropriate time to be eaten.

Aunt Verne was dutifully helping Grandma while her twenty-two-year-old husband Orley Stoumbaugh and Uncle Voyde sat at the table drinking coffee. The room was alive with laughter, and everyone was doing their best to divert Uncle Bill and Mom's attention from the back of the house, when suddenly, from out of nowhere, Santa Claus appeared. Mom was so excited! . . . but also just a little afraid. But her fear soon ended when Santa reached down and lifted her to his lap and asked, *"What do you want for Christmas, little darling?"*

This was the essence of pure Christmas joy and a scene she would always cherish, but it wasn't until many years later that she realized the voice coming from Santa was that of her father.

After the holidays, Grandpa finished the work he was doing in Stratton, and they decided to try their luck a little farther south. They packed everything they owned, and in a scene straight from The Grapes of Wrath, moved to another farming community somewhere in northern Oklahoma.

Oklahoma isn't famous for a lot of things, but it is known for its tornados, and they learned that lesson all too well in the spring of 1927 when a tornado stormed its way through their property and destroyed a grain silo right next to their house. After a quick family meeting, they all agreed it was time to move back to Colorado.

They settled into a small house inside the town of Stratton, but soon discovered there was very little work to be found, so in the last months of 1927, when Mom was five-years-old, they moved to Seibert, Colorado.

●

Seibert was just another of many small country burgs along U.S. Highway 24, sitting midway between Flagler to the west, and Stratton to the east. At the time it boasted a population of about six-hundred residents, and was the business center for several neighboring farms. Its small commercial development within its 6x7 block city limits was home to a bank, hotel, restaurant, barbershop, service station, and general store. It was also home to a very colorful man by the name of Fitzpatrick, who, in addition to publishing the town's equivalent of The New York Times, gave saxophone and coronet lessons to any-one in town who was interested.

He was originally from Craig, Colorado, and told stories about The Wild Bunch Gang coming to his ranch when he was still just a boy. Their visit was probably innocent enough; a random way station on their way to Wyoming; maybe once, maybe routinely; that was never made clear. But he knew who these outlaws were, and thought it was an honor to have them in his home. As they'd make ready to leave, he'd saddle up and ride side-by-side with them as far as the fence line of his property, and liked to brag that he once rode with Butch Cassidy and the Sundance Kid. All the kids in town were very impressed.

In later years Uncle Duane set type and operated the manual printing press for him. It was a long time before automation reached the free press in Seibert.

Mom's parents had been frugal with their earnings over the years, so shortly after arriving in town they were able to open The Russell Inn Café, inside the Blake Building on the northwest corner of the two main streets of town . . . Second Street and Colorado Avenue. Second Street ran east and west through town, and was also U.S. Highway 24, so in addition to the local business they enjoyed, they also benefited from all the tourist and commercial traffic that traveled through this part of the state.

Grandpa did all the maintenance and labor around the restaurant, but our strong willed Grandma pretty much ran the business herself. She had a great mind for business and was a fabulous cook, so the restaurant soon became a popular meeting place for most of the people in town.

Their living quarters were in a small storeroom adjacent to the restaurant, but because it wasn't designed to be used as a residence, there was no bath or toilette in the building. Left with no other options, the family was forced to walk across the street to the barbershop each Saturday night for a much appreciated hot bath. That actually sounds pretty bad, but in reality, personal hygiene was an important part of the family's normal routine. Mom once told me there were a lot of good reasons for people to be poor, but there was never an excuse for them to be dirty . . . and sponge baths were a daily occurrence for everyone in the family.

By the fall of 1929, they expanded their business by moving to a building on the southeast corner of the same intersection. They kept the name The Russell Inn Café, but were also now the proprietors of a four-room hotel. This was a big step up for them, and since the hotel had the added luxury of a single bath, they no longer had to make their weekly trips to the barbershop.

It was a bold move, and should have been a great one as well . . but timing is everything in life, and theirs couldn't have been worse. On Tuesday, October 29th, 1929, the stock market crashed and for the next twelve years, America would reel from the debilitating effects of the Great Depression.

Farmers suffered from reduced crop prices and incomes for everyone were drastically reduced. But the Oldsons were well liked by everyone in town, and friends splurged as often as they could to enjoy the charm and good company at their favorite little hangout. And a big part of this charm was the kindness and unassuming nature of Grandpa Oldson.

I never knew him, but based on family descriptions and the pictures I've seen of him, he reminded me of Percy Kilbride, the mild-mannered actor who played Pa Kettle in the Ma and Pa Kettle movies of the 1940s. Everyone who met him liked him, and he was called Doc by most everyone in town. Mom didn't quite know why he earned this nickname, but thought it was probably because he was the one who'd delivered her into this world (and many of her siblings as well), and was always the one who treated the family with home remedies whenever they were sick or injured.

And he never lacked for opportunities to show off his medical skills. "No Shirts, No Shoes, No Service" was never a rule in their restaurant, but on the day Mom ran barefoot across their old wooden floor, she wished it had been. The screaming and crying brought her dad running when she buried the biggest sliver she'd ever seen into the fleshy meat of her big toe, but no matter what he tried, he just couldn't get it out. He finally wrapped it with a poultice he'd made from bread and milk, and by the next day the sliver had worked its way through the skin, and the protruding blunt end of her torture was now ready for extraction. No professional consultations, x-rays or CAT scans were required and he was able to remove the sliver without incident.

Things were going reasonably well for everyone (considering the horrible state of the economy), but in the fall of 1932, when Mom was ten-years-old, tragedy nearly struck her family in a very big way. Mom was spending the night with her sister and her four kids in their two-bedroom cabin in Seibert while Uncle Orley was away, busy shucking corn for a neighbor at a nearby farm. It was unseasonably chilly that night, and just before bedtime, Aunt Verne stoked the fire on the coal stove and closed the flue (hoping to make the heat last longer), then she,

Mom, Ray, Bill, Clarice, and Pudge, cuddled closely together under the warm and cozy blankets of their beds and quietly settled in for the night.

Sometime just after dawn, Aunt Verne woke up in a stupor and realized something was terribly wrong. She struggled to get up and staggered across the floor inside the tiny cabin, but couldn't quite make it to the front door. Mom awoke to the sounds of moaning and watched in horror as she saw Aunt Verne's eyes roll back in her head as she fell to the floor. Mom would drift in and out of consciousness and awaken to the sounds of even more moaning, but the fire had consumed most of the oxygen in the room and its absence made her too weak to move. Aunt Verne finally got up from the floor and opened the front door to allow fresh air in, then collapsed again on the ground in the front yard. Mom finally managed to get out of bed and stumbled toward the front door, but by the time she reached an inner doorway, she wet herself and passed out; falling limply to the floor.

Neighbors saw Aunt Verne on the ground in front of the cabin and ran to tell Grandma and Grandpa Oldson. They called for the town doctor, Dr. McBride, but when he arrived, he said it was just something they'd eaten and told them to take a dose of castor oil. Not happy with his diagnosis, they called for Dr. Keene (in Stratton), who told them that given the circumstances, they probably just needed a lot of fresh air. He was right, because in a short period of time, they fully recovered and returned to a normal life.

But normal in a small town was usually quiet and uneventful, so on occasion a little ingenuity was needed to liven things up. Uncle Orley, who thrived on attention and was notorious for his pranks, was quick to devise new ways to shock his family and friends, and on a cold and bitter Halloween night, he got another chance. As the rest of the town slept, he and his fellow school bus driver, Martin Rasmussen, joined forces with their co-conspirators, realtor Francis Fingato and Professor Brown (the head of the schools) and worked until the wee hours of the morning loading outhouses onto a header barge (flatbed wagon) and moved them to the front steps of all the businesses on the main street . . . including the Russell Inn Café. By morning, all the kids in town had a great laugh over this prank, but the merchants weren't at all amused.

I don't know if it was reported to the Sheriff or not, but Mr. Fitzpatrick seemed to have it all figured out when he ran the following tongue-in-cheek news report in the Seibert Settler: *"No one knows who did this dastardly deed, so no action can be taken against the culprits, but with all the "Stumbling" and "Mussing" it up "Brown" going on in our town, better keep your "Gates" locked from now on."*

●

On Thursday, May 6th, 1937, the German airship LZ129 Hindenburg crashed while attempting to land at the Lakehurst Naval Air Station in Manchester, New Jersey. Twenty-two crewmembers, thirteen passengers and one ground crewman were killed during the crash, but miraculously, sixty-two people survived. This was a major event in America's history and received an extraordinary amount of photo and newsreel coverage, as well as the on-the-scene eyewitness radio report by a very distraught Herbert Morrison. Mom was so intrigued by the sensational newspaper accounts, that she was inspired to start her own scrapbook of the more exciting world events . . . but little did she know that in the next two months, she'd be the very next entry.

By July 1937, when Mom was fourteen-years-old, her siblings were already married, with the exception of her brother, Uncle Bill. Because they were nearly the same age, they were much closer with each other than with their other siblings, and as a result, spent most of their time together. On this warm summer day, she and Uncle Bill rode with his friend Ed Hesse to a dance in Flagler, where Uncle Bill knew a girl he was kind of sweet on. Ed's father was the railroad depot manager in Seibert and was apparently considered to be a big shot in town, so it was quite a treat for them to be hob-knobbing with the rich and famous.

When Ed decided it was time to leave, Uncle Bill wasn't quite ready, so he had Mom return to Seibert with Ed and told her to bring the family car back to him. But when Mom got home and asked Grandpa for the car, he told her no. Mom pleaded with him until Grandma finally intervened and said, *"Go ahead and let her take it. After all, you let everyone else drive it."*

On her drive back to Flagler, she was stopped by the local marshal and ticketed for being an unlicensed driver. This was a serious enough violation to get her name in the Crime Stoppers section of the local newspaper, but not serious enough to prevent her from continuing her trek back to Flagler.

Oldsons—Left rear: Ella, Sadie, Lizzie, Russell, Lottie, Clara
Front: Great Grandma Elizabeth, George, Great Granddad George,
and John

Left rear: Verne, Voyde, Dan
Front: Russell, Duane & Edith

Grandpa Russell Oldson &
Grandma Edith Oldson

Mom's friends in front of the Russell Inn Café

Mom in front of the Russell Inn Café

Inside the Russell Inn Café

Seibert, Colorado

Mom is third from the right in the front row

CHAPTER 3

"The Union"

As the school year ended in the summer of 1938, Dad was about to embark on a journey that would change his life forever. Granddad Aumiller's cousin Jerry lived in Seibert, and invited Dad to stay with him and his family for the summer. My eighteen-year-old dad had never been more than a few miles from his home before, so the idea of traveling to another state sounded like a great adventure to him. But as he boarded the Greyhound bus in Selden and said his farewells to his family, he was filled with a great deal of apprehension. This was the first time he'd ever traveled by himself, and in spite of how grown up he liked to think he was, he was very nervous about being on his own.

After traveling through town after town for what must have seemed an eternity, he began to fear he'd missed his stop. He finally gathered the courage to approach the driver and asked if they'd passed Seibert, but the driver just chuckled and assured him they still had a long way to go. Dad returned to his seat and quietly watched as an endless landscape of fields and farms raced by. He had no idea the world was so big.

When he finally settled in with his new summer family, Jerry took him for a tour of this grand little metropolis. Dad was well traveled now and felt a certain amount of independence and maturity for the first time in his life, so when they went to the Russell Inn Café, Dad sat at the counter with his cousin and ordered a ***real*** man's cup of coffee. It didn't take long to notice the young girl working inside the restaurant, and when she'd moved out of ear shot, he asked, *"Who's that little freckled faced girl?"* Jerry answered, *"That's Margie Oldson. You want to meet her?"*

Dad spent a lot of his time in the restaurant over the next few days, and after much flirtation, invited her to go skating with him in nearby Arriba. Overwhelmed by his good looks and manly appearance, she willingly agreed.

Dad had very little experience with driving, but Jerry agreed to let him use his car so he could properly woo his new girlfriend. With jackrabbit starts and grinding of gears, they began their snail paced twenty-one mile drive. Never exceeding thirty miles per hour, Dad kept the radiator cap on the center of the road, and just hoped he didn't meet any other cars coming his way. Mom secretly laughed about this, because by now she was already a well-seasoned driver.

Mom had been to this roller rink many times before and was somewhat proficient in the art of not falling down, but for Dad, it was a brand new experience. Shuffling along like an old man in slippers, he made his way around the rink, and for the next few hours, they laughed . . . and they played . . . and they flirted . . . and they fell. It was a wonderful day!

Dad even bought them a banana split to share, even though he never cared for sweets. Mom was pretty sure he was just trying to impress her, but it didn't matter. They were having the time of their lives!

Apparently, this wasn't the only time Dad borrowed Jerry's car for recreational purposes, because by September, they had some *really* big news for the family.

When the gnashing of teeth and wails of despair finally subsided, Uncle Duane and Aunt Alice invited them to live with them in Fleming, Colorado until arrangements could be made for their wedding.

On Wednesday, September 21st, 1938, Uncle Duane and Aunt Alice drove a very nervous young couple to the county court house in Sterling, Colorado, where amid the splendor and subtleties only a courtroom can offer, they were declared husband and wife by the honorable Judge H. Lawrence Hinkley. Pretty strong titles for an eighteen-year-old boy and a fifteen-year-old girl.

***Side Note**: Grandma Oldson's brother, Orbin Boggs, had once been the Mayor of Sterling, thus reaffirming the grandeur of her side of the family.*

After returning to Fleming, they spent the next few weeks trying to figure out what they were going to do with their lives now that they were responsible young adults.

Uncle Duane owned a small print shop in town, and hired Dad to set type and sell subscriptions for his newspaper. It was Dad's first job away from the farm and he realized if he was going to do more with his life, he probably needed to return to school. Mom, who'd always done very well in school, didn't have a choice. In those days, pregnant girls weren't allowed to attend school and she was forced to drop out. Her future had been determined by default.

By early November, Uncle Duane drove them back to Seibert, then they continued their trip to Selden with Jerry and his wife Gladys. They lived in the tiny little house with Granddad and Opal, Aunt Rainie, Aunt Beulah, Aunt Annavate, Uncle Lyle, and Dad's two half-brothers, Orley and Truman. Mom became very close with everyone (no pun intended) and this was the beginning of a loving and lifelong bond between Mom and the Aumiller family.

The depression had been in full swing for nine years now, and the effects were staggering for most of the country. Grandpa and Grandma Oldson turned their weakening business over to Uncle Orley and Aunt Verne, then opened The Flagler Inn in nearby Flagler. The new business didn't do well, so Grandpa and Uncle Dan decided to move to the western slopes of Colorado to build new homes. Grandma, Uncle Bill, and Uncle

Dan's wife Edith stayed behind to work the restaurant, but within a very short period of time, Grandma was forced to sell the last restaurant they'd ever own and move on to a brand new life. By now, the men were working in Steamboat Springs, so the three stragglers from Flagler moved there to join them.

The mountains in northwest Colorado were breathtaking and provided a welcome and dramatic change from the flatlands of eastern Colorado. They quickly settled in and didn't waste any time finding work. Grandpa continued his work as a carpenter, Grandma worked as a cook at a local restaurant, Aunt Edith waited tables at another restaurant, and Uncle Dan went to work for the forest service. Things went pretty well until Uncle Dan buried an axe in his wrist while clearing trees in the forest, and nearly bled to death before he could get to a doctor. But like most of the tougher men of his generation, he quickly recovered and went right back to work.

By the end of the year, the family learned of a new and much more rewarding opportunity. The Bureau of Reclamation was building a new dam at Green Mountain near Kremmling, and the Chicago based Warner Construction Company was looking for hard working men. That's all they needed to hear! By February 1939, they pulled up stakes and moved their caravan to the next oasis. Uncle Bill stayed with friends in Steamboat Springs until he graduated from high school in the spring, then gleefully rejoined his family in their new home.

Mom & Dad in Seibert, Colorado
before they were married

My eighteen-year-old Dad

CHAPTER 4

"Green Mountain"

Construction on the new dam began on Thursday, December 1st, 1938, so the work camp was still in its infancy when they arrived. Housing originally consisted of twenty-five bunk-houses, a commissary, mess hall, warehouse and field offices, and it didn't take long for the camp to fully evolve. In an attempt to comply with sanitary regulations, the Warner Company built a small town on the left bank of the Blue River, 1,200 feet upstream from the construction area, and trailers, small shacks and tents soon sprang up all around this brand new town called Heeney.

Grandpa found work as a carpenter on the dam project and soon opened a dime store in the center of town. Grandma ran this business by herself, while the rest of the family found their own means of support. Uncle Dan worked as a laborer on the dam, his wife, Aunt Edith, worked as a waitress in the camp restaurant, and Uncle Orley and Aunt Verne (who'd soon move to Heeney), operated the town's Laundromat. Or more correctly, Aunt Verne ran the laundry business while our spunky bantamweight Uncle Orley worked as a night watchman at the local pool hall. The self-service laundry had four Maytag washers, a Mangle (whatever that was), a centrifugal dryer and a log burning stove to heat the water, and their $300 per month rent included their three-room living quarters on the second floor. Since this was the only laundry in town, they actually made a good living.

Grandpa and Grandma moved into a small two-room cabin on the side of the mountain, and it quickly became a favorite meeting place for the rest of the family. While Grandma's father (Great-Grandpa Boggs) was visiting for the summer, he dug a cave on the side of the hill and built a food storage locker for her canned fruits and vegetables. This was a necessity for any self-respecting rural wife in those days, but the locker also served as a Time-Out Room for misbehaving grandchildren. From all accounts, it was a great deterrent against repeat offenders, and was definitely preferred over the alternative whip'n they could receive behind the dreaded woodshed.

Mom wanted to be with her parents when she had her baby, so in early March, Jerry and Gladys picked her up in Selden and drove her back to Seibert. She rode the rest of the way to Heeney with Uncle Orley and Aunt Verne, who I believe were in the process of their move to join the rest of their family. Dad stayed in Selden to finish his 10th year of high school.

The work was long and relentless, but in the evenings, the families would all get together to relax. Rehashing the day's events, they'd sit and enjoy the family's all-time favorite pastime . . . playing cards, and amid the laughter and joy of this simple pleasure, Aunt Verne would stop to fix something for a late night snack. Pancakes and homemade syrup were always the leading favorite.

The end of Mom's pregnancy was rapidly approaching, but because she'd gone her entire term without seeing a doctor, she didn't really know what to expect. Then on Wednesday, April 26th, 1939, she developed severe stomach cramps, and had no idea she was in labor. Thinking she was suffering from something she'd eaten, she went to the outhouse for relief. When Grandma heard her crying, she knew exactly what was happening, and called for the company doctor.

The doctor arrived within minutes, and in the stark and unsanitary conditions of this rustic two-room cabin, brought Anna Laura June Aumiller into this life. But contrary to the story June would like us to believe, this impoverished and humble abode wasn't really a manger, and she wasn't nearly as divine as she claimed to be.

Word of her arrival quickly spread throughout the entire camp and Uncle Orley soon proclaimed that she was the first white baby born in Heeney. This claim was later amended to her being the first damn baby born in Heeney, in reference to the new dam that was built at Green Mountain. It was a play on words, but as a child, I enjoyed telling the story without getting in trouble for swearing.

It took a few days before Mom could get out of bed, but when she was finally able to get back on her feet, she and Grandma took June to the grocery store in town and weighed her on the meat scale. Grandma wrote to Dad and told him he was the proud father of a 7½ pound daughter.

But the excitement of this birth was soon replaced by unrest and fear when, on Wednesday, July 12th, 1939, disgruntled union workers went on strike. Local unionists phoned Denver's AFL headquarters and asked for reinforcements, and, according to newspaper accounts, "dozens of cars and trucks, carrying an estimated 500 Mexicans, Negroes and hard cases" were sent to join the strikers.

The Warner Company hired its own strikebreakers, and according to another newspaper report, "strikebreakers were jumping from their cars, driving the picket force aside by sheer force of numbers." At the end of the day, two picket lines had been broken, but only one strikebreaker was injured when his head fell victim to a flying rock.

In the following days, however, the situation became much more volatile, and on Friday, August 4th, Governor Ralph Carr called out the Colorado National Guard. Scores of soldiers equipped with rifles and machine guns, and supported by two tanks, soon arrived. Martial law was declared and strict curfews were enforced. Then on Tuesday, August 22nd, the Warner Company and the AFL reached an agreement, and the strike officially ended on Friday, September 15th. Life returned to normal, but in later years, family members talked of those days in reverent awe.

•

When Dad received his letter from Grandma, reality finally set in. He knew it was now time to join his wife and provide for his new child, so when he finished his tenth year of high school, he took another Greyhound bus from Selden and met with Uncle Orley and Aunt Verne in Seibert. The three of them then drove back to Heeney.

Because he was only nineteen-years-old and too young to work at the dam, he found work on a ranch owned by "Cully" Culbrath, just southeast of town. They lived in a small one-room apartment, which was an add-on extension of the main ranch house.

In addition to his chores with the livestock, Dad's job also required him to do a certain amount of driving, so on Tuesday, June 13th, 1939 he got his first Colorado Chauffeur's License, listing his address as the Heeney Camp in Kremmling, Colorado. Apparently his driving skills had dramatically improved since his courtship days.

Because Dad was so shy and timid around the Oldson family, Uncle Orley gave him the nickname "Tim." It may have been a fitting name during those early years, but it certainly didn't apply when he got older! But nicknames have a tendency to hang on and he was stuck with it for the rest of his life. The only people who still called him Kennedy were the Aumillers and my mom.

Following his twenty-first birthday on Thursday, February 13th, 1941, our family moved into the town of Heeney and Dad began his new and lucrative job as a laborer on the dam project. They lived in a one-room tarpaper cabin, with a monthly rent of only ten dollars. He worked five days a week and made sixty-two and a half cents an hour. His paycheck was an incredible twenty-five dollars each week, minus the twenty-five cents he begrudgingly gave up for Social Security.

Granddad Aumiller was still living in Selden and making thirty dollars each month working on the WPA (Works Progress Administration). When he learned how much money Dad was making, he was in awe. He told Dad if he made that kind of money, he'd save half of it each month, and even though it was good advice, I'm not sure that Dad was disciplined enough to do it.

That spring, Dad borrowed Grandpa Oldson's car and on his two days off, drove nearly four hundred miles back to Selden, just to help Granddad Aumiller and Opal move to Denver.

When he finished in Denver, he continued his arduous trip back to Heeney and barely arrived in time for another grueling day of hard labor. And he did all of this in only two days!! This is the stuff only men of the Greatest Generation and my brother-in-law Bob Brown are capable of. I can't go to the bank and grocery store in that length of time.

On Thursday, June 12th, 1941, Dad bought Uncle Orley's well-worn 1936 Ford, and even though it was already an old car when he bought it, it served its purpose. Our family was finally self-sufficient and no longer had to rely on the kindness of others in order to get around.

Building a dam in the high altitude of Colorado's mountains was punishing work, especially for someone who was used to the flat fields of Kansas, but Dad quickly adjusted and worked shoulder to shoulder with some very tough men. One of these men was Bill Wiley, who was from the mountain town of Dillon, about sixty miles southeast of Heeney. An exceptionally bright, good-looking, brawny young man, he was just four days older than Dad. The two of them soon became best friends, and shared that friendship for the next fifty-two years.

On Monday, September 1st, 1941, when Grandpa Oldson was just fifty-six-years-old, he suffered a heart attack while working on the spillway at Green Mountain Dam. There was an ambulance already on site because of the dam construction, but despite the immediate medical care he received, fate still intervened.

While en route to Denver just west of Idaho Springs, Grandpa sat up in the back of the ambulance and said, *"I feel pretty good now. Why don't we turn around and head back?"* The ambulance driver replied, *"Oh, Doc, let's just go on into Denver and have you checked out."* He silently laid back down, and without uttering another sound, he quietly died.

The funeral was in Denver and he was buried in Lot 111, Block 37 at Fairmont Cemetery. It was probably the hardest thing Mom ever experienced, and she once told me that every time she goes to a funeral, she sees the casket lid being closed on her daddy. She never forgot the pain.

Work camp at Green Mountain Dam
1939

Work Camp at Green Mountain Dam
1939

Heeney, Colorado—Circa 1940

Uncle Orley inside the town of Heeney

Grandpa Russell & Grandma Edith Oldson

Uncle Voyde, Mom, Uncle Bill, Grandma Oldson, Uncle Dan, Aunt Edith and Bob (Spike), on October 11, 1942, the day before Mom's 20th birthday, and the day before Uncle Bill went in the Air Force

Mom & baby June beside the
Tarpaper Shanty they called home

Dad & June
In front of the "house" where she
was almost born

Mom & June - 1939

Mom & Dad on a trip to
Seibert from Green Mountain -
1939

Our "Tim-id" Dad

The Proud Parents

Mom, June & a friend

CHAPTER 5

"Denver"

The work never stopped at Green Mountain while the dam was being built, but when the harsh winter of 1941 brought it to a near standstill, non-essential workers were laid off. Unfortunately, Dad was one of them, and with nowhere else to go, he and Mom decided to move to Denver. Dad was certain he'd be able to find some kind of work in the big city, and by now, I think he probably missed being with his side of the family.

At the time, Denver's population was just over 322,000, with its city limits roughly extending north from Evans Avenue to 52nd Avenue, and east from Sheridan Boulevard to Yosemite Street. This was an area of about 77 x 140 city blocks, with much of the outer areas of the city sparsely populated, and for the most part, undeveloped. It couldn't even begin to compare to the monolithic giants like New York City or Chicago, but it was enormous for this part of the country and a place we were always proud to call home.

The downtown grid of streets were laid out at an opposing forty-five degree angle from the remainder of the city's north-south/east-west streets, so it's a little hard to describe its actual dimensions. But, generally speaking, its downtown section extended sixteen blocks west from Broadway to Wynkoop Street, and eleven blocks north from West Colfax Avenue to 23rd Street. Most of the buildings in this area were from four to eight stories tall, but the 372-foot Daniels and Fisher tower at 16th and Arapahoe Streets was, indeed, worthy of skyscraper status.

Denver was founded in 1858, and from its inception gained notoriety as a wide open, anything-goes kind of town, and its most renowned street was still very much alive and well in

1941. Larimer Street was rife with flophouses, restaurants, rowdy dance halls and seedy bars, but none of Denver's bars were more infamous than Casey's Reno Bar on the northwest corner of 17th and Larimer Streets . . . and none of its restaurants were sleazier than the misnomered Sanitary Cafe, just three doors down.

But there were other, much more refined restaurants in town. The Ship's Tavern in the Brown Palace Hotel, the Manhattan at 1633 Larimer Street, the New Edelweiss and Navarre restaurants are some that come to mind, and they mixed gracefully with a variety of other less cosmopolitan restaurants and saloons. Among the more notorious of these were the Denver's Oldest Bar at 16th and Market Streets, and the Flying Dutchman at 18th and Curtis Streets, where only the toughest or truly masochistic men dared to go.

There were grocery stores and other small businesses throughout the neighborhoods of Denver, but until the first shopping mall opened its doors at the original Cherry Creek Shopping Center in 1953, downtown Denver was still the favorite place to shop for clothing, furniture, fine jewelry, and all your sporting good needs. Storefront windows at The American Furniture Store, The Denver Dry Goods, The May Company, Gano-Downs, Joslins, Neissners, Neusteters, Mayer's Jewelry, Gart Brothers, Dave Cook's Sporting Goods, and Woolworth's Five and Dime, prominently displayed nearly every type of goods imaginable, tempting thousands of shoppers each and every day . . . except on Sundays. Because of the religious based Blue Laws that were still in effect, stores weren't allowed to conduct business on the Lord's Day, and if there was something you desperately needed just to survive the night (like cigarettes or medicine), you were just plain out of luck.

Dignified brick and stone office buildings also adorned the downtown business district and included the City and County Building, State Capital Building, U.S. Mint, U.S. Post Office, Denver Public Library, Denver Auditorium, Denver Gas and

Electric building, Kittredge, Boston, Republic, and Equitable buildings, the Mining Exchange Building, U.S. National Bank, Central Bank, Colorado National Bank, and my favorite, the Denver Police Headquarters building at 1245 Champa Street.

Denver's Theater Row stretched from 14th to 16th on Curtis Street, and in its heyday, was saturated with movie theaters on both sides of the street for the entire length of these two blocks. Theaters included the State, Victory, Rialto, Isis, Colorado and Empress, with each theater trying to outshine the other with their ostentatious display of white lights, and with over 10,000 light bulbs brilliantly on display, Curtis Street was purported to be the brightest street in America.

But movie theaters weren't limited to Curtis Street. The Orpheum at 1537 Welton Street, Paramount at 1621 Glenarm Place, Denver at 510 16th Street, Broadway at 1756 Broadway, Denham at 1810 California Street, and the Tabor Grand Opera House at 16th and Curtis Streets added to the grandeur of modern entertainment facilities in Denver and were supplemented by several neighborhood theaters that included the Mayan at 110 Broadway, Webber at 119 South Broadway, Ritz at 1912 South Broadway, Ogden at 935 East Colfax Avenue, Aladdin at 2000 East Colfax Avenue, and the Bluebird Theater at 3317 East Colfax Avenue.

Stapleton Airport (named after Mayor Benjamin F. Stapleton) sat in the middle of wide-open fields at East 32nd Avenue and Quebec Street, which at the time, was the farthest northeast section of the city. It opened to a limited number of flights in 1929, but passenger flights didn't really get started until Saturday, May 15th, 1937, when United Airlines began flying two daily transcontinental flights to San Francisco, Chicago and New York City. The twin engine DC-3's brought the wealthier businessmen and tourists to town, but the incredibly busy Union Station railroad hub at 17th and Wynkoop Streets, literally brought thousands of people from all over the country.

Among the many hotels that helped accommodate these visitors were the Brown Palace, Shirley-Savoy, Oxford, Barth, Cosmopolitan, Adams, Kenmark, Burlington, Albany, and Bean hotels, but thanks to the urban renewal demolitions that took place during the 1970s, the old Burlington Hotel at 2205 Larimer Street (now residential lofts) and the elegant Oxford and Brown Palace hotels are the only three that survived.

The city provided other avenues of entertainment and recreation for its citizens with the Museum of Natural History at Montview and Colorado Boulevards, the beautiful old Elitch's Gardens at West 38th Avenue and Tennyson Street, and the Lakeside Amusement Park at West 46th Avenue and Sheridan Boulevard . . . and picnics and family outings were common in the lush grounds of City Park, Cheesman Park, Washington Park and the Greek Theater near downtown Denver.

But the leading form of entertainment for Mom and Dad came in the form of dancing. For the next several years, friends and family would get together for nights of big band revelry at places like the Rainbow Ballroom near 6th Avenue and Broadway, The Aeroplane Nite-Club in the 3500 block of Morrison Road, and the Trocadero Ballroom at Elitch's Gardens.

The Tivoli-Union Brewery (formerly the Milwaukee Brewing Company) and the nearby Coors Brewery in Golden supplied spirits for the entire region, and if you felt the need to drink and drive, you could finish your day at your choice of Denver General, Colorado General, St. Joseph's, St. Anthony's, St. Luke's, Presbyterian, Lutheran, National Jewish, Mercy, or Porter hospitals.

Public transportation wasn't great, but it wasn't too bad either. Miles of tracks were laid throughout the city, and the Denver Tramway Corporation's electric streetcars ran on most of the major streets leading into and out of the downtown area. There was no such thing as a comfortable seat on a streetcar, and the cars weren't heated during the freezing days of winter. Transferring to another streetcar at the Central Loop at 15th Street between Lawrence and Arapahoe Streets was always a welcome relief when you could go inside the terminal and warm yourself beside the overheated potbelly stove and drink a hot cup of coffee (or in my case, a steaming cup of hot cocoa), or just read about the world in general as you browsed through the magazines and newspapers at the shelter's well-stocked newsstand. And if the streetcars didn't take you where you wanted to go, there was a reasonable chance the city's motorized or electric busses could . . . as long as you didn't mind finishing the last few blocks of your journey on foot.

●

Aunt Rainie and her cousin Anna Lou were living in an apartment at East 12th Avenue and Pearl Street when Mom and Dad moved to town, and when Anna Lou moved out to get married, Mom and Dad moved in. It was a little awe inspiring for these country bumpkins to be living just ten blocks from the heart of the city, but the move opened a whole new world of opportunities for them that made them permanent residents for the rest of their lives.

By now, Mom was already two or three months pregnant with Darlene and was thrilled to be living somewhere with steam heat and indoor plumbing. Dad was getting $12.50 per week in unemployment; Aunt Rainie made $6 for her five and a half day workweek with Dr. Esposito (a local dentist), and Mom swept the halls of the apartment building in exchange for their $6 per month rent.

The Japanese invaded Pearl Harbor on Sunday, December 7th, 1941, and on December 8th, President Franklin D. Roosevelt declared war on Japan. Three days later, Adolph Hitler declared war on the United States, and America began its four-year battle of World War II.

The war had an incredible impact on our country, both in the loss of life and the depletion of our natural resources, and nearly every American made huge sacrifices to help with the war effort. But for our family, life continued to go on pretty much the same as it had before the war even started. The extreme food and gas rationing that took place for the duration of the war didn't really change our lifestyle, since we never had that much money for food or gas in the first place.

When Dad's unemployment benefits ran out, he decided against going back to the mountains. He claimed he'd hauled and personally secured each and every rock on that dam . . . all by himself . . . and that was more than anyone could have expected from him.

He managed to find various construction jobs around town, and even though the family was just barely surviving, they were always happy. With a good portion of the Aumiller clan already living in Denver, there was never a lack of good company to help brighten their day, which included Dad's new best friend from Heeney.

When Bill Wiley finished working on the dam, he moved to Denver to go to barber school. He didn't know many people in town, but he did know my dad, and was anxious to meet the rest of his family. When he came to visit the Aumillers one night, Dad introduced him to Aunt Rainie, and what I always thought was love at first sight apparently was not. Turns out Aunt Rainie wasn't that impressed with him in the beginning, and it took another two or three years before they really started seeing each other, and by then, he'd already joined the navy.

That was a tough way to start a new relationship, but he didn't let the military stand in his way. When he came home on leave between assignments, he took Aunt Rainie to one of his favorite little nightspots for a romantic night of dancing, and during the enchantment of the evening, asked her to marry him. She laughed and said, *"We barely even know each other, Bill...*

and besides, you're too drunk to know what you're saying." He agreed that he was probably drunker than he should have been, but told her he'd ask again when he was sober. Well, that gave her plenty of time to think about her answer, and when he finally sobered up enough to ask her again, she told him yes. Near as I can tell, he must have been one hell of a good dancer.

But the war had its own agenda, and he soon had to return to his Unit. He was a Pharmacist's Mate in the navy but served as a Marine in the Pacific Theater of Operations. After this tour of duty, he returned to naval duty in the United States and was assigned to a submarine unit in New London, Connecticut. Aunt Rainie took the incredibly long train ride to Connecticut and arrived on Saturday, April 1st, 1944, then, on Friday, July 7th, they were married. She stayed in Connecticut until January 1945, then they both returned to Denver where she'd continue to live, while he moved on to his new assignment in San Diego. In October 1945, he was honorably discharged from the service and returned to Denver to meet his son Rocky for the very first time. They had two sons: Rocky, who was born on Friday, May 11th, 1945, and Randy on Wednesday, November 26th, 1947.

When Uncle Bill went on the Denver Police Department on Tuesday, April 16th, 1946, the Aumillers were proud to have such an important man in the family, and as he steadily progressed to the rank of Captain, the family competed with one another for his favor. He had an extremely outgoing and confident personality and was a larger than life hero to me, and truth be told, he was the reason I wanted to be a policeman when I grew up.

•

Mom learned a valuable lesson about the lack of prenatal care when June was born, so we now had our own family doctor. Dr. Michael Bograd shared his practice with his brother Nathan at 1934 South Broadway and was our doctor until well into the 1970s. He was a rotund gruff sounding and unkempt old man, who always had a foul smelling cigar in his mouth . . . but despite his appearance and coarse bedside manner, he was, indeed, a great doctor. Throughout the 1940s and 50s, he'd make house calls whenever he was needed and treat us at home for any illness or injury that didn't require hospitalization.

During Mom's second pregnancy, he guided her through her prenatal care and was quick to respond to Presbyterian Hospital on Wednesday, June 24th, 1942 for the delivery of my sister Darlene Aloha Aumiller.

Sometime before Darlene was born, our family moved to an apartment at 711 Humboldt Street, but by August, they couldn't afford to pay their rent and had to move in with Granddad and Opal at 745 Lafayette Street (just across the street from Mamie Eisenhower's childhood home at 750 Lafayette).

By this time, Granddad and Opal already had their first four children: Truman LaVelle, who was born on Sunday, February 23rd, 1936, Orley Kale (Duck) on Tuesday, September 7th, 1937, Rochella Leota on Sunday, June 23rd, 1940, and Autrie Millrex (Autie) on Wednesday, June 3rd, 1942 (plus Uncle Lyle and Aunt Annavate), but fortunately, they were living in a very large house, and their quarters really weren't any more crowded than everyone was already used to.

Granddad and Opal would later have three more daughters: Roberta Ann (Bert), who was born on Saturday, February 15th, 1947, Romona May (Mona) on Friday, May 13th, 1949, and Roxanna Kay (Roxie) on Sunday, June 22nd, 1952.

Shortly before the war began, Aunt Rainie went to work as a reinspector and timekeeper at the Remington Arms Denver Ordnance Plant, and by the end of February 1942, Dad, Granddad Aumiller, Opal and Aunt Beulah were also working there. Granddad Aumiller was a fireman . . . Dad and Aunt Beulah made ammunition, and Opal made K-Rations for the military.

The Remington Arms Plant (now called the Denver Federal Center) had been contracted by the government and was built near West 6th Avenue and Kipling Street. At the time, it was considered to be *waaay* out in the country. It covered 2,040 acres, and employed up to 23,000 workers. Work was conducted twenty-four hours a day, seven days a week, and during the war, production never slowed down.

Since Mom and Dad could afford to live on their own again, they moved into an apartment at 916 Downing St. This was actually a large two-story house that had been converted into three separate apartments (two on the ground floor, and one on the second floor). Our family lived on the main floor and shared the upstairs bathroom with Opal and Mike Weller and their two little kids, the tenants of the second floor apartment.

Fortunately, Remington Arms provided Blue Cross/Blue Shield health insurance for our family, because when Dr. Bograd delivered me at Presbyterian Hospital on Sunday, February 20th, 1944 at 2:47 pm, there were serious complications with my birth. Because I was so premature, the delivery nearly killed both my mom and me.

When I was born, Dr. Bograd quickly put me aside and worked to save Mom's life and didn't return to me until she was stabilized. After several hours he told Dad there was a very good chance that neither of us would survive. Imagine how Dad must have felt with the prospect of raising June and Darlene on his own. Darlene, sure . . . ***But June???***

I only weighed four and a half pounds and was barely able to breathe on my own while I was confined to an incubator for the first three weeks of my life. Mom was in such bad shape, she didn't even see me for that first week, but by then, she was well on her way toward a full recovery and was able to go home. And through all this extra care, the insurance company paid everything but $25. *Oh, the good old days of health care!*

If I didn't already have enough working against me, I was also butt-ugly. I was born with a single Bucky Beaver style tooth in the center of my mouth; had long white hair all over my body, and was as wrinkly as an old man (the real Benjamin Button). They didn't even name me for the first several days and coldly referred to me only as Boy. But by the time I left the hospital, I was officially named. ***Dignity, at last!***

Dad wanted to name me Lyle LaVate after his brother Lyle and his dad LaVate, but Mom thought it would be a much better idea to name me William after her dad and brother, and LaVate after his dad and brother. This was a compromise even Dad couldn't refuse. But the rest of the family thought there were too many Bill's in the family (Bill Wiley; the two Bill Oldsons, and Bill Stoumbaugh), so they continued to call me Boy for the first year of my life.

Three was the magic number of kids for my parents, and it's probably a good thing they stopped with me. With quirky names like Anna Laura June, Darlene Aloha and William LaVate, there's a pretty good chance my next sister would have been named Beulah Carburetor, and I just couldn't have lived with that.

Dad   Mom
Kennedy (Tim) Murray   Edith (Margie) Marguerite

Anna Laura June   Darlene Aloha   William LaVate

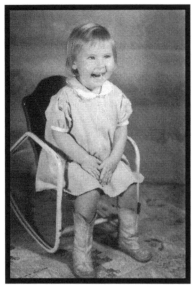

June

Dad, Mom & Darlene

Glenna (probably),
June & Darlene

June & Darlene

FOUR GENERATIONS:
Cora, LaVate, Dad & June

Granddad & Opal

Uncle Lyle in front of his home
in Selden

Granddad Aumiller & Dad in
Denver

Aunt Annavate

Aunt Lorraine (Rainie)

Aunt Ruth

Ruth, Annavate, Beulah, Rainie

Dad

Dad & Mom
at Granddad & Opal's home

Uncle Lyle

Dad and Uncle Lyle

Mom   Mom

These pictures of June were taken on the same day at 916 Downing Street - The one on the right was taken after spending the day with our neighbor "Auntie Vi"

74

CHAPTER 6

"The War"

By the spring of 1944, the war in Europe had grown even more intense for our American troops, and as preparations were being made for the June 6th D-Day invasion in Normandy, the Selective Service was calling up men who'd previously been at the bottom end of a very long list. Dad wasn't too thrilled with the prospect of going off to a war he thought would mean certain death for him, and felt with a wife and three little kids to take care of, he should move back to the less populated Green Mountain area in Grand County where he'd be less apt to be drafted. He wouldn't resist if he was called, but he wasn't about to volunteer to serve on his own.

There weren't a lot of jobs available in this part of the state once the dam was completed in November 1943, so when Dad returned to Heeney to find a new job, he went to the ranch where he'd worked before. Cully was more than happy to have a good man like Dad working for him again; so he quit his job at Remington Arms; packed everything we owned into the back of our old Ford, and moved us back to the mountains just as soon as he could.

The new job paid far less than he was making in Denver, and now instead of working a forty-hour week, he worked twelve hours a day, seven days a week. Well, that's almost true. He "only" worked six hours on Sunday mornings, then had the rest of the day off to enjoy as he saw fit — *Let the Good Times Roll*. But he was okay with that. Hard work wasn't something Dad was ever afraid of, and at least now the family was still together, and hopefully, would remain that way throughout the remainder of the war.

Cully had two or three log cabins scattered around the wooded hills of his property, and to augment the meager wages he was paying, provided our family with one of the smaller cabins to live in. A tiny one-room cabin pathetically furnished with only a small sofa, bare-bones kitchen table and chairs, and a bed sitting next to the old wood burning stove, it wasn't much of a house (by anyone's standards), but it was our own private little home where my sisters could romp and play without disturbing any of the Culbrath family.

On a day just like every other, Dad finished his long day at work and was home playing with June and Darlene while Mom was busy fixing dinner. She'd just finished boiling a bucket of water she'd later wash dishes with and moved it to the floor behind the rear corner of the stove. I was asleep in an old wooden dynamite box (my childhood crib), and at three months old, was much too young to be included in this kind of rough play even if I was awake. The girls were running and giggling as they tried to keep out of Dad's reach, when Darlene suddenly stumbled backward and fell bottom-first into the scalding bucket of boiling water. She shrieked and screamed as Mom and Dad raced across the room to pull her from her unbelievable torture, but they were much too late to save her from the excruciating pain she'd now have to endure.

She was burned so badly the skin on her tiny two-year-old bottom blistered and peeled within seconds. She was in **SO** much pain, and Mom and Dad were nearly panic stricken with fear. They were in the middle of the mountains and miles from the nearest doctor or hospital, so left with very few choices, did everything they could to comfort her and nursed her the only way they knew how.

Dad had a tin of Raleigh's Salve he knew worked really well on cow's chafed udders, so they smothered her bottom with this soothing salve and wrapped her with the cleanest cloth they could find.

As the evening drew on, Darlene finally cried herself to sleep while Mom held her as close to her as she could . . . comforting and caressing her with a mother's tenderness each time she whimpered from her nightmares and pain . . . fearful that her precious little daughter could actually die from the severity of her burns.

And her fears weren't without merit. Her oldest brother Voyde and his wife Iva lost their little boy just a few months earlier when he'd done the very same thing at their home. It was just that serious.

It was a very long night, but when the light of a more hopeful new morning filled the room, Darlene was stabilized and able to walk. They continued their treatment over the next several days, and in time, the burns completely healed. Her pink little butt stayed the same rosy pink it had always been, and she was lucky enough not to suffer from the scarring they feared most.

As it turned out, Dad's plan to circumvent the draft didn't work out at all. He received his draft notice by late that fall, and we moved back to Denver to live with Grandma Oldson in a little house in the 100 or 200 block of West Archer Place. Shortly afterward, we all moved to another house at 182 West Bayaud Avenue, which was just a few blocks north of the old white, eight story Montgomery Ward Store on South Broadway and Virginia Avenue . . . where we bought nearly everything we owned.

On Monday, November 27, 1944, Dad became one of more than 11,500,000 other young men who were drafted into the service during World War II when he began his military career with the U.S. Army at Fort Logan, Colorado. He served as a Private First Class with the 15th Engineer Battalion . . . his serial number, 37 713 867, was a number he was proud to remember for the rest of his life.

He went to boot camp at Camp Hood (later named Fort Hood), about sixty miles southwest of Waco, Texas, and after four rigorous months of Infantry Basic Training, set out on the first leg of his journey to the devastation of war-torn Europe.

A very long train ride took him from central Texas to New York City, where he spent just enough time to be overwhelmed by the sights and clamor of the most famous city in America. He toured the streets of Manhattan with several of his army buddies, and ended up in the Empire State Building, which, at the time, was the tallest building in the world. He only made it to the observation deck on the 86th floor before he found the place he really wanted to be, and in spite of his fear of the upper floors swaying in the wind, he managed to enjoy his afternoon drinking beer in one of the city's favorite tourist bars.

On Tuesday, April 24th, 1945, Dad sailed from New York City aboard the small, overcrowded, and remarkably unstable liberty ship, The Panotoc.

For the next thirteen days the tiny little ship bobbed like a cork . . . up and down . . . back and forth . . . over and over and over again. He got sick before they even left the harbor, and stayed that way for most of the trip. His only relief would come during those brief moments of calm seas, which, as he remembered, didn't happen that often. It was probably just as well though, because when he wasn't begging to be shot and put out of his misery, he'd worry about where he was. Since he'd never learned to swim, he had an inherent fear of water, and being in the middle of the ocean was a living nightmare for him.

Standing on the deck with no land in sight, he asked a crewman, *"How far do you think we're from land?"* Without even flinching, the sailor answered, *"Only about a mile."* Dad looked all around but couldn't see anything in view, then said,

"Yeah, in which direction?" "Straight down," the man replied, and Dad immediately got sick again.

On Monday, May 7th, 1945, their convoy arrived in LaHavre, France, and as the soldiers made their way down to the docks, everyone was pretty nervous about what they'd encounter. They knew the war was drawing to a close, but what they didn't know was that Germany would formally surrender the very next day and the war in Europe would be over.

Dad spent most of his time based in Garmisch, Germany, but traveled through several other German cities as well. These included Oberammergau, Augsburg, Nuremberg, Ingolstadt, Stuttgart, and Munich, where he saw more carnage and destruction than any civilized man could imagine . . . but his most memorable stop was just outside the quaint little town of Dachau, about ten miles northwest of Munich.

The Dachau Concentration Camp wasn't the most infamous of Germany's concentration camps, but it was the very first to be built. Completed on Wednesday, March 22nd, 1933 by the National Socialist (Nazi) Party, it was built to house political prisoners and any others who weren't sympathetic to Hitler's regime.

It wasn't designed to be an extermination camp, so compared to more than a thousand other death-camps that sprang up in other Nazi controlled territories, it was considered to be one of the most humane of them all (if that could even be a term to describe the atrocities that occurred there), with probably the fewest number of casualties. It housed more than 200,000 prisoners over the next twelve years, and by unofficial accounts, 31,591 prisoners died from disease, malnutrition, torture, hangings, shootings or suicide. This number included (as I remember) 6,000 Russians who were used as target practice by prison guards, and 15,000 others who tragically died in the last six months of the war.

The camp was rectangular shaped, covering an area approximately 750 feet wide (from east to west) and 2,700 feet long (from north to south). The entire perimeter was secured by concrete walls and dual electrified barbwire fences. Guard towers were spaced at intervals that allowed constant and complete views of the compound, and soldiers armed with machine guns never hesitated to shoot anyone who approached the walls.

A huge two-story administrative building nearly covered the entire width of the grounds at the bottom of the compound (the south end) and faced the assembly grounds immediately to the north. A deceptively serene looking tree-lined avenue ran north from the center of the assembly area and extended to the top of the camp. As you faced north from the assembly area, seventeen long rows of prisoner's barracks lined up from east to west on both sides of the avenue, with the thirty-four overcrowded barracks extending all the way to the north end of the camp.

A gravel road near the top of the camp exited the west side of the main compound and took you about 300 feet to the crematories. An irrigation ditch ran south through this road just inside the prison walls, with a small bridge that crossed over the ditch and allowed access to the crematory grounds.

The original crematory was built in 1940, but it soon became obvious that it was too small to handle the large volume of bodies, so in 1943, a new five-chamber crematory was added.

On Sunday, April 29th, 1945, Dachau was liberated by the 42nd Infantry Division of the American Seventh Army, and by the time Dad arrived nearly two weeks later, the camp was still filled with dead and dying prisoners. Even though the camp had been cleared of many of the diseased prisoners and its structures, it was still a horrific sight!

When Dad finally worked his way to the northwest end of the compound and crossed the irrigation ditch leading to the crematories, he watched as the slow moving water ran red with blood. When he reached the crematories, he found human bodies stacked four to six feet high along the east wall of the newer crematory, and took pictures of these unimaginable images on black and white film with a camera he bought shortly after arriving in Europe. He later gave these pictures to me, but they, to my eternal regret, were lost following my second divorce in 1984.

●

On Thursday, April 12th, 1945, the entire free world was stunned by the news that President Roosevelt died of a massive cerebral hemorrhage while visiting his favorite retreat in Warm Springs, Georgia. He was a hero to most Americans (at least to the Democrats) who, among other things, brought the nation out of the Great Depression, and now, after being elected to an unprecedented fourth term of office, was leading our country to a complete and unconditional victory over Germany and Japan.

His death was a great loss to our country, but couldn't begin to compare to the personal grief hundreds of thousands of individual families suffered through during the course of World War II. No American family seemed to be immune to the tragedy of war, and ours was no different.

On Thursday, May 24th, 1945, just forty-two days after President Roosevelt died, and seventeen days after Dad landed in Europe, Dad's brother Lyle, a Corporal in the United States Marine Corps, was killed during a bombing raid by the Japanese on the little known island of Okinawa. It would be more than a month before Dad learned of the horrific loss of his cherished brother, and now, alone, half a world away from the rest of his family, he grieved in solitude. It had an enormous impact on him, and as a child in the early 1950s, I can remember watching tears stream from his eyes whenever he talked about his brother. It was a horrible loss!

On Tuesday, March 1st, 1949, Uncle Lyle was returned to Denver from his temporary burial ground in Okinawa, and was buried in Block 38 at Fairmount Cemetery.

•

Dad was in Europe for five months as a Rifleman, and four months working as a mail clerk for his Company. With the war at an end, it was a far safer environment for the troops to be in, but there were still hard-line Germans who weren't happy with the results of the war, and it was still a dangerous place to be (much like the situation in Iraq in 2003—we won the war, but were still taking fire). For the next several months our soldiers were warned to keep alert to the dangers from snipers and other rebels, so to protect himself, Dad carried his M1 Garand nearly everywhere he went, and if he didn't have his rifle with him, he carried a confiscated .380 Walther semi-automatic pistol. He really wanted to see his family again.

Before finishing his tour of duty, he helped build emergency bridges with the 15th Engineer Battalion, 9th Infantry Division, and earned the European / African / Middle Eastern Service Medal; World War II Victory Medal, Rifle Marksman Medal, and a Good Conduct Medal. He was never in battle, but his memories of the complete destruction and death he saw in Germany stayed with him throughout his life.

On Saturday, January 26th, 1946, he began his eleven day journey home from LaHavre, France, and arrived in New York City on Wednesday, February 6th . . . two days quicker than his trip abroad . . . two fewer days of seasickness, *Thank God!*

America lost 418,500 soldiers during World War II, and Dad was always afraid he'd be one of them. He struggled with this fear until he was honorably discharged at Fort Logan, Colorado on Wednesday, February 13th, 1946 . . . his 26th birthday. After being away from his family for fourteen months and seventeen days, this truly was a ***great*** birthday present!!

We were still living with Grandma Oldson at 182 West Bayaud when Dad returned home, but she sold this house soon after he arrived and bought another small home at 429 South Stuart Street. We all moved into this house and lived there for the next several months, until our eventual move to the projects.

Dad: Ready to go to War - 1945

Dad in Germany 1945—He looks happier to be there
than he was!

Dad   Dad (left) & Army buddy

Uncle Lyle—Circa 1945

1945-1946

Me, on South Stuart Street

June & Darlene   Me

Mom, Darlene & Me   Mom -- a little less frazzled

Darlene & Me

88

Darlene, Me & June - Just before the body slam

Me on Stuart Street—
"Don't Ask; Don't Tell"

Pictures Mom sent to Dad in Germany
June, Darlene & Me

CHAPTER 7

"The Fire Department"

Dad spent the next several months working as a laborer at various construction sites around town until he learned the City of Denver was looking for a few good men for its police and fire departments. He applied for work through the Civil Service Commission, and after scoring high on the written, physical agility and oral tests, was hired on Thursday, May 1st, 1947. At that time the testing process was the same for both the police and fire departments, so just before he was sworn in, he was given the option of working for either department. He chose wisely.

The fire department paid far more than he was making in the construction business, and because his work was no longer seasonal, he now had the security of a guaranteed pay check on the 15th and end of each month. The fire department also offered a retirement plan that would allow him to retire at 50% of his salary after twenty-five years of service, which included an escalator clause that provided annual pay raises equal to those given to active members. If they'd get a 3% pay raise, he'd get a 3% pay raise, thus assuring he'd always stay ahead of inflation. In those days this was considered to be very sound financial planning.

Dad worked 24-hour shifts, followed by 24-hours off, and for the first few years of his career, never had two days off in a row unless he was on his eighteen day vacation or fifteen days of accumulated sick leave. For the remaining ten months of the year, he literally spent as much time with his co-workers as he did with his own family. But after a few years, the fire department initiated a new policy that gave the firemen a "Kelly Day," which (as I recall) was an extra day off every third week. This was a great new benefit for Dad because it gave him a three-day weekend once each month, and he was finally able to do the kinds of things normal people did on their days off, including sleeping in every once in awhile. Before that, he had to get up each and every morning at 6am (either to get ready for work at home, or to stand his 7am end-of-duty roll call at work), and never had enough days off in a row for even a simple weekend fishing trip.

Dad worked at Fire Station #8 (or 8s as the firemen called it) at 1616 Park Avenue, and may have worked at 13s at 600 South Broadway for a brief period of time, but these were assignments he'd had early in his career, and stations I'd never been to (at least that I can remember). Most of the first fourteen years of his career were spent at 15s at 1080 Clayton Street; a station I was very familiar with.

This ornate two-story graystone fire station sat at an angle on the southeast corner of the block, with its two bay doors facing northwesterly into the intersection. The tradition breaking all-white hook and ladder and pumper fire trucks backed into their parking spaces on the station's main floor, and the remaining great room was furnished with a small classroom area for in-service training, a sofa, two or three stuffed easy-chairs, a ping-pong table, and a clunky old wooden card table and chairs for nightly games of pinochle. In later years, the men all chipped in and bought a black and white television set, and replaced the sofa with three rows of surplus airliner chairs. In the 1950s the seats were a lot wider and more comfortable than those cramped little seats most of us ride in today, and were actually a pretty good place to lounge around and watch TV.

The kitchen was at the rear of the station and each shift had their own designated chef. Legendary meals were prepared in this kitchen, and if you never had their famous firehouse spaghetti, sausage and meatballs, you missed out on one of life's truly great pleasures!

Rows of single dormitory beds lined the oversized bedroom on the second floor, with bunkers resting beside each bed. When the alarm sounded in the middle of the night, the firemen jumped into their bunkers, pulled the suspenders over their shoulders, slid down the fire pole and were out of the house within seconds.

Each fireman had his own wooden locker in the hallway where he stored extra uniforms and toiletries, and the community showers and toilets were at the end of the hall.

During the course of their 24-hour shifts, the firemen worked together as a team in everything they did. Responding to emergency calls was always their first priority, but during the rest of the day, a strict regimen of duties was willingly complied with by every member of the crew. Beds were always made, floors were swept and mopped, the bathroom and kitchen were always kept clean and sterile, fire trucks were washed and polished, and all their gear was properly maintained and ready for service. When the chores were finished, time was allocated for daily in-service training, but after that, the remainder of the day was dedicated to personal recreation. Recreation included playing cards, pumping iron, playing ping-pong, shooting hoops, or working on their cars in the alley alongside the building. But by the early 1960s, the department felt this was an inappropriate practice and ended Dad's favorite pastime activity.

The station had one pay phone on the wall the firemen shared for personal calls, and in the evenings, they'd each take their turn so they could at least talk with their wives while they were gone for the day. To avoid paying for his calls, Dad would call home and let the phone ring twice, then he'd hang up. That was our signal that he was calling, and Mom would immediately call him back. We didn't do it often, but God help us if we answered the phone during those first two rings. Dad would lose his dime and we'd be in trouble for a month!

Dad had a lot of friends throughout the fire department, but the only men I remember were Jack Jaynes, Bill Levenhagen, Don Searcy, Bob (Pinky) Sparlan, Jim Jordan (the Department's premier Arson investigator) Jim Wolke, William Heddenskogg, Bob Burke and Bill Kellog. They were constantly "jobbing" each other with creative pranks, and no unlocked personal locker was ever safe from invasion or booby traps. And because Dad was so goosey, he was especially vulnerable to their attacks.

Late one night while he was walking the short distance from the bathroom to the bedroom, one of his co-workers stepped from the shadows wearing a full-face rubber mask of a grotesque and scary looking old man. Dad drew back his fists in fear, ready to fight for his life, and his bloodcurdling scream woke every person in the neighborhood. He was so impressed by the realism of the mask that he borrowed it and brought it home the next day to scare his family. (This was in the mid-1950s and we were living in our house on South Bryant Street).

He quietly snuck in the front door so he wouldn't wake any of us . . . donned the mask, and chuckled to himself as he walked into the bedroom to wake Mom. When he gently nudged her awake, she quietly turned over and sighed, but instead of being frightened like he was, she just looked up at him and smiled. Undaunted by her reaction, he went into our bedrooms and woke each of us, one kid at a time. But none of us were scared by this horrible face . . . we just thought he was having a really bad day.

Later in the morning, Dad laid down for a short nap. When Mom went into the bedroom an hour later to wake him, she put the mask over her head, carefully stood a safe distance away from the bed and called his name. He opened his eyes, drew back his fists in fear, ready to fight for his life, and his blood-curdling scream woke every person in the neighborhood.

When our relatives came to town, their visits almost always included a tour of the firehouse when Dad was at work. While showing the fire trucks to a group of our Oldson cousins during one of these visits, the shrill blast of a fire alarm suddenly pierced the air. *"Get out of the way!"* Dad screamed, but our elderly Aunt Daisy just froze in front of the truck. He ran to her, physically picked her up by her arms and set her aside, then jumped behind the wheel of the pumper, ready to impress everyone with the roar of the siren as he'd race away from the station. He started the engine, turned on the emergency lights and sat there in disbelief when none of the other firemen joined him. Precious seconds ticked away . . . crickets chirped . . . but no one moved. Dad frantically looked around for the rest of his crew and finally realized he'd been "punked" when he saw them all standing near the bay doors behind him, snickering over the success of their latest practical joke. There was no call . . . just another great prank played out at his expense, and all of my relatives just howled when they realized what had happened. *Dad was **SO** easy!!*

There were a lot of calls for service at 15s. Most of them for minor household fires, medical emergencies or extractions from wrecked cars, but in those days, the city was still filled with old run-down businesses and warehouses, and there were all too many working fires for the firemen to battle. When they responded to their next three-alarm fire, they were always willing and eager to risk their own lives in order to save the lives and property of complete strangers, and because they all knew their very lives could depend on the response from their fellow firemen at the next burning building, they formed a unique bond with one another that made them a true Band of Brothers, with a level of camaraderie unheard of in most jobs.

But waiting around the station for the next call could be a long and boring process, and on one particularly quiet evening, the serenity of their shift was abruptly interrupted by a very non-fire related event.

While some of the firemen were sitting around the card table playing their latest round of pinochle, and others were silently reading their books or newspapers, two firemen came walking down the stairs, and judging from the tone of their voices, they were very upset with each other. Because arguing or fighting was absolutely unheard of at the station, it caught the attention of everybody in the room and they all stopped what they were doing and turned to see what was going on. Two firemen got up from the card table and started toward them to intervene, but before they could reach the two arguing firemen, one of them yelled, *"I've had it with your bullshit,"* pulled a gun from his pocket and shot the other fireman point-blank in the center of his chest. As he fell to the floor, everyone froze in their tracks or jumped for cover, and Dad fell backwards in his chair, hitting his head against the wall as he desperately tried to get out of the line of fire. Before anyone could recover from the shock of the murder they'd just witnessed, the *"victim"* got up from the floor and the two arguing firemen busted out laughing. The gun turned out to be a .22 caliber blank starter pistol, and was totally incapable of firing a real bullet. When everyone finally understood what had just happened and managed to get all the *"What the fuck were you thinking?"* and *"You miserable assholes"* out of their systems, they all laughed and laughed, then judged it to be the greatest prank ever pulled at this station. This was just one more example of the fun they had together, but in the overly sensitive environment of the work place today, that same prank would probably have ended the careers of these two young firemen.

In 1951, Dad completed his first four years on the job and attained the rank of first-grade fireman. He was now eligible to apply for promotional exams, and in 1952, he tested for the rank of Engineer . . . a position that would allow him to handle the mechanics and hydraulics of the pumper. He passed on his first test.

In 1955, when the Department announced they'd be testing for the position of lieutenant, Dad decided to give it a try. Once he applied for the exam, he had ninety days to study the required books, and devoted all of his free time to this study, both on and off duty. He was even tutored by his good friend and Captain, Jack Jaynes.

On the day of his exam, he rushed through the questions, walked from the examination room, and was confident he'd aced the test . . . but when he received his letter from the Civil Service Commission, he was stunned to learn he'd failed by a mere fraction of a point. He was allowed to review his test, and much to his chagrin, discovered he'd missed questions he clearly knew the answers to. It was a huge disappointment for him, and unfortunately, set the tone for all of his future tests.

He completed his second test in 1957, and even though he was comfortable with his efforts, he wasn't as confident as before. He'd get so anxious and nervous during the tests that he'd rush through each question and just hope he could finish before his time ran out. He'd read the first part of the multiple choice questions, and when he saw an answer he was familiar with, he'd quickly mark it as the correct answer without checking any of the other options. Within days, he learned he'd failed this test, too, and again, by only a fraction of a point.

In 1959, he took his third and final exam, and this time he was ready. On the morning of the test, he took a doctor's prescribed tranquilizer that was guaranteed to keep him relaxed, and calmly meandered into the exam room.

Does anyone else see the flaw in this plan?

It was a mellow day . . . no worries . . . no panic attacks . . . and, unfortunately, no dice. This time he breezed through the exam and finished before anyone else, and when he walked from the room, he didn't even care how he'd done. When he received the test results, he wasn't disappointed to learn he'd failed by mere hundredths of a point . . . this time it was by several points. That was enough for him . . . he'd never go through that much time and energy again just to suffer from the humiliation of another defeat. But Dad was okay with that. He was still more than content with the job he already had, and for the remainder of his career, prided himself in being the best fireman he could possibly be.

When Jack Jaynes was promoted to Assistant Chief, he asked Dad to be his aide-de-camp and driver. Jack was probably the best friend he had on the job and he jumped at the chance to work with him again.

In 1961, he transferred to 23s at 850 South Federal Boulevard and worked there for the next seven years. We all liked it when Dad worked so close to our homes, because whenever we heard the sound of sirens, we knew he was hard at work, and probably rushing to help save someone's life.

In 1968, he moved to 10s at 3201 Curtis Street. This was the busiest station in the city, but it turned out to be a horrible assignment for him. It seemed like his entire shift was spent running from one call to another, and even the late evening and early morning hours were busy. Someone was always pulling a corner fire alarm in the middle of the night, and since false alarms were answered with the same urgency and adrenaline rush as real calls, getting back to sleep when he was finished wasn't always that easy to do. I kind of liked it though, because I was a new patrolman in his district and would cover most of his calls after three in the morning.

It didn't take long for the firemen to notice my name tag, and when they'd find out I was Dad's son, they'd ask why I didn't become a fireman too. *"That's easy,"* I explained. *"Firemen are crazy people. They jump through a hole in the floor and slide down a greased pole to a floor a full story and a half below them . . . they climb up ladders that are way too tall for any sane man to climb, and whenever they find a burning building, they stupidly rush straight into the middle of it instead of running away. Only a crazy man would do something like that."* They all agreed this was all probably true, but pointed out that none of them were crazy or stupid enough to chase after a man with a gun. I guess you just have to pick your own level of insanity.

When the firemen finished looking for any signs of a fire and reset the alarms, I'd follow them back to their station to enjoy a cup of coffee. Halfway through our break, another call would come in and we'd all rush off to the next false alarm. After the second call, I'd had enough. When they returned to their station, I stayed behind, hiding in the shadows and anxious to make my next arrest. I never caught anyone pulling an alarm, but at least Dad and his friends got to finish their night's sleep.

He worked at 10s for only about a year, then transferred to 26s at 7045 East 38th Avenue, just west of the airport. He got a lot more sleep there.

In 1971, in preparation for his retirement, he stopped driving Chief Jaynes and transferred to the Fire Prevention Bureau at 12th and Champa Streets, just south of the police headquarters building. This was a good move on his part for two very good reasons. First, because it came with a promotion to the rank of Technician, and secondly because his upcoming pension would be greater because it would be based on his current salary. It also offered a drastic change in his working conditions, and now instead of working twenty-four hour shifts, he worked from 8am to 4pm, Monday through Friday, and the department gave him a take-home car to drive back and forth to work. He liked the change in his routine, and it kind of helped him ease into the unfamiliar territory of sleeping at home every evening.

On Tuesday, January 16th, 1973, after twenty-five years, eight months and fifteen days of dedicated and honorable service, my fifty-two-year-old dad finally pulled the plug. It was a spur of the moment decision, but one I'd later completely understand. There comes a time when you know you're ready to retire, and when it happens, ***it's time to go!***

I have very few regrets in my life, but my greatest is not going to Dad's retirement party. I'd already committed to an off-duty job on the night of his party, and told him I wouldn't be able to make it. Dad had an incredible work ethic and taught me to always do my very best at work and honor any obligations, so I was sure he'd understand why I couldn't come and would be proud of my dedication to my job.

But I was wrong.

He later told me it really bothered him when I didn't join in his celebration, and hearing him say it almost broke my heart. He was always there for me, and I should have been there for him.

Definitely my biggest regret in life!

Dad - A brand new fireman 1947

Dad & friend waiting for the next call at 15s

Denverite Burned When

Firemen William Levenhagen, left, and Ken Aumiller of Engine Company 15 inspect a charred closet door in the bedroom where Mrs. Madeline Gardner was critically burned Sunday. The fire gutted the bedroom. Fire officials said the blaze may have been caused by careless smoking.
—*Rocky Mountain News Photo by Bob Talkin.*

Fire at 4101 E. 3rd Avenue on February 26, 1956
The caption says "Ken" Aumiller is on the right, but he's actually on the left. Bill Levenhagen is on the right.

Dad & co-worker cleaning the rigs at 15s

Work, work, work

1950 Company photo in front of 15s at 11th & Clayton
Dad is kneeling in the middle of the left group

Dad in the center, Jack Jaynes top right, and their
traditional firehouse Dalmatian

I believe this was taken when he worked at 10s
Circa 1968

The last picture of Dad as a fireman
Fire Prevention Bureau—1971

CHAPTER 8

"The Projects"

Soon after the war ended, the government dismantled some of the army barracks at Camp Hale near the Colorado mountain town of Leadville, and moved them to a new Veterans Housing Project in north Denver. They were managed by the Denver Housing Authority, but unlike most other housing projects in the city, they weren't dedicated to low-income level families, and I think every man who lived there was gainfully employed and fully capable of paying his own rent.

When I was three-years-old, we left Grandma's home on South Stuart Street and moved into these new "Projects" (as we lovingly called them) and lived at 1340 West Alice Place-A. Mom couldn't remember exactly when we made the move, but knew it was shortly before Dad went on the fire department on May 1st, 1947.

There were eight barracks in our projects . . . two barracks long between Lipan and Pecos Streets (from east to west) and four barracks deep between West 47th and West 46th Avenues (from north to south), exactly where the Denver Police Department's new District One substation now sits. The unadorned wood framed two-story buildings were trimmed with a shoddy drab-gray shingle siding and were just about as ugly as they could possibly be. Our apartment (a euphemism for stark living quarters) was in the east block of barracks, and we lived in the middle section of the second row from the north.

A large graveled playground sat just across the road from the east end of our barrack and was equipped with three rows of those hard black rubber-seat swing sets, monkey bars, a set of elevated horizontal ladders, a chin up bar, a very tall slide, and a flat metal stand-on Merry-Go-Round. Since child safety wasn't really a major concern in those days (it was "proper neglect") we all had our fair share of scrapes and bruises from the unregulated joys of childhood play . . . but we didn't care. We were all just normal little kids; playing hard and having fun, just like all little kids of my generation did.

The barrack complex was the largest part of our community, but was augmented by several small metal Quonset huts that less than graced the dirt lot just east of the playground. One of Denver's busiest railroad yards sat immediately east of these huts, and the blare of train whistles and clanking of rolling trains were heard at all times of the day and night. But the sounds became pretty routine to us, and over time, we hardly even noticed them.

But what we never got used to was the disgusting stench from Denver's thriving stockyard compound, just two miles east of our home. If air conditioning even existed in those days, we certainly weren't privileged enough to have it, and with our windows wide open during most of the summer months, we were consumed by the vile aroma of recycled wheat and hay.

The skyline of downtown Denver was clearly visible just southeast of our neighborhood and was a constant reminder of our urban roots. A large triangle-shaped red neon Conoco sign sat on top of one of the tall buildings in the northwest part of the city, and by evening, drew your attention to the majesty of old town Denver. The seemingly endless rows of buildings, and especially the 21-story Venetian inspired campanile at the Daniels and Fisher building, proved that Denver was, indeed, a city of distinction . . . and in my mind, far superior to that little town of Selden.

There were no trees, shrubs or lawns in our entire community. Each barrack was separated by an asphalt road, leaving dirt voids between the road shoulders and each barrack. Parking was allowed in this area in front of our unit, but the dirt frontage area on the backside of our building was pretty much used by the kids to play in. It wasn't really as bad as it looked, but some of the few pictures we have of us playing in front of the projects look like photos of child inmates in the Nazi era concentration camps.

Clothes lines were stretched between wooden poles and the barracks at various points along the front side of our building and were available to all the tenants on a first come, first served, basis.

The front door of our home faced south, and this entry was accessed by a five-step wooden stairway. Once you entered the unlocked outer door, you found our closed front door on the right, or the long stairwell leading straight up to the second floor apartment. Jackie and Paul Bobeck, and their three children, Sonny, Gloria, and Charlotte . . . and Anna Mae (a niece Paul and Jackie also raised) lived in the apartment just above us and soon became some of our very best friends.

The back door and landing faced north, and our back steps were covered by a large wooden two-story fire escape. We only used this back door when we were going outside to play or walk to the grocery or Five & Dime Store in the Chaffee Park Shopping Plaza at West 48th Avenue and Pecos Street.

The interior of our home was really pretty simple. When you came through the front door, you entered our kitchen, and as you looked straight across from the door to the east wall, you saw a small gas stove to your left and the kitchen sink and cabinets directly in front of you. A large white wooden potato bin, refrigerator and portable ringer washing machine sat against the front wall to your right (south), and our retro chrome metal kitchen table and chairs sat immediately to your left.

The kitchen extended to the north (much like the long interior of an empty trailer), and with no visible signs of separation, merged directly into the living room. A cheap brown cloth sofa backed against the east wall, with an even cheaper coffee table sitting directly in front of it. A small dark cushioned side chair sat against the north wall, with an end table and lamp to its left (east); and our furnishings were completed with a tall old 78-rpm record player that backed against the west wall. The walls were all painted with a non-descript off-white, almost yellow color, and if we had any pictures hanging on our walls, none of them come to mind.

A doorway midway between the kitchen and living room on the east wall (to your right), led to two bedrooms and our bathroom. The bathroom, on the right as you walked through the doorway, had a shower stall, sink, and toilette (in that order), and, as I vividly remember, a razor strop hanging from a hook on the back of the door. There was no bathtub.

Each room had a single screw-in light fixture on the ceiling with a 100 watt light bulb that was turned on and off with a drawstring (long enough for each of us to reach). There were no wall switches or decorative light globes in any room of our house.

An alcove at the northwest end of the living room took you west past the backside of the second floor stairwell to your left, and the back door of the apartment to your right, and into the third, much larger bedroom.

Before we bought our first refrigerator in 1950, we had an old rustic icebox that sat in the little cubbyhole below the stairwell, and when our supply of ice ran low, Mom would put a white square posterboard placard in our kitchen window to alert the iceman that she needed more. A motorized flatbed ice truck made routine deliveries to our community, and when the delivery man saw our placard, he'd stop; grab a couple of large blocks of ice with those heavy metal tongs and haul them directly from his truck to our icebox. While he was busy making his deliveries, we'd climb into the bed of his truck and steal chips of ice until we'd see him walk back out of the barracks. He'd yell, *"Get away from that truck,"* and we'd

110

scamper like rats . . . still sucking on our stolen booty; giggling with each step of our escape. He always acted like he was mad at us, but, in reality, I think it was as much of a game to him as it was to us.

•

In the evenings, we'd all gather around our radio that sat on top of our refrigerator in the kitchen, and listen to our favorite radio shows. Through the magic of rudimentary sound effects, terrifying women's screams, and suspenseful music, we could easily imagine just how each of the characters and their sur-roundings appeared as we cringed in fear at the high drama of radio broadcasting that played out before our very ears. Our imaginations ran wild with the thrills of such classics as The Inner Sanctum, Dragnet, The Shadow, Superman, Sergeant Preston of the Yukon, Sky King and the B-Bar-B Ranch, and The Green Hornet; and we'd giggle and laugh at the comedy of programs like Amos and Andy, Fibber McGee and Molly and The Jack Benny Show.

When our nightly shows ended, we'd gang up on Dad in the middle of the living room floor and try to wrestle him to the ground. We never won, of course, but it wasn't because of a lack of trying. When he'd get tired of wrestling, he'd get on his hands and knees and we'd scramble to be the first on his back for a wild bucking bronco ride. As he bucked and twisted and thrashed about, we'd hold onto the back of his T-shirt with everything we had; laughing and screaming in absolute glee until we were gracelessly hurled to the floor. When one of us went flying, another would jump on; urging him to buck even more. Mom would sit on the couch and watch . . and laugh . . as she diligently darned our worn out socks. A mother's work is never done!

On other nights, Dad would teach me how to fight. He knew fighting was a part of growing up for little boys and wanted me to be prepared for the bullies I'd meet when I started school. He'd get on his knees in front of me and say, *"Put your duke's up,"* then quickly (but gently) slap my face with his open hands. I'd block his punches as best as I could, then charge into him with a barrage of failed punches; never quite able to get past his long arms to reach his face. It was always a one-sided contest until Mom finally stepped in and said if it was going to be a fair fight, Dad's arms needed to be as short as mine. She stepped into her bedroom for a few seconds; returned with her terrycloth bathrobe; removed its long belt and tied it tightly around Dad's upper arms and chest, leaving only his forearms and hands to fight with, then said, *"Okay . . . now fight."* It was wonderful! Dad couldn't get his short little Tyrannosaurus Rex arms up high enough to defend his face, and I'd smash his chin and nose with as many punches as I could throw before he finally managed to jump to his feet, laughing and screaming, *"Stop It . . . Stop You Little Shit!"* And I learned my very first cuss word.

On Sunday mornings, we'd sit on the kitchen floor in front of the radio and spread the comic pages of the Denver Post in front of us and listen intently as radio personalities acted out each colorful panel. Overacting celebrities with cartoon voices added a whole new dimension to the antics of our favorite funny page characters and made this a time worth waiting for.

Dad sold the old Ford before he went into the army and we were still without a car. When Grandpa Murray died on Sunday, February 8th, 1948, Dad had to borrow Aunt Rainie's car so he could go to his funeral in Selden, and when he returned home, decided it was time to buy another car. He bought Uncle Voyde's old maroon 1941 Ford, and once again, we were independently mobile.

We went to a lot of movies in the days before television, and during the summer months, we'd usually go to the drive-in movies. Since our entire family could get in for about the same price as one adult at the downtown theaters, this was definitely the place to go. Whenever a new movie opened, Dad would load the family into the car and we'd drive to the North Drive-

In Theater at 7300 Federal Boulevard, or the West Drive-In Theater at 601 Kipling Street. Dad would find a parking spot and pull forward and backward on the parking hump until we were in the perfect position for everyone to see the screen, then the three of us kids would run to the playground at the base of the big screen while we waited for the sun to set. Mom and Dad stayed in the car and listened to the pre-movie music on one of those tinny sounding car speakers.

As the sun set over the mountains, they'd project a game onto the screen to entertain the men. Most cars had spotlights in those days, so the men were challenged by the bright image of a cartoonish looking character named Spot, who dared them to follow him as he quickly moved from one spot to another. When the game ended and the advertisements for the concession stand began, we'd scramble back to our car so we wouldn't miss any part of the movie. Dad would lean as far to the left as he could and Mom would lean to the right, and we'd huddle together in the center of the back seat and watch the best fare Hollywood had to offer.

These were family nights, but on weekends, we'd visit Grandma Oldson and Aunt Daisy for our weekly kids day movies. We'd walk the ten blocks from their home at 424 Galapago Street to the Mayan Theater at 110 Broadway, where we'd buy our popcorn, milk duds and coke before the show began, then settle in for an afternoon of pure joy. A newsreel showed the latest news of the week, followed by two or three cartoons, then a cliffhanger serial adventure would begin. The show always ended with someone in extreme peril, so we never wanted to miss the next episode to see how they survived. When the pre-shows were finished, we'd sit back and watch a Bowery Boys, Abbott and Costello, Laurel and Hardy, or Bob Hope and Bing Crosby movie.

And if we still hadn't seen enough, the housing authority set up a theater at the west end of our barrack, and on summer weekend nights (weather permitting), the entire neighborhood could sit down and watch an all-star array of old 16mm films that were projected onto the west end of our barrack. Simpler times, but wonderful memories!

●

Uncle Bill Oldson (Mom's brother), Aunt Wanda and our cousins Glenna, Terry and Sherry moved into the Quonset huts sometime during the late 1940s, and lived there for most of the time we were at the projects. Uncle Bill was a mechanic with the Rio Grande Motorway trucking company, and worked for them from Tuesday, February 28th, 1950, until they went out of business in 1976. We'd spent a lot of time with our cousins long before they moved to the projects, so they were already good friends by the time they arrived. Our other childhood friends included the Bobeck kids, Robbie and Billy Marsh, who lived across the street in the barrack just south of us, Billy and Stevie Tan, and Jackie Sue Craven, who lived in apart-ments just east of us.

On the day I met three-year-old Billy Tan, he shyly asked his mother what my name was, and she answered, *"Why, he's Billy, too."* He looked a little confused but knew what he'd heard, and from that day on called me "Billy Two." It was an endearing name that I always liked and was much, much, nicer than a similar "Number Two" name my three ex-wives would later call me.

The two Billy's were my best friends, and Jackie Sue was my absolute heartthrob. She was about five years older than me, and was an ***incredibly*** beautiful little girl. I saw her about six years after we'd moved from the projects, and by that time, she'd grown into an even prettier version of Marilyn Monroe. Believe me, you can't get more beautiful than that! If the law had allowed it, and she was interested in a moonstruck fifteen-year-old dirty young boy, I would have married her on the spot (or at least given her a new house like I'd later do with most of my future wives). She was just that beautiful!

114

Some of my greatest childhood memories include the warm and peaceful summer evenings in our poor little corner of the world, where under the faint glow of the occasional incandescent street light, the neighborhood kids would gather in the middle of the street and play games like kick-the-can and tag, while the adults sat on old bus stop benches in front of our apartment and laughed and talked and carried on. There was always a feeling of warmth and safety as we embraced the innocence of our youth under the protective umbrella of our loving parents, and to me, those childhood images are truly reminiscent of classic Norman Rockwell paintings.

We all have special stories from our childhood years, and some of my favorites come from those poor and innocent days in the projects with my sisters . . . snippets of family lore that have been repeated and laughed about by my family for the past sixty years . . . stories that begin with the hot summer day in 1948 (or somewhere thereabouts) when June and I were at the playground (probably fighting with each other), while Darlene stayed at home to help Mom with dinner. Darlene was always trying to emulate Mom's finest characteristics and was a natural when it came to domestic duties. When they were nearly finished, my precocious six-year-old sister turned to Mom and said, *"We're not going to call those little bastards to supper, are we?"*

Mom was stunned!! But because she was so tickled by such an outrageous statement from such a precious little angel, Darlene didn't get into trouble . . . and the little bastards were called to dinner.

Dressing up in Mom's clothes was always a great treat for my sisters when they were little girls. They'd each put on one of her full-length slips and pretend they were dressed in wonderfully sophisticated evening gowns, then "delicately" highlight their faces with makeup. With serious applications of mascara, rouge and bright red lipstick, they were transformed into elegant and enchanting ladies . . . or cheap looking sluts, depending on your point of view.

Darlene was so enamored by a pair of Mom's fancy red high-heel shoes, she once asked if she could have them when Mom "kicked the can." Darlene was always such a good little girl, but no one ever really knew what was going to come out of her mouth next, and I don't think she understood Mom would actually have to die in order for her to get those shoes.

June was *much* older than me, and by now was really quite a vixen . . . it seemed like all the boys were after her. When she was probably only eleven or twelve years old, she was allowed to go with a boy to a show at the "Q Center," the neighborhood Community Center just southeast of our home. After the show, they walked to the Sunny Side Drug Store at 4600 Lipan Street for a cherry coke (and anything else she wanted), and Darlene and I snuck around behind them to watch everything they did. We peeked through the west window and were amazed to see that this boy had two whole dollars to spend on his date. That was a lot of money for a kid in those days.

Going to the playground alone in the projects was a common occurrence for us kids, but on one unusually eventful summer afternoon, the entire family was there. As the sun began to set, we could hear the mumblings of a man who was standing on the south side of a three-foot metal fence that protected the south end of the playground from the road. Even though it was pretty clear our parents were with us, the man began yelling, *"Billy, come here,"* probably learning my name after hearing the repeated chant *"Billy, stop being such a brat"* from my mother and sisters. Not understanding how inappropriate this was, I started walking toward him. Dad yelled for me to stop, then walked to the man and asked why he was calling me. But instead of apologizing or giving any excuse, he challenged Dad to a fight.

That was such a mistake!

Dad just loved a good fight, and in the next few seconds, in a flurry of punches, had this probable child molester beat to the ground. I'd never seen a man hit so many times in my life, and to me, it was absolutely awesome! Mom found a short 2x4 lying on the ground nearby and came running toward Dad; swinging it like a bat. At the time, I thought she was coming over to hit him for fighting again, but later learned she was only coming over to help kick some serious butt.

It soon became very clear to Darlene and me, that as responsible children of a *real* fireman, we should learn to practice the elementary basics of fire safety. With the help of two or three of our little friends, we climbed into the crawl space below our apartment and began starting controlled fires with kindling wood we found lying throughout the underbelly of the barrack. After each fire, we'd sound the alarm, then rush over and smother the flames with dirt. We thought we were heroes.

A neighbor lady who was outside hanging laundry, saw smoke pouring from the access door and called the fire department, and within minutes, we were whisked outside by several disgruntled firemen.

Mom was so embarrassed!!! She told the fire captain Dad was a new fireman on the department and assured him he'd punish us when he got home the next day. Thankfully, the captain accepted her word and released us with only a warning, but the moment they left, Mom turned to us and said, *"Just wait till your father gets home!!"*

OH MY GOD!!! THE HORROR!!!

We knew how grouchy Dad could be, and the anticipation of facing him the next day was almost unbearable!

Neither of us slept much that night, and in the morning, we heard Dad come into the house. We could hear the muffled tones as Mom was talking with him, and even though she was probably telling him not to be too harsh with us, what we heard was, *"Beat them half to death!"*

When Dad finally called for us, we were so afraid we could barely move. A soulful voice sang *"Nobody Knows The Trouble I've Seen"* as we inched our way into the living room; holding each other's tiny little hands and dragging our Teddy Bears behind us. Angels wept for our souls, for doom was surely near. *Oh, the humanity!*

When we tearfully looked up at the towering figure of our very serious father, he broke into laughter. What we were going through was far worse than anything he'd planned, and he couldn't bring himself to punish us any further. He later told us it looked like we'd been on a two-week drunk and were just too pitiful to punish any more. We didn't get spanked, and promised we'd never do anything like that again . . . ever!

But the most vivid memory for me occurred when I was just five years old. My sisters and I were playing in the street in front of our home when we saw a Denver police car driving west toward us from the playground. We stepped into our dirt yard to get out of its way, and watched silently as the old black and white humpback '48 Ford slowly cruised closer and closer. When it reached our side, it stopped. The tough and mean looking policeman on the passenger side leaned his head out of the window and gruffly asked, *"Are you Billy?"* My heart dropped a full two feet to the ground as I quietly whispered, *"yes,"* then the car door opened and the biggest policeman I'd ever seen stepped out and told me to get in the back seat (I had no idea why I was being arrested, but I was pretty sure I was guilty). I scooted to the center of the massive back seat, my skinny little legs sticking straight out in front of me, my tiny little feet barely breaking the edge of the seat. I sat there quietly, trembling, trying to look as innocent as I possibly could. As the car started to drive away, I wondered if I'd ever see my family again, then suddenly, my sisters started jumping up and down, screaming, *"Uncle Bill, Uncle Bill."* The driver stopped the car and turned to me . . . and laughed. It was my Uncle Bill Wiley.

I'd never been so relieved in my life, and from that day on, I wanted to be a policeman. Who else could have that much fun scaring little kids and get paid for it? *They were absolutely awesome!*

●

Winters in the projects always seemed so bleak. There were no graceful snow-flocked trees or sculpted bushes to beautify the landscape, and the contrast of the drab colored barracks against the snow and mud covered grounds gave the illusion of a bitter and forsaken military outpost. On the coldest of days, smoke from the Public Service Company power plant, residential coal or oil-fueled furnaces and burning backyard trash incinerators smothered the city with a degree of pollution unheard of in modern times.

Driving through the snow and ice with our threadbare recapped tires was always treacherous, and unless it was absolutely necessary, we'd stay at home. Street clearing and snow removal were minimal compared to today's standards, and cars were constantly getting stuck on some of the hills throughout the city. To help compensate for this failing, the city placed green-colored fifty-five gallon barrels of sand on the sides of the steepest roads to help stranded motorists. Drivers could scoop sand under their rear tires and were almost always able to get the traction they needed to move ahead.

But even without the snow, the short days and long nights of winter seemed very harsh, and the freezing temperatures only fostered our growing boredom. With city parks no longer hospitable, drive-in movies closed for the season and our play-ground equipment too cold to play on, we'd bide our time and patiently wait for the arrival of spring.

Dad filled his winter days by working his three or four 24-hour work shifts each week, working an occasional part-time job somewhere, or meeting with friends for a beer or two at one of his favorite little bars. Always the perfect housewife and devoted mother, Mom spent her weekdays cleaning our home, washing and ironing clothes, getting us ready for school in the mornings, and taking care of us when we got home. She made most of the clothes for herself and my sisters, and spent a lot of her time at her manual push-pedal sewing machine.

Since Dad drove to work every other day, the only way Mom could have the car was to take him to work in the morning and pick him up the next day. We'd always ride along with them, and when we'd get to the station, Dad would take us inside and show us his great firefighting equipment. I'd put on his bunkers and helmet and wield one of his axes; pretending I was the one crashing through that burning door to save little babies and kittens and anyone else who needed to be saved. When I was finished, Dad would thrill us all by jumping through that big round hole in the second story floor, and sliding quickly down the greased fire pole to the hard rubber mat on the floor below. He'd let us climb into the front seat of the hook and ladder truck, and he'd tap the siren just enough to hear a short burst, then turn on all the emergency lights so we could imagine ourselves racing to the next blazing fire.

A white metal brace stood up from the center of the windshield and supported three short white metal arms that resembled an airplane propeller. A large red light was attached to the end of each arm, and when the lights were turned on, this "propeller" would slowly rotate. There were white spotlights on both sides of the windshield, and a large bright oscillating white light and siren on the hood of the truck. The lights weren't as effective as the strobe lights of today, but the deep toned Four Mile manual siren always got everybody's attention.

It was such a thrill to visit Dad at the fire station, and as we'd slowly drive away, we'd look back and wave; proud that we were the children of Denver's finest fireman!

On weekends, we'd visit Grandma and Aunt Daisy at their home at 424 Galapago Street, or go for a Sunday morning breakfast at Granddad and Opal's house at 1007 Ogden Street. But during the school week, our afternoons and evenings were spent inside the boundaries of our apartment.

My sisters and I were generally well behaved, but when Dad was at work, we'd constantly push the limits of Mom's patience with an overabundance of childhood energy. She'd usually let us play as hard as we wanted, but as the evenings wore on, she'd set us down to listen to the radio, color in our coloring books, or have us help put together a jig-saw puzzle. Around 7:30 each evening, she'd make us take our showers, then with a sigh of relief, send us off to bed. She'd end her day by sitting down with a civilized cup of hot tea while she worked the newspaper's daily crossword puzzle.

Mom was always so much more forgiving of our antics than Dad, and on the days he was home, we'd try our best to act like well-behaved children. Sometimes it worked, and sometimes it didn't. Most of the time we couldn't help but resort to our true personalities and Dad would be forced to rein us in. He was a very strict disciplinarian, and even though I don't remember him ever using it, we always feared the razor strop hanging from the bathroom door.

●

I started school in the fall of 1949, and joined my sisters at Garden Place Elementary School at 4425 Lincoln Street. During the remainder of our years in the projects, Darlene and I attended this school, but when June started the seventh grade, she moved on to Horace Mann Junior High School at 4130 Navajo Street.

Garden Place was built in the old Globeville section of the city, which was generally inhabited by older Slovakians and Poles who'd outgrown the need for an elementary school. To help justify the school's existence, the School Board bussed kids in from the projects to fill the half empty classrooms, but unlike the court-mandated bussing that began in the 1960s, our being bussed had nothing to do with integration. In those days, most white Americans were still very comfortable with their prejudices, and racial equality didn't seem to be an issue.

The three-story red brick building was probably only a dozen years old, but looked much older to me (actually, all buildings in the 1940s looked old to me). The rooms and hallways were painted with that asylum colored pale green paint, but were accentuated with intricately trimmed dark wooden doors, windows, and framed classroom blackboards (which in those days were actually black). Sputtering steam radiators struggled to heat the cold high ceiling rooms, and the unmistakable bouquet of dank cellars filled the air. Rows of old fashion wood/iron desks with pigtail dunking ink wells lined each room and faced straight ahead toward the teachers large foreboding desks. Banners showing the written alphabet in perfect script ran the full length of the wall above the blackboards, with an American flag standing just to their left. Before our first class began each day, we'd stand at attention and face the flag as proud and patriotic young American children; put our tiny right hands over our hearts, and dutifully recite the Pledge of Allegiance. It made us feel all grown up.

The fifteen-minute drive on our bus gave us plenty of time to play with friends before school, and we'd usually get there early enough to play a game of box hockey in the courtyard or inside the main foyer before our classes began.

Waiting for the school bus at the west end of our barrack was also a good time to play, but in a world full of bullies, playing's not always the order of the day. For reasons I can't remember, Sonny, our upstairs neighbor, started shoving me around during one of our short waits, mercilessly goading me into a fight I couldn't possibly win. Make no mistake . . . I liked to fight when I was a kid. I was in the Principal's Office at least once a week for fighting (or so it seemed), where our matronly old principal Mrs. Holmes would glare at me through her tiny round Gestapo wire framed glasses, pen my name in her notorious Big Black Book, and write, *"He did it again—see the last 90 pages for details."* Actually, I never saw what she wrote, but I'd love to see that book today.

But fighting Sonny was not something I wanted to do. He was five years older and much bigger than me, so I cowered away in fear, trying my best to keep out of his reach. Then suddenly, from out of nowhere, June stepped between us and punched him square in the nose.

Blood spewed everywhere!

He backed away in disbelief, completely embarrassed by being beaten by a girl, and listened repentantly as she made it quite clear that picking on me was her job, and no one else had that right. I didn't care... *because on that day, she was my HERO!!*

•

As December rapidly approached, winter took on a whole new meaning. Bleakness gave way to the spirit of Christmas as we prepared for three of the most important events of the season. The first was going downtown to see the Christmas lights, the second was decorating our Christmas tree, and the third was the holiday itself.

By the first of December, the holiday season officially began when the Christmas lights were turned on at the City and County Building, a structure that filled the entire city block at 1437 Bannock Street. As many as 30,000 colored lights washed over the building's facade and clock tower, with red and blue floodlights softly illuminating each of the forty vertical four-story Greek colonnades. The grounds were sprinkled with lush Evergreen trees, liberally trimmed with brightly colored Christmas bulbs, with a life-size Nativity scene gracing the front steps of the building. But the greatest sight for us was the full sized model of Santa and his sleigh being pulled by eight reindeer, with Rudolph at the lead. This was one of the most spectacular Christmas displays in America, and being there on a cold winter's eve was a very special time for our family.

When Mom and Dad could finally persuade us to leave, we'd walk over to 16th Street, where for the next several blocks, every light pole and traffic light was adorned with Christmas lights and garland. The sidewalks were crowded with families who'd come to see the wonderful animated Christmas scenes in the street level windows of The May Company and The Denver Dry Goods, and we'd *"ooh"* and *"ahh"* over all of the toys prominently on display.

A week or two later, we'd drive to the nearest Christmas tree lot and carefully inspect each and every tree they had to offer. When we were sure we'd found the perfect tree (in our price range), Dad would load it in the trunk or tie it to the top of our car, then take us back home for our second greatest joy of the season . . . decorating our Christmas tree.

Dad would trim the stray branches from the bottom of the trunk and firmly secure the base to the tree stand, while Mom made hot chocolate and marshmallows so we could properly toast this wonderful family celebration. We listened to 78-rpm records as Bing Crosby sang Silent Night and White Christmas, while Mom and Dad finished stringing Christmas lights around our tree. When they were finished, we'd hang our store bought red, blue and green white-striped ornaments and our handmade decorations from all the branches we were tall enough to reach, then step back and bask in the beauty of our tree before beginning our clumsy ritual of lobbing handfuls of tinsel all over the tree. We always thought we did such a wonderful job, but if you compared our work with the perfect strands Mom carefully laced on the upper branches, our efforts looked pretty pathetic. But it didn't matter. To us, it was the most beautiful tree in the world!

But Christmas itself was indeed, the most magical time of the year for our impoverished little family. We'd rarely get anything frivolous during the rest of the year, but on Christmas, all our fantasies would come true. Mom would usually get a dress or two; Dad would get some kind of tool to help him work on his car, and my sisters and I always got at least one special toy we just couldn't live without.

The one toy I remember above all others was the red metal and tan wooden Flexible Radio Flyer snow sled I got when I was about six years old. I'd seen young boys racing their sleds down wintry slopes in movies like It's A Wonderful Life, so I knew what to expect when I dragged my new treasure out the front door and down the steps to the street.

It seemed like we had snow every Christmas, and this one was no exception. Bundled in my full-body snowsuit, goulashes, knit hat and mittens, I had visions of soaring at great speeds on the snow-covered street in front of our barracks. I plopped the sled in the center of the road, laid firmly on its top, and waited for the surge of power as I'd be swept away. *But nothing happened!* No one explained that I had to run with the sled and throw myself on its frame to make it glide across the painfully flat ground, and I was stunned by the laughter from my family as they watched the confused and disappointed look on my face as I laid motionless in my tracks. Mom finally walked over and gave me a big hug, then showed me how it was supposed to be done.

I had hours of fun on that sled . . . well, at least for the next two or three snowstorms. Mom and Dad were constantly reminding me to put it away when I was through for the day, but like most little kids my age, I had a very short span of attention and left it beside the road one too many times before retiring for the evening. The next morning I was heartbroken when I learned my Uncle Orley Stoumbaugh had run over my most prized possession with his milk truck while making his neighborhood deliveries, and completely destroyed the only decent toy I owned. Poor me! He claimed it was an accident, but judging from the smirk on his face and that ornery look in his eyes, I was convinced he'd done it on purpose. Mean him!!

I've always loved Christmas, especially when the snow was still falling and the neighborhood was covered with four or five inches of fresh new powder. I know what you're thinking: *"Who doesn't love Christmas?"* Fair enough, but to me, Christmases in the 1940s and 50s were even more beautiful and special than they are today. I may have grown up in the city, but when the cold dark clouds of winter pressed closer and closer to the already snow-covered grounds, our cozy little neighborhood seemed to grow smaller and smaller, taking on the flavor of small town America; not unlike the storybook yuletide neighborhoods of Selden and Flagler.

The days felt like weeks as the holiday grew nearer, and each anxious day I'd ask my mother, *"Whad'ya get me for Christmas?"* while shaking one present after another. *"A silver wish and golden wait awhile,"* she'd smile and say. God, I hated that answer!! Frustrated, but still undaunted, I'd rattle the boxes even more; always thankful to hear the satisfying "clank" that guaranteed a new toy instead of clothes.

I loved the smiles on my parents' faces when they watched me and my sisters open our presents on Christmas morning; the same smile I'd later wear on those mornings my children opened their own gifts; the same smile and memories most of you shared with your families.

•

Christmas always ended too soon for us kids, but the brand new year had its own reward. During the first week or two in January, The National Western Stock Show and Rodeo opened at the old National Amphitheater, just half a block northwest of East 48th Avenue and Humboldt Street (immediately north of where the Denver Coliseum would be built in 1952), and for the next two weeks, crowds were thrilled by one of the very few winter activities the city had to offer.

Because of the enormous crowds that swarmed the complex, the city required a large contingency of emergency personnel to be on hand. The stock show promoters hired moonlighting off-duty police officers for security and firemen to monitor and enforce fire safety regulations. Dad worked as many of these shifts as he could.

On a weekend day when he wasn't working, Dad would load up the entire family and drive us to the show. When we arrived at the complex, Dad would flash his badge and we'd all get in for free . . . we felt just like royalty!

We'd walk the halls of the arena and marvel at all of the concession stands and exhibit stalls. Vendors sold food and drinks, clothing, agricultural equipment, saddles, and just about anything else that could be related to the lure of the West. The halls teemed with crowds of the young and old, with big-bottomed girls and skinny assed cowboys everywhere you looked. If we'd ever had any questions about this being a cow town, they were definitely answered here!

The godawful stench of animals we dreaded so much in the summer months suddenly seemed right as we walked from the arena to the livestock pens. There were cows and bulls, pigs and sheep, chickens and rabbits, and every other kind of farm animal that could possibly soil the grounds.

Livestock competitions were held and judges awarded the best of the best with blue, red, yellow or green ribbons. On the last day of the stock show, the prized blue ribbon steer was auctioned off and sold to the highest bidder, which, as I remember, was usually the Joe "Awful" Coffee Ringside

Lounge at 1120 17th Street, or the Brown Palace Hotel at 321 17th Street.

When we returned to the arena, we'd find seats in the general admission section and settle in for the show. Vendors walked the aisles selling their wares, barking *"Hot dogs, hot dogs for sale"* or *"Coke, get your Coke here."* Dad would call them over, and with no disrespect to my mother's incredible cooking, we'd thoroughly enjoy this dining out experience. It was a rare occurrence and always a special treat.

When the rodeo started, the crowd roared as cowboys began their daring feats of bareback riding, tie-down roping, steer wrestling, barrel racing and bucking bronco and Brahma bull riding. Clowns took center stage between these events and brought the crowds to their feet in laughter with their comedic routines.

When the stock show was in town, our school had a special Rodeo Days theme all its own, and on this one special day of the year, we were allowed to come to school dressed as our favorite cowboy. The girls usually wore blue jeans and bright plaid shirts, but the boys sported their absolute best cowboy attire. Wearing my white cowboy hat, black faux leather chaps, blue cowboy shirt with white piping, and my cowboy boots and spurs, I'd strut through the halls with my six-shooter slung low, waiting for the first of a hundred gun fights I'd have that day.

These were definitely simpler times. Can you even imagine children being allowed to bring toy guns into school today? I think not!

When the rodeo closed its doors, the last glimmer of winter's fun ended, and all we could do now was wait for the inevitable recycling of seasons and the warmth and promise of a brand new spring.

●

Monday, December 4th, 1951, was just another typical winter day in Denver. It was cold outside, but the sky was blue and the grounds at our housing projects were clear. I'd been in bed all weekend with a really bad cold, and despite my pleas to go to school (yeah, right), Mom made me stay home until I felt better. In those days, cold medication for seven-year-olds was nearly nonexistent, so Mom treated me by rubbing plenty of Vick's on my chest and erected an improvised sheet tent over my bed so the vaporizer could channel the steam where it was most needed. She was always such a doting and loving mother, but was especially caring when any of us were sick.

By noon I was feeling a little better, and she got me up for lunch. She had tomato soup simmering in a pan on the stove and was busy mixing the ingredients for a truly great tuna sandwich. While I was waiting at the kitchen table, Dad came home from work. He was usually home by 8am, but was late today because of an airplane crash and fire he'd worked since the day before. As Mom and I listened, he told us about the crash.

A B-29 bomber flying toward Denver was having mechanical problems and was trying to make it to the Lowry Air Force Base for an emergency landing. It lost power about two miles southwest of the airfield and crashed into five homes in the upscale residential neighborhood near East Alameda and Jasmine Street. The plane completely destroyed two of the homes and caused serious damage to the other three. Eight of the fourteen crewmen were killed, but fortunately, no one on the ground was injured. I listened intently as Dad described the devastation of the crash site and how he and his partner struggled to carry one of the charred bodies from the airplane. Stumbling through the smoke and over the rough terrain, they managed to get only a few feet from the scene when one of the victim's arms pulled loose from his body, and they dropped him to the ground.

It was a graphic story and made me feel a little queasy, so I was glad when he started talking about something else. But I wasn't prepared for the rest of his story.

It soon became obvious the rescue and cleanup efforts were going to take several hours, so the Red Cross set up a truck nearby and provided coffee and food for all the police and firemen. After all the emergency duties were completed, Dad and some of the other firemen went to the truck for a break. As Dad was drinking his coffee, one of the firemen standing beside him was eating a roast beef sandwich and picking at his teeth with his finger. He asked Dad if he had a toothpick, and when Dad said no, the fireman said, *"I've got a piece of dead meat stuck in my teeth and I can't get it out."* Collective moans and laughter followed this dark humor, but everyone there understood this was the kind of humor men resort to when they're trying to cope with overwhelming circumstances.

But when I heard it, I almost gagged. I'd just taken a big bite from my sandwich, and for years associated the taste of tuna with that joke and with the image I still had in my mind of the "dead meat" stuck in that fireman's teeth.

•

The principles of television date back to the late 1800s, but television itself wasn't recognized outside the scientific community until Tuesday, January 26th, 1926, when it was publicly demonstrated by John Lorgie Baird in his laboratory in London, England. It took another twenty years before it arrived in the United States (1946), and another six years after that before it came to Denver.

On Friday, July 18th, 1952, our cosmopolitan little cow town finally emerged from the dark ages. Television had at long last come to Denver, and Channel 2, KFEL-TV, was the first and only station to air televised programs.

Grandma and Aunt Daisy were the first in our family to get a TV, and they got theirs just in time for us to watch the best television programming of the day . . . the 1952 National Democratic Convention. *Oh, Boy!* We'd visit Grandma and Aunt Daisy at their home on Galapago Street and watch the screen for as long as the program was aired, then sit and stare at the test pattern when it was over.

Five months later, just before Christmas, Dad loaded the family into our car and drove through the flurry of a fresh new snow to the Valas TV & Appliance store on South Broadway. I don't remember Mom being with us, and my best guess is that she was working a temporary job somewhere to help with the Christmas expenses.

We were so excited! Think about it . . . we were about to buy a device that could actually snatch living pictures from out of the air and project them onto a screen within the privacy of our own living room. The real science of science fiction was finally a reality, and we were there to witness it!!

We looked around the show room floor, but there really weren't a lot of different sets to choose from in the early days of television. As I recall, you had a choice of brand names like Magnavox, Zenith, Emerson, Motorola, Philco, Admiral, and General Electric, but big console TVs with small black and white screens were all this store had to offer.

Dad found a set that both suited his desires and wallet, so amidst great adulation and joy, a very proud father signed the paperwork and made three young children very happy.

With the help of the salesman, Dad loaded the cumbersome television into the trunk of our car, then we drove to a nearby greasy-spoon Rocky Built Diner near Alameda on Broadway where we celebrated our new lifestyle change with hamburgers and chili. *It was one of the best days of my young life!!*

When we got back to the projects, a neighbor helped Dad set our "enormous" new 16" Emerson TV against the wall next to our record player in the living room, and we all sat back and reveled in the beauty of the best piece of furniture we'd ever owned.

In the evenings, we'd huddle around our television and watch such classics as The Milton Berle Show, Ted Mack's Original Amateur Hour, The Honeymooners, Your Show of Shows, with Sid Caesar and Imogene Coca, Your Hit Parade, The Jack Benny Show, and one of my favorites, The Red Skelton Show.

It was an incredible experience to watch those truly great old television shows, and because everything was live in those days, we always got to see our favorite bloopers as they were happening. The reception was only as good as the rabbit ears antenna allowed, and our shows were frequently interrupted with a "Technical Difficulties" notice, but we didn't care . . . *We Had Television!!*

•

Sometime around 1952, the Denver Housing Authority started building the Quigg Newton low-income housing projects near West 44th Avenue and Mariposa Street. Mom would walk us over to the new construction site and we'd be amazed by the beauty of the new two-story brick apartments, and mentally compare them with the gruffness of our own projects. They were so much nicer than our homes, and at the time, we thought they were luxury condominiums. I think the new complex was built to replace our military projects, and by the spring of 1953, our community was scheduled for demolition.

We stayed in the projects until the last possible moment, and when we were evicted, we moved in with Grandma Oldson and Aunt Daisy at 424 Galapago Street.

Uncle Orley and Aunt Verne bought this house for $2,500 when they left Heeney; sold it to Uncle Orley's nephew Russ

Meade in 1945, and in the last months of 1946, he sold it to Grandma and her widowed sister Daisy and divorced sister Fern.

Soon after their move, Aunt Fern suffered from uremia (kidney failure), and because of her devoted faith as a Christian Scientist, refused to be treated for her ailment. She died on Sunday, February 23rd, 1947 at the age of fifty-three. I have no memory of her, but my earliest and fondest childhood memories of Grandma and Aunt Daisy centered around this house.

An old two-bedroom red brick home on the east side of Galapago Street (about a quarter block north of West 4th Avenue), it sat on the north side of an alley, with a large vacant lot between the alley and West 4th Avenue. The long narrow tree-filled backyard was secured with a three-foot chain-link fence, and the small front yard was bordered by one of those great old Victorian Age spiked wrought iron fences; the kind you see around gravesites from the 1800s.

The living room was at the front of the house (west), followed by a dining room, kitchen, and an enclosed back porch. The tiny bedrooms were to the left of the living and dining rooms, and a small bathroom with an antique footed bathtub was just to the left of the kitchen (north).

A tall black oil burning heater sat at the east end of the dining room floor, with a stove pipe venting up for about a foot, then running horizontally into the back wall. The kitchen was pretty big for such a small house and had a stove and refrigerator on the west wall, a large butcher-block table in the southwest corner, cabinets and kitchen sink in the southeast corner, and a white wooden table and four chairs just north of the sink. A large white metal pantry backed against the east wall, between the back door and the bathroom, and another open built-in wooden pantry lined the north wall, between the bathroom and Aunt Daisy's bedroom.

133

Most everyone who came to visit parked in the vacant lot next to their house and came in through the back door. Grandma and Aunt Daisy took in laundry to support themselves, so whenever you came into the hot and humid sweatshop they called their back porch, the washing machine and clothes dryer were running full steam. The dryer had never been properly vented and the hot exhaust and lint fed into an old nylon stocking tied to a port on the front of the dryer.

With seven people living within the confines of their small home, it was always crowded and busy. If they weren't cleaning or cooking, they were constantly ironing clothes for their clients. My sisters and I tried to stay out of their way as much as we could, and would sit in the living room and watch The Price Is Right, or those godawful live performances of As The World Turns and The Days Of Our Lives. When we'd get bored with the shows on television, Darlene and I'd go outside and play in the backyard or vacant lot, or swing on the large gray wooden swing that hung from the covered front porch. June was fourteen by then, and I don't really remember her spending that much time playing with us, but knowing the state of her raging teenage hormones, I suspect she spent most of her time enticing all the teenage boys in the neighborhood.

In the evenings, we'd sit around the dining room table and play cards or help Grandma and Aunt Daisy piece together their latest jigsaw puzzle. The puzzles were always a big family affair and could keep us entertained for days.

When it was time for bed, Darlene and I slept on a red pull-down sofa sleeper in the living room, and a roll-a-way bed was set up for June. Grandma and Aunt Daisy slept in the front bedroom and Mom and Dad in the other, and no one ever complained about the sleeping arrangements. It must have been a huge imposition to have us living with them, but they always made us feel welcome.

On Monday, July 27th, 1953, the three-year war with Korea ended and America once again looked forward to a peaceful and prosperous future. Mom and Dad were swept up with this newfound sense of euphoria, and at the ages of thirty-three and thirty-years-old, decided it was time to take advantage of Dad's veteran's benefits and buy their own new home.

Their search began and ended in the Green Acres subdivision in southwest Denver, where they found a Carlson-McClelland home they really liked. The house was priced at $11,300, with a monthly payment of $62.81 per month. This was probably more than they could afford, so before they applied for the loan, Mom found a "permanent" full time job with Sears and Roebuck . . . just to be on the safe side.

By now Dad was spending far too much time and energy working on our old car, and was certain the family was going to need a change soon; probably sooner than later. They knew they couldn't risk buying a new car while waiting for the home loan to be approved, so they patiently waited and just prayed the car would last a little while longer.

On Tuesday, September 8th, just days after our VA loan was approved, they bought their first new car from Elwood Edwards Auto Sales, 1027 South Tejon Street; a 1953 cream colored Chevrolet Bel Air with only twenty-one miles on the odometer. It cost $2,363.85, but after the $900 trade-in for our old car and another $100 cash deposit, they ended up financing $1,363.85. The twenty-four monthly payments of $72.25 were high, but still manageable.

When the new school year began, we were still living with Grandma and Aunt Daisy, but knew we'd be moving to our new home within the next two or three months. To avoid the inconvenience of having to change from one school to another in the middle of the semester, Mom enrolled Darlene and me at Goldrick Elementary School at 1050 South Zuni Street, and June at Kepner Junior High School at 911 South Hazel Court.

For reasons I've never understood, I finished the third grade at Garden Place and started the fifth at Goldrick; completely skipping the fourth grade.

Since there were no school busses to pick us up at the end of the block, getting to school became quite a challenge, and with no other means available, we were forced to rely on the public transportation system. We'd get up bright and early every weekday morning and walk seven blocks to West 4th Avenue and Broadway, where we'd catch our first city bus. We'd ride to Alameda Avenue, then transfer to another bus that took us to Exposition Avenue and Vallejo Street, where Darlene and I'd get off and walk another six blocks south to our school. We'd usually get there about half an hour early, so we'd go to Aunt Rainie and Uncle Bill's house at 1060 South Vallejo Street and wait there until our classes began. June continued her bus ride to West Kentucky Avenue and South Federal Boulevard, then walked the remaining two blocks to school.

Me, far left, and Darlene sitting in the chair by the back porch

Me, June & Darlene,
in front of the
"Concentration Camp"

Me—in all my splendor

Mom on laundry day

Darlene & June

Mom beside our old Ford

Darlene, Jackie Sue Craven & June

Darlene, June, Me & Dad

Darlene, June, Jackie Sue & Me

She could have been the next Marilyn Monroe

Grandma Oldson, Aunt Verne & Aunt Daisy

My family in the back yard at Grandma's house
424 Galapago Street

Mom & Me -- Christmas at
Grandma Oldson's home

The family -- Probably at
Granddad Aumiller's house

Darlene, Me, Mom & June -- Looks like Easter

CHAPTER 9

"Bryant Street"

On Saturday morning, November 7th, 1953, we left the aston-
ishingly generous and loving company of Grandma and Aunt
Daisy, and moved into our brand new 990 square foot, three
bedroom traditional ranch-style home at 1432 South Bryant
Street. It didn't matter that we were filling our new home with
our Goodwill style furniture from the Projects; I thought we
were rich!!

Our sleek ultra-modern new home sat at the top of a steep dirt
terrace, and the bright two-toned green shingle framed house
was the most beautiful house I'd ever seen! It was a symbol of
the Aumiller's success, and for the next fifty-three years, stood
as the only constant in the ever-changing dynamics of our
family.

The front steps and sidewalk brought you to a long covered
porch on the west side of the house, and the front door led into
our "huge" 17'x12' living room. If you continued directly east
across the living room floor, you came to a north/south
hallway, which was the access to our three small bedrooms and
our only bathroom. The largest 12'x10' bedroom sat at the
south end of the hall, with the bathroom immediately to its left
on the east side of the house. A small coat closet faced west
just north of the bathroom, and a linen closet faced south at the
north end of the hall. The second and third smaller bedrooms
were in the northeast and northwest corners of the house.

A 10'x8' dining area monopolized the southwest corner of our
home, with an adjoining 10'x16' kitchen immediately to the
east. Our old white refrigerator; new white doublewide stove
and white washing machine sat against the north wall, with a
row of small white metal cabinets lining the wall just above
them. Larger white upper and lower metal cabinets, a long

green linoleum covered counter top, and a doublewide white porcelain sink sat against the south wall. The kitchen floor was the same green linoleum as the counter top, the bathroom floor, red linoleum; the only rooms in the house that didn't have hardwood floors. Only the wealthiest of families had wall-to-wall carpeting in those days, so we were stuck with those beautifully polished hardwood floors that were only fit for the lowly working class families. Who knew in another thirty or forty years, hardwood floors would be the designer's choice in some of the most expensive homes?

There were light switches and light fixtures in every room of the house, except in the living and utility rooms. There were no ceiling lights in the living room, so the wall switches only worked with lamps, and the bare overhead light bulb in the utility room was turned on and off with a drawstring, just like the lights at the projects. Writing about such trivial details may seem strange to most people, but to me, having light switches and decorative light fixtures in our home was just one more example of our new and better class of living, and proved to me we weren't poor anymore.

Our back door faced south at the east end of the kitchen, and a door just to its left on the east wall led to a small utility room. Mom used this room as an ironing room for the first few years we were there, but when Dad bought a new clothes dryer and freezer, most of the space was used up and Mom was forced to do her ironing in the kitchen.

Not to brag, but our house was so modern, we even had a garbage disposal!! *Who else in our family could make that same claim?* It eliminated the need for the traditional filthy garbage pail, but we still had to deal with our other trash in the conventional manner. We'd separate the cans from the paper and I'd haul the flammable trash to our concrete incinerator at the end of our long backyard sidewalk, and on burn days, I'd satisfy my latent pyromaniac desires and fill the skies with clouds of smog producing smoke. We'd put all the other trash in large tin cans and I'd carry them down to the curb every Tuesday morning for collection by the City's garbage men.

True to Mom and Dad's plans, Mom quit her job shortly after we moved into our new house, and returned to being a stay-at-home mom. But it didn't take long to realize there wasn't a lot of money left over once their new mortgage and car payments were made, so Dad found a part time job with Dick's Wholesale, and for the next several years spent most of his days off from the Fire Department delivering vending machine snacks and cigarettes to bars and restaurants along Santa Fe Drive, ending his southern route at Bud's Cafe & Bar at 5453 Manhart Street in the rural little town of Sedalia.

Dad loved that little bar (well, actually, he loved every little bar), and in his opinion, they served the best cheeseburgers in the entire Denver metropolitan area. To its credit, this 1948 no frills hometown cafe is still proud to offer that same quality of burger even to this day.

Because Dad spent so much of his life living in poverty, he became fanatical about the care and maintenance of everything he owned, and to make sure those elegant hardwood floors weren't needlessly damaged by the hazards of everyday wear and tear, *everyone* who came to our house was ordered to take their shoes off the second they walked through the front door. Dad correctly reasoned the absence of shoes in the house would keep the floors both pristine and scuff-free, and they'd be buffed and polished by our bare socks while we shuffled from one room to the next.

Today our old neighborhood feels like it's practically in the center of the city, but in those days, we were about as far removed from the city as we could possibly be. The frame homes to our south and across the street to our west, and the brick homes in the block just north of our home were already finished, but the remaining areas were still vacant fields. A small farm house and horse stables maintained their country

145

status just south of Florida Avenue at the south end of our block, and the area just behind our home was still wide-open pastures . . . so rural I could hunt rabbits and magpies with my BB gun without worrying about breaking someone's windows with an all too frequent misdirected shot. When they finally started building homes in the fields behind our home, my new neighborhood friends and I took full advantage of the construction sites and laid siege to what we perceived to be bombed-out buildings and bomb-cratered basements whenever we'd play my favorite game of War. Dad's boyhood heroes were Cowboys; mine were World War II American Soldiers . . . real men; tough men; men of great honor . . . just like my dad and his brother Lyle.

Like all new neighborhoods, ours was devoid of lawns and trees. We suffered through the mud and dirt for the remainder of the winter, but in the spring of 1954, Dad and a few of his firemen friends installed a three foot chain-link fence around our back yard, then Dad prepped the ground for a new lawn. Stacking heavy concrete rain gutter drains on a rope tethered dual framed length of 2x6 boards, he leveled the ground by dragging it behind him like a horse drawn plow. If sod was even available in those days, we certainly couldn't afford it, so Mom and Dad spread their grass seed by hand. Because the terrace was so steep, they had to secure gunny sacks to the ground with long metal spikes in order to keep the seeds from draining to the street every time they watered the lawn.

They planted a vegetable garden in the yard directly behind our house and we raised our own carrots, lettuce, corn, onions, turnips, and radishes. In the evenings, we'd sit down to watch television and snack on those wonderfully sweet raw onions. They were *so good*, but by the next morning, we could barely stand to be in the same room with each other.

After a couple of years, they replaced the garden with grass and added shrubbery and trees. I remember lying on the ground and gently pulling individual blades of grass from the yard as I marveled over the fact that we actually had a lawn. *Opulence was a wonderful thing!*

Until my sisters and I were a little older, Dad did most of the yard work himself. For the first summer or two, we were under strict watering restrictions and were only allowed to water every other day. Dad would spend his entire mornings dragging garden hoses and sprinklers from one spot to the other, giving each new section a twenty-minute dousing. After dark, he'd set the hose on any dry spots and let a slight trickle of water soak into the ground. He wouldn't use a sprinkler head so the water police couldn't see the spray while they were patrolling the neighborhood, and since there were no water meters in those days, the Denver Water Board never really knew how much water we were using and our lawn always got the water it needed.

Dad mowed the lawn with a push mower and manually trimmed the edges with a pair of hand clippers, and because he was so meticulous with his work, our lawn became a virtual showcase . . . and with very few exceptions, was off-limits to absolutely everyone.

Whenever a neighborhood boy lost his senses and walked across any portion of our lawn, Dad would jump from his kitchen chair and pound on the window or run out the front door and scream, *"Get Off The Lawn!"* He was a crotchety old man well before his time.

Our home soon became "the" social gathering place for the family, and on most of Dad's nights off, someone would drop by for a visit. They were always invited to stay for dinner, and if they accepted, Mom would "just throw an extra potato in the pot," then spend the rest of the night tending to everyone's wants and needs. She was always the perfect hostess.

After dinner, the grownups sat at the kitchen table for hot games of Pinochle, Canadian Canasta, Crazy-Eights, Oh Hell, or Nuts, while the kids sat back and watched and cheered or jeered, depending on who was winning. Dad had long since outgrown his shyness, and his great sense of humor, quick comedic delivery, and moan provoking puns made him the life of every party . . . you never heard such laughter! This was the kind of fun families are supposed to have.

During the summer months, Pinky Sparland (also a Denver fireman); his wife Lee and their boy and girl from the house to our north, and our south side neighbors John and Marilyn Warren and their two boys Mike and Paul would come to our home for an evening of pure entertainment. Mom and Dad lined the front porch with card chairs and the adults would sit and have a drink or two while Dad loosened up for yet another night of his special blend of comedy. The kids played in the front yard (with Dad's permission), or sat around the porch listening to the adults while everyone laughed at Dad's great stories and jokes. Pinky had one of the most outrageous and contagious laughs I've ever heard, and even if Dad's jokes weren't really that funny, his hee-haw laugh was enough to make us all laugh. Those were truly great times!

We lived in a happy, quiet little neighborhood, where on week-ends everyone mowed and trimmed their lawns and washed their cars, careful to make sure they looked as good as they possibly could. Everyone was proud of what little they owned, and it definitely showed. The wars had all ended and the world as we knew it was a good and just place to live, but the innocence of this era was shattered when Denver suddenly became a place infamously known around the world.

On Tuesday, November 1st, 1955, when I was eleven-years-old, John Gilbert Graham, a neighbor who lived at 2650 West Mississippi Avenue (just four and a half blocks from our home), packed a bomb in his mother's suitcase and drove her to Stapleton Airport. She boarded United Airlines flight 629, and at 7:03 pm, eleven minutes after the Portland/Seattle bound DC-6B left the airport, it exploded over the farmlands near Longmont, Colorado, killing all thirty-nine passengers and five crew members. This wasn't the kind of terrorist attack we all worry about today, but the specific and premeditated murder of his mother Daisie King. (This crime was depicted in the opening segment of Jimmy Stewart's 1959 movie, The FBI Story).

He was held in the old stone Denver County Jail at West Colfax Avenue and Kalamath Street until he was tried and convicted in Denver District Court for the sole murder of his mother (before this happened, there was no federal law that made it a crime to blow up an airplane), and on Friday, January 11th, 1957, he was put to death in the gas chamber in the Colorado State Penitentiary. It didn't bother him that he'd also killed forty-three other people while murdering his mother, and in fact, made the following statement to the press before his execution: *"As far as feeling remorse for these people, I don't. I can't help it. Everybody pays their way and takes their chances. That's just the way it goes."*

I'd read all the accounts of his arrest in the Rocky Mountain News and watched the reports on television, and knew this was a very serious event in our local history. And through it all, I'd see pictures of this monster surrounded by the police, and was once again reminded why I wanted to be a policeman when I grew up.

●

I had a lot of cousins living around town who kept me entertained while I was growing up, but my absolute favorites were Rocky and Randy Wiley (Uncle Bill and Aunt Rainie's two young boys); Terry, Glenna and Sherry Oldson (Uncle Bill and Aunt Wanda's kids), Rodney, Tina and Melody Bailey (Aunt Beulah and Uncle Clinton's three oldest kids), followed by Jeff and April Taylor (Glen and Clarice's kids), Sharon and Lora Bullock (Pudge and Bud's girls) . . . plus all seven of the young aunts and uncles I had from Granddad and Opal's large brood. My cousins who really weren't old enough to be my childhood friends were Chris Kennedy and Lisa Bailey (Aunt Beulah and Uncle Clinton's two youngest kids); David, Danny and Tommy Johnson (Merna and Bob's three boys), Mike and Marci Stoumbaugh (Ray and Phillis' kids), and Lee and Mona Stoumbaugh (Bill and Betty's two kids).

Clearly I didn't lack from a shortage of family members I could call my friends, but most of my regular childhood friends were those I'd either met at Goldrick Elementary or Kepner Junior High School. These included my nearby neighbors Tom Maniatis and Ricky Rapue (both sons of Denver Firemen); Dale Woods, Freddie Inselman, Ralph Olinger, Tom Wulf, Mike Ferguson, Mike Sennett, Ronnie Johnson, and Bob Cavelier.

Tom Wulf, who'd grow up to become a Colorado State Patrolman, was my closest friend in this group, and the only one I'd see socially beyond my high school years. Mike Ferguson, at 6'5" was the tallest, best looking and rowdiest of my friends, but grew up on the wrong side of the law and became a violent and intimidating looking young man.

Most of the cops in southwest Denver had at least heard of Mike during the 1960s, and many of them had arrested him at one time or another. He was still pretty active when I came on the job in 1967, and it wasn't long before I joined that long list of officers when I was forced to jail him for his latest assault. I later heard he'd been killed in a fight at a cowboy bar on West Colfax Avenue, but recently learned from retired Sergeant Jim Lindsey that his demise was only a rumor. At least at that time. He'd actually survived the barroom brawl, but wouldn't survive a later shooting when his wife blew his face off with a shotgun. That was a tough way to go.

Mike Sennett, Tom Maniatis and Ralph Olinger were the studious ones in our group, while the rest of my friends were the same academic slugs that I was. Mike became a respected dentist in town and Tom became a renowned research scientist and current Professor of Biochemistry and Molecular Biology at Harvard University. Ralph worked at the Coors Brewery, but I have no idea what paths my other friends took.

Chumming around with my buddies was the only thing I had any interest in doing when I was still a little boy, but when I reached that magical pubescent age of twelve-years-old, things really started to change . . . and the girls I'd shied away from for fear of getting their cooties, suddenly became very desirable to me. I didn't fully understand all the new urges and physical changes to my body, but I was quick to welcome them with open arms.

I had a variety of childhood flings (losing my virginity to a very friendly girl when I was just thirteen), but by the time I was fourteen, I met a young Catholic girl I was sure I'd marry someday (who could resist that little Catholic school girl uniform?) Carol Mauser lived just up the street from me, and at fourteen-years-old, had the exciting figure of an eighteen-year-old woman and the haunting good looks of Groundhog Day's Andie MacDowell. **Oh, my!!**

It didn't take long before we were overcome by the thrills and agonies of an emotional teenage love, but since I went to West High School and she went to St. Francis, we'd only see each other after school and on weekends, and usually at her home. Her dad fell victim to polio while he was a Captain on the Denver Fire Department and was forced to retire with a medical disability pension years before his time. He was pretty slow moving, but got along remarkably well with the assistance from his metal leg braces and forearm crutches, and I was sufficiently intimidated by the gruffness of his formidable Raymond Burr's Perry Mason stature whenever I was there.

Her parents Ed and Dorothy wouldn't let her officially date until she was sixteen, so for most of the first two years of our relationship, we were severely hampered by the limited amount of freedom they'd allow. Our parents would drop us off at the roller rink or movie theater, or allow us to go to chaperoned teenage dance parties at friends' homes, but our more intimate (but always virginal) moments were shared when I'd sneak over to be with her when she babysat the neighborhood kids.

I became friends (to one degree or another) with her sisters, Rosalie, Donna and Celeste . . . with their next door neighbor, Roberta Hagan, and Tom Wulf's girlfriend, Sharon Tavenner (daughters of Denver policemen Merle Hagan and Russell Tavenner), and her ravishing neighbors from across the street, Donna Graiko, and her even more stunning older sister, Cynthia. I was blessed to have so many good friends.

Our Brand New Home - 1432 South Bryant Street
Note the dirt yard and street - 1953

This is how Dad did it
in the olden days

Always working

CHAPTER 10

"Family Vacations"

We'd take an incredible thirteen-day trip to California in 1958, but prior to that time, most of our summer vacations were spent visiting with family in Kansas, Utah or Nebraska, and these trips usually only lasted four or five days. Selden was always my favorite place to visit, because it felt like we were stepping back in time a hundred years . . . to a time when the world was still seen in black and white, and everyone walked like Charlie Chaplin.

We rarely ventured too far from home when we still had our old Ford (better described as Fix Or Repair Daily), but with the security of a mechanically reliable new car, Dad was no longer afraid to take us on long road trips. So, in the summer of 1954, we took our first trip in our very first new car and returned to Selden for our second long weekend visit with Grandma Aumiller. We were anxious to see her again, but probably more anxious to show off our new car and brag even more about our beautiful and exciting new home. Being a fireman in the big city already made Dad a *huge* success in the eyes of our Selden family, and these new assets were just more icing on the cake.

We left home late one Friday evening and drove across town to Colfax Avenue, then continued our journey east on U.S. 40. This was the most direct route at the time, since the concept of an interstate highway system through Colorado didn't even exist until October 1956, and even though the Denver portion of Interstate 70 opened on September 12th, 1964, the continuing route to the Kansas border wouldn't be completed until 1971.

Dad preferred to drive at night when we were still little kids; partially because there'd be less traffic to contend with on those narrow two-lane rural highways, but mostly because he

155

knew we'd sleep for the greater part of the trip. A sleeping family rarely whines about having to stop for bathroom breaks, and that was just the way Dad liked it. Once he was on the road he hated to stop, and firmly believed if he didn't have to pee, no one had to pee.

But he was wrong. By the time we reached Goodland, Kansas, I was wide-awake, squirming in my seat, and begging Dad to stop. He finally pulled into a truck stop for gas, and while he filled his tank, I emptied mine. It was *"a good thing."*

Since we were already stopped, Dad decided we could all use a break, and pulled across the lot to a slightly smaller version of a Gunther Toody's restaurant. When we took our seats inside, our veteran middle-aged blond kiss my grits kind of waitress took one final satisfying drag from her cigarette, snuffed it out in an ashtray next to our booth, then pulled the stub of a pencil from behind her right ear and said, *"What'll you have, Darlin?"* Dad ordered a cup of coffee; Mom had her usual hot tea, and my sisters and I had milk and cherry pie while we fed nickels into the Seeburg record selector at our table and listened to three or four of our favorite songs. We only stayed long enough for Dad to stretch his legs and recover a little from the monotony of late-night driving, then we were back on the road again.

We arrived in Selden just after daybreak and parked in the dirt on the south shoulder of U.S. 83, directly in front of Grandma's house. The ancient wood framed house looked much older than it really was, and probably hadn't seen a fresh coat of paint in more than twenty years. The weathered grey siding blended perfectly with the dirt that surrounded the old house, and the scene looked just like an old tintype picture from the Civil War Era. A sidewalk led to the front door and was bordered by two 3' concrete "snowman" shaped columns that sat on either side of the pathway. The columns were encrusted with colorful old cat's eye marbles that gave the home a certain fairy tale kind of appeal.

Our eighty-four-year-old grandma met us at the door and hugged us like only a great-grandmother could. She was a tiny frail little woman, with the physical stature of Yoda, and the heart and soul of a saint. As we walked into the kitchen, it was as though we'd traveled back in time even more. The house still had the same old fixtures from the early 1930s, and with the exception of a recently installed secondhand sink, probably hadn't changed since the day she moved in.

A doorway directly across the room from the front door led to a small storage room (south), with a large cast-iron wood burning stove sitting against the wall immediately to its right, and an old white refrigerator (with the exposed coils sitting on top) against the wall to its left. The "new" kitchen sink on the east wall only supplied cold running water, but was a vast improvement for Grandma, since she no longer had to go outside in the middle of the freezing winters to pump her water.

A rustic old kitchen table and battered wooden chairs sat along the front wall (north), with a floor-to-ceiling dark wooden cupboard standing against the west wall. A doorway to the left of the cupboard led to the living room, with a small bedroom to the left, and a larger bedroom straight across the living room floor (on the west side of the house). A big potbelly stove sat at the south end of the living room, and the remainder of the room was furnished with two old couches, a stuffed chair and an antique wooden rocking chair.

We were welcomed by our ancient slow moving fifty-eight-year-old Uncle Warren (Granddad LaVate Aumiller's brother—dressed in his usual bib-overalls), then silently greeted by his fifty-one-year-old sister, Aunt Ossie (Oca), as she briefly smiled at us from her rocking chair in the living room. But her smile was short-lived, and she immediately returned to the privacy of her own little world. As a result of her life-long bouts with epilepsy, she grew up to be an extremely shy and special woman, and for the remainder of our visit, sat huddled over in the security of her rocking chair, muttering unintelligible words to herself as she rocked back and forth, knitting an imaginary sweater with imaginary knitting needles.

She'd lived with her mother since birth, and Uncle Warren had been with her since his wife Alice died of a heart attack on the streets of Selden in 1937. He later married a mail-order bride, but the spark just wasn't there, and she quietly faded away into the sunset.

None of the Aumillers in Selden had a phone, but in typical small town fashion, word of our arrival soon spread like wildfire. Within minutes, the entire Aumiller clan arrived to greet us, and the real fun of our family reunion began.

Uncle Glenn (Granddad Aumiller's youngest brother); his wife Aunt Margie and their five young kids were the first to arrive from their house across the highway (Dad's childhood home). Uncle Glenn was only fifty-one-years-old, but looked like an old Fred Astaire. He was completely deaf and didn't have a tooth in his mouth, but was filled with a vibrant and youthful energy that kept him on the move for most of the time we were there. If you were facing him, he could read your lips as well as most people can hear, and had no trouble following the conversations. Understanding him, however, was a little more difficult. Aunt Margie was a short slightly overweight forty-three-year-old woman who wore an old grey dress and scarf, and looked like a stereotypical Russian peasant woman from the 1940s. She and her two pretty young daughters Nova and Alice stood in the background and silently watched and listened to everything that was going on in the room.

Their son Poncho (Claude) was probably about sixteen-years-old, followed by his ten-year-old brother Ohio, and his eight-year-old brother Gary. Most of the family was pretty shy and laid back, but Gary was just as gregarious as his dad, and genuinely seemed excited to see us.

We were soon joined by our fifty-five-year-old Uncle Wynn (Winslow), yet another of Granddad Aumiller's brothers; his fifty-three-year-old drunken wife Aunt Zola and their handsome twenty-four-year-old drunker son Dwight. Uncle Wynn was hard of hearing and really didn't have much to say, but Aunt Zola more than made up for his silence. Dad told us she was a real knock-out when she was a young woman, and remembering her big blue eyes and broad friendly smile, I can see how that could have been. But the years and alcohol were not her friends, and she looked like the down-and-out alcoholic that she truly was.

She wore a dirty blue housedress and red scarf, similar to the kind Hattie McDaniel wore in her role as Mammy in the movie Gone With The Wind. She was missing all but two or three of her front teeth; had a large mole on her face (with the obligatory long whiskers), and probably hadn't suffered from the indignation of a bath for several weeks. With this visual in mind, imagine how we all felt when she hugged us and tried to give us a big sloppy wet kiss. We'd grimace and try to pull away, but in the end, she got her kiss.

She wasn't shy about asking for a bottle of wine, and Dad learned years ago that if he'd just stop and buy her one on the way into town, she'd quickly slip away from the family and find someplace more secluded for her respite. Dwight was even more of an alcoholic than his mother, and usually disappeared with her.

While Mom and my sisters stayed at the house with Grandma to do whatever women do when men aren't around, Dad took Ohio, Gary and me on a walking tour of the town so I could take in all the highlights of up-town Selden. We went into every shop on Kansas Avenue, looking for anyone Dad might still know, and ended up at Bart's Service Station alongside the highway on the northeast end of town. Bart's was the favorite meeting place for most of the idle men in town, and near as I could tell, was the only bar within miles. The service station lobby was lined with cases of beer the men used for benches while they sat and drank their brew; smoked their cigars and cigarettes . . . cussed and spit every now and again, and talked about fast women, faster cars, and corrupt politicians.

By early that evening, all of us kids walked to the old movie theater in the center of downtown. It was only open on holidays and weekends during the summer months, and on this Saturday night we saw Alfred Hitchcock's new thriller, The Rear Window. When the movie ended, we had to walk the long, eerily quiet five blocks back to Grandma's house . . . all alone and in the absolute dead of night.

Single 200-watt streetlights hung over every intersection, but the dim lights quickly faded to darkness, and by the middle of each block, we could barely see our own goose bumps. We laughed and joked as we briskly walked through the darkness, but were certain Raymond Burr would leap out at any moment and kill us all. The walk back home felt a lot farther than the walk to the theater, and we were really relieved when we finally got back to Grandma's house.

The following morning I awoke to the welcoming aroma of freshly percolating coffee, and could hear the muffled chatter of my family drifting in from the kitchen. By the time I strolled into the warmth of the cozy little kitchen, I saw my grandma frying eggs and bacon in cast-iron skillets on the hot surface of the old stove, and knew at once this was going to be a very special breakfast.

I said my good mornings as I walked across the room; still in my pajamas and rubbing the deep sleep from my eyes. Suddenly my arms started to itch, and within seconds the itching spread to my entire body. I knew something was terribly wrong and looked to my mother for help. She unbuttoned the front of my shirt, then gasped when she saw my entire chest and stomach covered with tiny red bumps. Since I'd already had the chicken pox and measles, she knew they weren't the problem, so we both walked back to my bed and checked for the next possible option. When Mom pulled the sheets back, we saw a virtual army of bedbugs scurrying in every direction. Grandma cried as she quickly found some kind of ointment to relieve the itching, but it didn't relieve the image I still had in my mind of the scores of bugs crawling all over my body, or take away the horrible pain my grandma felt for her little Billy Bumps, the name she gave me that very day, and lovingly called me for the remaining years of her life.

When the girls finished washing the dishes and everything was put away, we took a drive around town. We stopped at Uncle Wynn and Aunt Zola's house so Dad could show us how the other half of the Aumillers lived. The front yard was filled with tall weeds that mercifully helped camouflage the rubble of discarded bottles and old tires, and a worn out sofa sat on the front porch of the dilapidated wood framed house, where the family would sit and drink on those incredibly hot summer nights. We went inside for a short visit and I was amazed to see the primitive conditions they lived with. The only pieces of furniture I can remember were a table and chairs in the living room and mattresses lying on the bare splintery bedroom floors. A potbelly stove sat in the living room, and was apparently used for both heating and cooking. The walls were unfinished rotting wood, and I could actually see the surrounding homes through the large gaps in the walls. They continued to live in these squalid conditions until 1966, when Aunt Zola was killed in a fire that totally engulfed their home.

She was asleep when the fire broke out, but Uncle Wynn was able to get her up and out of the house before it was too serious. They were safe now, but as the flames began to rapidly spread, Aunt Zola suddenly remembered she had some money hidden inside the house, and tragically ran back inside in a failed attempt to save it. The fire was raging by now, and in the next few seconds, she fell victim to the thick black smoke and was consumed by the blazing inferno. Uncle Wynn survived for another ten years, but I have no idea where he lived after the fire.

When we got back to Grandma's house, we settled in for a quiet visit. We were going home later that night, so Mom and Dad laid down for a short nap so they could be awake for the long drive back to Denver. Darlene and I played checkers with Grandma for most of the afternoon, and every now and again she'd feel sorry for us and surreptitiously let us win a game. Watching our precious little great-grandmother sitting so still in her high-back wooden chair was like watching James Whistler's mother pose for the fourth most recognized painting in the entire world. But unlike Whistler's Mother, our Grandma Aumiller had the tender sweet smile of an angel; the angel we all still think of today.

Our cousin Orris Aumiller and his wife Bernita also lived in Selden, but I don't remember visiting with them on this trip. I think Orris may have still been in Korea following his tour of duty during the war. He was Uncle Warren's son; a soft-spoken good looking young man, who always reminded me of Audie Murphy, the most decorated American soldier of World War II and future Hollywood movie star.

We made three more trips to Selden during the next seven years, and if we missed them in 1954, we always visited with them on our subsequent trips. We were there for Easter in 1958; for Uncle Warren's funeral in 1960, and our last trip was for Grandma's funeral after she died on July 30th, 1961.

Before we arrived in 1961, Orris and Bernita told their seven (soon nine) little kids that Kennedy was coming to visit, and they were absolutely ecstatic when they heard the wonderful news. They were so proud and honored that such a great man would come to their house, and bragged to all their friends of the upcoming visit. Imagine their enormous disappointment when Kennedy Aumiller parked at their curb instead of President John F. Kennedy.

These were the best behaved kids I'd ever seen, and when you sat in the warmth and comfort of their little home, you never heard a peep from any of them. Orris and Bernita must have been very proud of them; I know I was!

●

Our cousins Donald "Doc" and his wife Joyce Wichers (daughter of Iva—Grandma Oldson's sister—and her husband Owen Bos); their daughters, Delores, Dorothy, Doris, and their son, Don, lived on a small farm just outside of Downs, Kansas, and our first trip to their home was a real treat for us all. My sisters and I'd never been to a farm before, so exploring the barn and climbing on the tractors and plows scattered around the outbuildings was kind of fun for us city slickers.

We'd toss horseshoes until our arms went limp, then stand beside the barn . . . kick dirt clods with our feet . . . chew on a long piece of straw . . . and say things like, *"yup," "nope,"* and *"looks like rain."* At the end of the day, we'd watch their dog round up the livestock and herd them into the barn, where we learned firsthand how to milk a cow. At night, we'd walk down the dirt road away from the house, and stare in awe at the incredible display of stars in the sky. We'd never seen the evening sky outside the glow of city lights and had no idea how vast it really was.

●

Our cousins Bill and Onita Jemison (also the daughter of Iva and Owen Bos); their daughters, Joyce, June, Jeannie and their son Ray, lived in Osborne, Kansas. Bill owned a jewelry store in town, and at the time, was probably the wealthiest member of my family. We'd have great family reunions at the city's park, and there was always plenty of great food and drink for us to enjoy . . . with aunts and uncles, friends, and more kids than I could count. It was pretty clear what people in small towns did when they got bored.

•

Going to Utah was always an adventure because of the perilous route through the Rocky Mountains. When the five-year Eisenhower Tunnel construction ended in 1973, driving over Loveland Pass could be avoided, but in the 1950s, driving the steep narrow serpentine highway was the only choice. Grossly underpowered cars and trucks snaked their way to the top of the 11,990 foot pass, and traffic only moved as fast as the slowest car. My sisters and I were always afraid of heights, and Dad never missed an opportunity to exploit our fears. When we'd look out the side window and whimper about how steep the embankment was, Dad would jerk the car to the right edge of the road and scare us half to death. We'd scream in terror and he'd laugh at our panicked expressions; always thrilled to spend this quality time "playing" with his kids.

Uncle Dan Oldson (Mom's brother), Aunt Edith and their six kids lived in Duchesne, where he worked for a propane company and she worked at one of the local diners.

Once we'd settled in for our visit, our cousins quickly separated us from our parents and took us outside to play. June and Darlene spent most of their time playing with our cousin Pickle (Laura), but Butch and Spike (Bill and Bob) didn't play favorites, and always included them in our boys club. While we romped and wrestled and played our big kid games, Ronnie, Rusty and Randy would dart around us like frantic little puppies at feeding time, but even though they were much younger than the rest of us, they were never excluded from joining in with our fun.

We spent most of our days hiking up the steep rugged foothills near their home on the outskirts of town, and played on the barren tabletop mesas. I don't know what adventures my sisters envisioned while we were there, but as John Wayne, I was always on the alert for an ambush from the Indians. It didn't occur to me at the time, but there really were a lot of Native

American Indians living in Utah, and even though they were probably used to the common prejudices of the times, I'm pretty sure they wouldn't have appreciated my own. But in my defense, political correctness wasn't yet a part of the American conscience, and my narrow little mind had already been heavily influenced by the hundreds of biased western movies I'd seen.

When we were finished on the mountain, we'd go back to their home and play in the yard around their house. There was always a shell of an old car or tractor sitting somewhere around their property, and when I climbed behind the steering wheel, my imaginary cowboy hat transformed into an army helmet as I drove my mighty Sherman tank across the battlefields of World War II Germany. *It was good to be a kid.*

In the evenings, we'd build a bonfire in the backyard, then tell ghost stories and other tall tales, while our parents sat at the kitchen table and played two or three hot games of Pinochle. Every now and again, we'd hear the sounds of whooping and hollering coming from inside the house when someone trumped an ace, and we'd laugh at their hysterics, knowing they were having just as much fun as we were.

We'd get up early on at least one day of our visit, and head to the beaver ponds for the best fishing you could imagine. I loved the beaver ponds, but not just because of the beavers who were there to entertain us. I loved them because the water was just shallow and clear enough to see where the fish were swimming, so we always knew just where to cast our line. I'd cast my spinner as close to them as I could, and dare them to take a bite of my lure as I slowly reeled in my line.

I think the adults were limited to ten trout per person, and the kids to only six. Our parents never seemed to have a problem catching their limit, but we hadn't quite mastered this sport of total relaxation, and rarely fared as well as the adults. And since we were only allowed to keep the fish longer than six inches, a lot of our time was spent in a catch and release mode. But by day's end, we always had enough for a dinner or two, and usually for breakfast as well.

Some of the best times of my life were spent fishing with my family and relatives, but fishing the beaver ponds in Utah was much more fun than fishing at Green Mountain, Jefferson, Homestake, Trappers, or Stillwater Lakes in Colorado, where we used worm-baited hooks and bobbers while we *endlessly* waited on the banks of the shore for that elusive tug on our lines. I never had much patience for that kind of fishing.

●

When we'd go to Nebraska, we'd visit with Uncle Duane Oldson (Mom's brother), Aunt Alice and their two boys Dick and Larry. Uncle Duane was a contractor who built commercial buildings and schools, and seemed to move back and forth quite a bit between Scotts Bluff and Broken Bow. Because the boys were so much older than Darlene and me, there was never anyone for us to play with, and we spent most of our time just hanging out with the grownups.

Mom and Dad always had a great time during these visits, and for a very good reason. Uncle Duane and Aunt Alice were the first to offer their help and support during their early years together, and still treated them like they were their best friends. We'd sit around the house while they reminisced about the good old days, and as I recall, great amounts of alcohol were consumed. Aunt Alice was a tough two-fisted drinker who could usually out-drink anyone at the table. But she wasn't an alcoholic like Aunt Zola . . . Aunt Zola drank as a substitute for life . . . Aunt Alice just drank for fun.

●

Visiting with Uncle Voyde Oldson (Mom's oldest brother) and Aunt Iva probably didn't qualify as real vacations, but we often drove to their home for one or two day visits while I was a young boy. They only lived in three places during all the years

I can remember . . . at Green Mountain Dam; in Loveland, Colorado, and finally in Greeley, Colorado. Uncle Voyde worked for the Bureau of Reclamation, and during their brief time at Green Mountain, lived in a small house in the Bureau Camp, just at the base of the reservoir spillway. It was probably safe enough; no one else seemed to worry, but I had a tough time sleeping at night knowing if the dam broke, we'd be the first to go (yeah, I know—too many disaster movies as a child).

They had four children: Merna, Iva Jean, Jim and Dennis, but I don't remember either of the girls being there during our early visits. The boys were young enough to keep me entertained, and I considered them to be my friends as well as my cousins.

In 1969, Jim married my first ex-wife Sandra, and even though we were no longer a couple (and our relationship was at best strained), it was good to still have her in the family. At least I could see her at family functions.

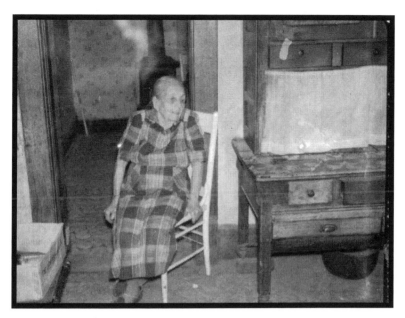

Our own Whistler's Mother

Grandma Aumiller & Aunt Ossie

The Oldson Family
Duane, Voyde, Dan, Bill
Grandma, Mom & Verne

The In-laws
Edith (Dan), Grandma, Orley (Verne), Dad,
Alice (Duane), Iva (Voyde)

CHAPTER 11

"Things Change"

Dad liked us when we were little kids, but by the mid 1950s, things started to change. We weren't really bad kids, we just weren't cute and cuddly anymore . . . well, at least June and I weren't. We were a lot more like Dad than he cared to admit, and our bull-headed stubbornness just made it that much more difficult for him to cope with us. As an adult I can understand how frustrating we must have been to him, but at the time, I just thought he was a grouchy old man.

But Darlene was still the best daughter a parent could ask for, and because she really was that good, we didn't mind that she was Dad's favorite child. She was always quiet and well behaved; did everything Dad asked without questioning why, and always did well in school. But June and I were just the opposite. We were loud and obnoxious . . . argued with everything Dad said, and only went to school because the law required it. We understood why Darlene was his favorite child, but neither of us were willing to be good enough to compete with her.

Dad and I rarely did any father/son things together in those days, so when he took me deer hunting when I was eleven years old, it was a huge deal to me.

On our first trip in October 1955, we headed to Green Mountain Dam with my Uncle Bill Wiley and two of my older cousins, Bud Bullock and Ray Stoumbaugh. We stopped for a break at the Mint Saloon in the original town of Dillon (now covered by the reservoir), where the men shot a few games of pool . . . drank far more beer than they should have, and shamelessly flirted with every waitress in the bar. The more Dad drank, the more he flirted, and the more he flirted, the more bags of potato chips and pork rinds he'd bribe me with to keep me from telling Mom when we got home. This became a standing joke for all of our hunting trips, but of course, I knew he wasn't serious about his flirtations, and never hesitated to tell Mom when our trips were over. Even at eleven-years-old I understood it was just harmless fun . . . that this was just Dad being his fun-loving self in the company of adults. He was always a lot of fun when he was with his friends, especially when he'd been drinking.

We left the bar after a couple of hours and drove into Heeney. We spent the night with the Hadeen's (old family friends from the dam building days), and just before sunrise the next morning, we drove to the base of Green Mountain.

Even though it was bitterly cold that morning, Dad dressed moderately. He knew it would get warmer later in the day, so the only clothes he wore besides his normal street clothes were his engineer boots, a light jean jacket, red vest and red hunter's cap. But not me . . . I was a wimpy little kid, and wore a heavy plaid coat, blue jeans, long underwear, fleece-lined boots, a red vest and red hunting cap with pull-down earflaps, and a pair of the warmest winter gloves I could find. The only thing missing from this scenario was that wascally wabbit, Bugs Bunny.

As we headed up the mountain, Dad told me to stay five steps behind him and to be *very, very* quiet. When I'd step on a dry leaf or twig, he'd turn and give me "the look" and I'd bow my head in shame and silently assure him I'd be more careful. As we continued up the hill, I watched each cautious step after the other, diligently avoiding anything that could possibly make the tiniest sound. But because I was so focused on my own two feet, I was completely oblivious to anything in front of me, and when Dad stopped every hundred feet or so to look around for any signs of movement, I'd walk right into the middle of his back. *If you thought I got "the look" before, you should have seen this one!* My cousins who were down the mountain from us later said it looked like we were connected by an invisible rubber band, and every time I bumped into Dad, they had a great laugh at this vaudevillian comedy that was my very first hunting trip.

I carried a long strand of rope (to drag the dead deer), a couple of plastic bags, and just to make me feel more like a man, Dad let me carry his hunting knife on my belt.

By midmorning, Dad spotted a small herd of deer about a hundred yards ahead of us. He picked out the only buck in the herd, and in one fluid motion, brought the rifle to his shoulder and fired. Hearing the incredibly loud bang of his old Winchester .30-30 and seeing the deer fall to the ground was the most exciting thing I'd ever experienced! We raced through the fields of sagebrush and found the deer struggling to get to its feet; barely still alive, and obviously in the last throes of its life. I was surprisingly comfortable when Dad slit its throat, and had no trouble at all when he showed me how to gut it out. He put the heart and liver in the plastic bags so we could take them to Uncle Bill Wiley's mother in Dillon, then tied the rope around the deer's hind legs and dragged it down the mountain to our car. I walked proudly beside him carrying those gross bags of organs.

For those of you who haven't already figured it out, this was as basic as a hunting trip could possibly get. There were no Fifth-Wheel RVs for us to camp in, no horses, Jeeps or ATVs to take us up the mountain or carry the deer back down when we were done. There were no custom rifles or telescopes involved in this hunt, just good military trained marksmanship and old fashion hard work. And we never hunted for trophies; it was always about the food. Mom, Dad, Grandma Oldson, and Aunt Daisy butchered the deer themselves on that big butcher-block table at Grandma's house, and we'd all have venison steaks for the next several months.

Hunting with Dad over the next few years was the most joy I had with him in my teen years, and was the prelude to the greatest bond and friendship a father and son could possibly share.

●

On Sunday, September 9th 1956, the Continental Paper Company at 1000 West Louisiana Avenue burned to the ground. With its demise, my Uncle Orley was suddenly without a job, and without his usual income, he and Aunt Verne were at risk of losing their small mountain home in the nearby town of Kittredge. Mom just couldn't let that happen to her sister, so she gave up her cherished freedom and found a full time job, just to help make their mortgage payments. She spent most of her life sacrificing for others, and this was typical of her kindness. When Uncle Orley finally went back to work, Mom realized just how much she enjoyed her job and decided to continue working. I was twelve-years-old by then, so we were all legally old enough to stay at home by ourselves, and the extra income propelled us into a lifestyle we'd never imagined possible.

Mom worked for The Monaghan Company at 500 Alcott Street, a company that manufactured medical instruments for artificial respiration and equipment designed for the treatment of lung disease. She was encouraged to bring home piecework for the family to work on as often as she could, and in the evenings, we'd all sit around the kitchen table and carefully trim the excess rubber from molded face mask harnesses (apparently, no one invented a machine that could handle this process and it had to be done by hand). We earned 15 cents for each harness we trimmed, and if we worked really fast, we could finish about ten masks in an hour. When we added our earnings from this to the three dollars we'd get each week for our allowance, we felt like we were practically rich.

Mom's innate abilities, extreme dedication to work and natural people skills were very much appreciated by the management at Monaghans, so when her boss Marie quit and moved to Los Angeles in 1957, Mom was promoted to the vacant supervisory position and continued to work in middle management until her retirement in early 1973.

Now that Mom was working, we became a two-car family for the very first time when Dad bought an old green 1948 Dodge pickup he used to get back and forth from work. It needed some work, but over the years gave Dad hours of pleasure as he restored it to a pristine condition in his free time in the alley beside the fire station.

By the end of September 1956, when the 1957 line of new cars hit the market, Dad bought his second new car. The new Chevrolets, Plymouths and Fords were sporting the innovative and provocative new big fin look everyone loved, but as enticing as they were, Dad decided against buying any of them. His philosophy was "if you can't buy it wholesale, don't buy it," which was especially true when it came to buying new cars. He went to see Jack Olson at Burt Chevrolet on South Broadway near Cornell Avenue, and found a beautiful red and white 1956 Chevy with a powerful V-8 engine he just couldn't live without. It was still a brand new car, but far less expensive than the 1957 models, and in the end, money talked, and the cheaper car was the only logical choice.

New cars were a huge source of pride for my dad, and were symbolic of the achievements he never dreamed possible. His rise from the depths of extreme poverty into the realm of what we considered to be an affluent middle class lifestyle wasn't exactly a classic rags to riches fairytale, but it certainly qualified as a rags to better rags success story.

Over the next few years, he bought three more new cars from Jack Olson: a black and white 1959 Chevrolet Impala, a blue 1963 Chevrolet Impala, a blue 1966 Chevrolet Impala, and finally in 1969, he bought a new blue Ford LTD he found on display at the airport.

A Ford??

I was stunned! Dad and Uncle Bill Oldson always had a feud over which car was better, and of course, Dad was adamant about the superiority of the Chevrolet. I guess he just liked the looks of the Ford that year.

When he retired in 1973, he was still happy with his car, and for the first time in over twenty years, he didn't have a monthly car payment to worry about. That was a very good way to start his retirement. In 1978, he sold his old Ford and bought a two-year old Cadillac from Charlie Dains (Aunt Annavate's second husband), and tenderly nursed it along for the next thirteen years. In 1991, he bought his last new car, a silver Chevrolet Lumina sedan. The car promised speeds of up to 120 mph, but in true old codger fashion, the needle on his speedometer rarely went beyond the 35 mph mark.

•

On Friday, April 26th, 1957, on June's eighteenth birthday, she married Tommy Wayne Blake at the Grace Brethren Church at 700 South Federal Boulevard and immediately moved out of our house. Apparently, she just couldn't wait another day to get away from the tyranny of Dad's iron-fisted rule. Darlene and I hated to see her leave, but when Dad raised our allowances from $3 to $5 per week, we forgot what she even looked like.

Darlene had her own bedroom now, and I shared mine with our cousin Poncho (Claude) who'd moved in with us just a short time earlier. He was Uncle Glenn and Aunt Margie's boy and had been invited to live with us so he could have more opportunities in life than Selden had to offer. He was six or seven years older than me, but from the very beginning, treated me like I was his very own brother, and included me in pretty much everything he did. He'd take me fishing . . . to the movies, and we even joined the Workman's Gym in north Denver so we could be all muscular and buff while we cruised 16th Street in his sporty 1955 red and white Ford convertible, looking for cheap and easy girls. We never found any, of course, but (we thought) we looked *really* good in the process.

For a boy who'd always been outvoted in a democracy of two sisters all his life, it was great to finally have someone on my side. Poncho lived with us until the spring of 1960, then went into the army. I never saw him again.

In the summer of 1957, when I was thirteen, I decided it was time to start working during my summer vacations. Aunt Annavate (who insisted we just call her Annie) was dating Charlie Dains, the manager of United Dairies at 646 Bryant Street, and with a little coaxing from her, Charlie hired me to work as a laborer in the plant.

Charlie was a big lumbering John Wayne kind of guy, who, in my opinion, was one of the luckiest men alive. Annie was a stunning redheaded temptress who could have easily been a movie star in the days when Hollywood was still famous for its beautiful actresses, but as gorgeous as she was, it was a real toss-up between her and Aunt Rainie. They were both *extremely* beautiful women, and I liked to delude myself into believing their genes were common among the Aumiller family.

Charlie just got luckier and luckier, and on Tuesday, November 12th, 1957, he and Annie were married . . . and my summer jobs were assured for the next three years.

●

Yes, things were really going well for the Aumiller family. With the extra income from Mom's job and one less child to support, my parents were able to afford many more luxuries in life, and in the spring of 1958, they announced their plans to take us to California.

OH, MY GOD!!!—CALIFORNIA!

Hollywood!! . . . Movie Stars!! . . . Disneyland!! . . . L.A. Freeways!! . . . the Pacific Ocean!! This was a vacation we could *never* have imagined, and we'd soon be rubbing elbows with the elite of America. I felt faint!

Dad borrowed $500 from the credit union, and early on Saturday morning, June 7th, 1958, we loaded the trunk with our luggage, then Grandma Oldson, Darlene and I crawled into the cramped back seat of our '56 Chevy, and we began our first and only real family vacation together.

Mom kept a journal of our trip so we could relive those wonderful memories whenever we wanted. It was an incredible vacation for our family, and reading about it now after more than fifty years, I'm amused by some of the comments she wrote. She seemed to have been just as excited about staying at motels and eating at restaurants as she was about all the other wonderful things we saw and did, but in all fairness to my (then) thirty-five-year-old mother, this was her first real vacation, too, and all of those things were as new to her as they were to us.

Her journal was brief . . . and as follows:

CALIFORNIA TRIP

June 7, 1958

28,795 Mileage
Left home 4:35 am
Returned home 4:36 am
Forgot road maps!

The sun is just barely up. Beautiful! Gassed up 11.4 gal $4.20. Ate breakfast at Poncha Springs about 7:30. Car is acting up – missing some – Fuel pump maybe. Arrived in Gunnison 9:30 am. Mileage 28,994 – 11.8 gal $4.49, oil .51.

Was the fuel pump! Left Gunnison at 10:40 am. Arrived in Montrose at noon. Discovered we have missed Wolf Creek Pass. We'll travel the million dollar Hiway.

Ate lunch at Ridgway. Good food. Mileage 29,086. Stopped at Ouray to see Box Canyon Falls. Cost $.50, but is worth more. It's beautiful. Scenery between Silverton and Durango is spectacular. Saw Twentieth Century Fox (4:00 pm) shooting movies at Haviland Lake. Didn't recognize anyone, but Bill thought he did.

Entered New Mexico at 5:17 pm. Mileage 29,192. There are many house trailers in this area – wonder why? Farmington 6:00 pm gas 12.2 $5.00. Mileage 29,221. Shiprock 6:45 pm.

Rented a motel here, Natoani Nez, and had dinner at restaurant of same name. All Indian help and I don't believe they understand English very well. Poor service, and food the same. We're all tired and ready to go to bed even though it's only 8:30. Got to bed about 10:00.

June 8

Mom was up at 4:30 – the rest of us at 5:30. Left the motel at 6:10. No place to eat, so will travel. 7:00 am. Still no place to eat. Just saw a Navajo reservation – small part of it. It covers 16 million acres in 3 states. Kennedy says he wouldn't trade a piece of our land wide enough to piss across for all 16 million acres.

Arrived in Gallup 8:05. Had breakfast at M&M Café. Real good. Mileage 29,344. Got car greased here, also new fan belt & oil changed. $8.17. Gassed at Painted Desert, 29,417 mileage 12.1 gals $4.70.

Went through Petrified Forest. All the trees are laying on the ground. Had dinner at Holbrook. Not so hot service or food. Mileage 29,567 $2.00 5 gal gas.

4:15 pm. Saw house trailer overturned in middle of hi-way on way to Grand Canyon. Saw canyon made by Little Colo. River and thought it was amazing, but the Grand Canyon is fabulous. So wide and deep and colorful. Gassed up at the top of park. $3.00 7.5 gal Mileage 29,655.

Saw two deer and took pictures. Later saw another deer – tame! People were feeding it. Around 7:00 pm when we left the park.

Williams – 8:30 pm. Tired, dirty and hungry. Found a nice room at Westerer Motel. Good eats & service at the Koffe Pot Café.

June 9

Left Williams June 9 4:05 am. Mileage 29,715.

Ate breakfast in Prescott, Arizona at Maxine's Restaurant. Poor coffee. Gas 10.7 gal $4.12 Mileage 29,826.

Crossed California line at 10 am. Mileage 29,946. Colorado river is really wide. Elevation 265 ft!

10:45 am. Saw two cars wreaked. They collided head on – road straight and wide. Remember seeing ambulance heading toward Blythe about half hour ago, 1 mile west of Desert Center. Mileage turned 30,000.

11 am – Stopped for lunch at Indio at noon. Tommy Barbers Café. Good food. Plenty hot here. Gas at White Water. Mileage 30,077. 11.6 gal $4.40.

Went thru Riverside at 2:30 pm. First pretty spot we've seen in California. Arrived in Pomona at 3:15 pm. Kenny is out of town and Helen is working till 9 pm. We're heading for L.A. on the freeway. Didn't get anywhere, but got there fast. (Gas 2.00 LA 4.00 11.9 Ventura)

180

Had supper at Mom's Café – good food, good service. Went back to Helens for watermelon and cantaloupe. Stayed all night at Eldo Motel.

June 10

Had breakfast with Helen – real good hot cakes. Left Pomona about 10:30 – back to the freeway. Got on Santa Ana freeway to go to Union Station, but somehow was going the wrong way and went 12 miles past the turn off before Kennedy realized we were going wrong. I'm turned around, so I didn't know any better. Got back to Union Station at noon and met Pinky & Lee. Had lunch at Hady's on Hollywood & Vine. Drove out Sunset Blvd. to the beach.

Real pretty homes on this drive. Saw Jeff Chandler driving out of a parking lot before lunch. Wow!

Took off our shoes and waded in the ocean. Cold! Went to Marineland. What an interesting place. The trained whale, porpoises and seals were wonderful. Had supper at a seafood place down by the amusement park. Good food. Back to Pomona and the Eldo Motel at midnight.

June 11

Had breakfast at Helens. No one home, so we fixed our own. Back to Los Angeles to meet Pinky's at noon. Goofed! Should have been there at 10 am. Met them at Disneyland at 2 pm. Some place, especially for kids. Back to Pomona and supper with the Ballon's. The kids went to a show and we played cards. We were going to Knotts Berry Farm, but it closed early. Slept at the Ballon's, too.

June 12

Had breakfast and bid our goodbyes to Kenny and Helen. Met Pinky & Lee at 10 am and called Marie. Met her at noon and had lunch with her on the beach at The Point. Sure nice to see her again. Stopped at Ventura to buy a bathing suit then drove down to the ocean for a swim. Not much swimming, but lots of fun. Had supper at Andersons in Buelton and stayed in the Deluxe Motel in Santa Maria. Pretty town and nice rooms.

June 13

Up at 8 am. Had breakfast at restaurant. Good food. We are following Hiway 1 up the coast. Elevation 50 ft in almost every town. Gassed up in Loma Vista.

14.6 gal $5.91. This is in the mountains – very pretty. Saw the Begonia Gardens. Beautiful! Ate lunch in Monterey at El Patio. Good food, nice waitress. Arrived in Frisco about 6:30 pm. Houses are wall to wall and no yards. Drove on to Stinson Beach and Sea Downs for a free beer. Got there about 8:30 pm and they were closed. Drove back to San Rafael. Had dinner at King Cotton (not very good food) and stayed at San Rafael Inn. Nice place. Called Dan to let him know we will be there sometime Monday.

June 14

Slept till almost 10 am. Had breakfast at King Cotton and are on our way. Gas in San Rafael 10.9 gal $3.90. Made a tour of San Francisco today by cable car. Saw famous Telegraph Hill, a little of China Town and Fisherman's Wharf. The smell! Took an hour cruise on the Sea King – her maiden voyage. Very interesting. Saw a refrigerator ship flying the flag of Denmark. Saw three flat tops, one of them the Midway. Didn't catch the other two names. Couldn't see the golden gate because of the fog banks there. Saw a cargo ship, a tanker and sea going tugs. Went under the Bay Bridge and around Alcatraz. Later we drove over Bay Bridge. Had lunch at Alioto's on the wharf. Good, but expensive. Coffee and tea $.25 a cup.

Left Frisco about six o'clock and drove to Modesto. Went to Auntie Vi's and she was gone. Stayed at the Phyl-Mor Motel and went swimming in the pool.

June 15

Had breakfast at the Lotus in Modesto. Went back to see Auntie Vi about 7:30 am. Had a real nice visit with her and a big delicious bowl of strawberry shortcake. Left at 11:25 am. Had lunch at Ranch Sierra Inn – Lousy service and overcharge – 1 mile high. Gas 11.5 gal $4.70 Mileage 31,445.

Stopped at Reno to play slot machines. Bill and Darlene invested $.50 apiece at Harold's Club and made $1.15 each.

I hit a $7.50 jackpot. Made $2.50. Only spent an hour there. Had dinner in Lovelock at "Carls Slaughter House," says Bill. Gas at the Two Stiffs gas station in Lovelock. 5.9 gal $2.49. Stayed at Winnemucca Nev. at the West End Motel. Terrible beds.

June 16

Gas at Battle Mountain 7.9 gal $3.45. Gas at State Line. Mileage 31,857, 8.7 gal. $3.50. Left Nevada and played our last slot machine.

Mom and Darlene came out ahead. Ate breakfast at the Star Casino in Winnemucca. Crossed the Great Salt Lake Desert. Not very warm because we got across it early. Got in Salt Lake about noon and it's real hot here. Had lunch at Morrison's – good food. Gas out of Heber City 10.4 gal $4.05 Mileage 32,036.

Mileage 32,138 gas 5.1 gal $1.93. Got to Dan's about 4 pm. Spent 2 days and had a nice time. Ate plenty and slept a lot. Played pinochle two nights. First night the men won all but one game. Last night we women skunked them three games.

June 19

Last leg of our trip. Started home at 9:30 am. Stopped in Vernal to do some shopping. Ate lunch in Artesia. Ran into a herd of sheep on the hi-way just out of Meeker. Heard the sheepherder tell some people there were 1000 ewes and 1400 lambs.

Mileage 32,315 7.8 gal $3.06. Gas in Rifle.

Ate supper in Dillon and learned Bus Wiley was buried yesterday. We drove to the cemetery on our way home. So Sad! They were both so young. (This wasn't in the journal, but Uncle Bill Wiley's brother and his wife were killed in an automobile accident).

Got home about 8 pm. Took Mom home first – no one there. Aunt Daisy and Maxine were out for a ride, but came home shortly after we got there. We came on home and again no one here. Guess Poncho is bowling. Home never looked so good.

●

By the summer of 1959, I'd reached that defiant stage in my life when I thought I was bigger, smarter and much stronger than my dad. I'd been lifting weights for over a year now and still working hard at the dairy. I was strong for a fifteen-year-old, 147 pound boy, and because of all the fights I'd had in my life, thought I was a pretty tough guy . . . definitely tougher than my "old" thirty-nine-year-old dad.

I was wrong!

Early on a Sunday afternoon, Dad asked me to help take a mattress to Granddad's home at 945 Emerson Street. It was usually difficult to find a parking space at Granddad's home, but when we arrived, we found one directly in front of his house. A car was stopped in the middle of the road half a block ahead of us, but at the time, we didn't pay much attention to it.

Dad parked at the curb, we pulled the mattress from the bed of his pickup, and as we carried it toward the front door, the car backed up next to our truck and the driver started screaming at Dad for taking his parking space. Dad turned and said, *"You were half a block away when we pulled in. How was I supposed to know you wanted to park here?"* He told the man we'd be finished in a couple of minutes and he could have the space when we left. But the man just got louder and more abusive. Dad ignored his rantings and we continued carrying the mattress to the front porch. By now, the man was out of his car; flailing his arms and fists and getting madder by the second. I was sure Dad was afraid of him . . . I know I was. *This guy was huge!!*

We set the mattress on the porch and Dad calmly walked back to the passenger side of his truck and opened the door. The madman yelled, *"Yeah, you better get a club, you little son-of-a-bitch."* Dad took his glasses off and set them on the seat, then walked around the back of the truck and said, *"I don't need a club for you."* He ran toward this towering giant and beat him like the dog that he was. He threw a right . . . a left . . . a right . . . another left . . . over and over again! He had the man trapped against the back of his car and he couldn't get away from the onslaught of Dad's punishing blows. The man begged him to stop, and after one final powerful punch, Dad stood down. Blood poured from the man's now battered face as he stood up and apologized, then crawled into his car and slowly drove away. I think he felt lucky to still be alive.

I couldn't believe my eyes! I remembered the fight Dad had in the projects, but this was even more awesome!! I would never again question Dad's authority or power. *He was the man!!!*

Working at Monaghans—Mom's sitting to the blonde's left

Mom happily at work

Mom (second from the left); her boss Marie on the right

CHAPTER 12

"Sandra"

Dad's physical superiority made me a much more respectful and obedient son, but my fear of him did nothing to curb my rampant teenage hormones.

Early in 1960, my two-year childhood romance with my first love ended, and by June, I met my future wife, Sandra Russell. A nineteen-year-old Ava Gardner lookalike hired as a key-punch operator at the dairy, she was the most beautiful girl I'd ever seen! . . . I think every guy at the dairy wanted her. I flirted with her at every opportunity, and was both shocked and elated when she agreed to go out with me. I was only sixteen, but convinced her that I was nineteen, which wasn't too hard to do since I always looked older than my age. It was a good thing back in the day, but not so great now that I'm sixty-eight. Anyway, we dated throughout the summer, and by the time she found out how old I really was, I had her hooked. What a guy!

Our flirtations at work apparently interfered with the good order of business and it was decided one of us would have to leave. Nepotism clearly prevailed, and when Sandra was dismissed, she immediately found work as a nurse's aide in a nursing home at East 11th Avenue and Pennsylvania Street.

We had a great summer and fall, but by early November, it all caught up with us when we learned she was pregnant.

We'd done an awful lot of kissing and stuff (like frenzied rabbits), so we really weren't too surprised when one of those rabbits died. But I didn't see it as a bad thing; in fact, I saw it as one of the best things that could have happened to me. Like most sixteen-year-old boys, I thought I was more grown up than I was and saw this as the perfect way to get away from the oppression of "Attila the Dad."

We dreaded telling my parents, but on the evening we sat down at their kitchen table and told them the news, we were relieved by how well they accepted it. It would be years before I did the math, but clearly any other response from them would have been the proverbial pot calling the kettle black; something they've never done, but many of my readers may be guilty of. And to those people I say, *"let he who is without sin cast the first stone."* Anyhooo . . . since abortions weren't legal in those days, we all agreed the only honorable thing we could do was get married.

On Friday, November 12th, 1960, five months after we'd met and seven months before I graduated from Lincoln High School (and still just sixteen-years-old), I married the second love of my life, twenty-year-old Sandra Lee Russell, in a civil ceremony in the living room of my parents' home. I wore a new black suit Mom bought for me at Montgomery Wards, and Sandra wore a wedding gown she'd borrowed from an aunt.

From the first day of our marriage, my relationship with Dad dramatically changed. In his eyes, I was now an adult, and from that moment on, treated me as an equal and not as his ward. He became my best friend, and for the next thirty-three years, we shared a bond of mutual respect and admiration unsurpassed by any other father and son.

We rented a tiny studio apartment in the basement of a house at 1001 East Asbury Avenue, and began what we knew would be a lifetime of marital bliss. Our rent was $45 per month, but with the $50 she made each week and the $1.10 an hour I made working evenings at the dairy, we had just enough to support ourselves.

By January 1961, Sandra suffered a miscarriage, and the independence I'd found in marriage was suddenly in jeopardy. Mom and Dad briefly considered having our marriage annulled, but decided against it when they saw how well we were doing together. I think they understood how difficult it would be for us to adjust to merely dating again, and knew it would be nearly impossible to keep me at home. Those days of innocence were gone.

Going to school and working every evening turned out to be much more than I could handle, and whenever I was too tired for school I'd stay home and sleep. It wasn't a problem (I thought) because when I'd return to school the next day, I'd simply take a note to the Principal's Office that read, *"Billy was sick,"* signed *"Mrs. Aumiller."* At the time I thought it was pretty cool because no one else in school had that much liberty, and I was relatively certain that I was the only boy in school who was having sex every day, at least with another person.

As the school year progressed, my history teacher took me aside and said if I didn't make some changes pretty quickly, there was a very good chance I wouldn't graduate. I knew if I ever wanted to be a policeman I'd need a high school diploma, so I quit my night job and concentrated on my grades.

As soon as I graduated from high school, we moved to a larger one-bedroom basement apartment at 332 South Canosa Court (in the same house that June and Tommy were renting), and I returned to work at the dairy.

Before I started delivering milk to the Westwood section of southwest Denver, I'd heard all these great stories about how housewives in their skimpy morning attire greeted their milkmen, and looked forward to these cheap voyeuristic thrills. I guess I worked the wrong route, because the only thrill I ever got during my stint as a milkman was the tingling of frostbite on the tips of my fingers from the icy chill of some very cold milk bottles.

It didn't take long to get tired of getting up at 3:30 every morning, so I quit my job with the dairy and found work as a mail boy at the Superior Oil Company at 1700 Broadway.

The Superior Oil Company occupied the entire nineteenth and half of the eighteenth floor in the 21-story Mile High Building, and their offices were the most elegant I'd ever seen. To keep with the professional decor of the business, I was required to wear suits to work, even though I was at the absolute bottom rung of the corporate ladder. I thought I looked just as professional as everyone else, and felt great pride in being a member of this organization.

I worked alone in the mailroom and immediately fell in love with my job. The chief geologists, geophysicists and corporate attorneys all had their own secretaries, who, with few exceptions, conformed to a strict guideline of sexuality and beauty. It didn't take long for them to take this innocent seventeen-year-old boy under their wings, and the prettiest of them always seemed to have business in the mailroom. Sexual harassment in the work place wasn't even a term back then and I was a willing recipient of daily hugs, pecks on the cheek, and blatant sexual innuendos. I thought it was a wonderful job.

I was biding my time until I was old enough to become a policeman, so I never gave a second thought about the limitations of this job. I made $175 per month, and Sandra was making nearly double that amount at her clerical job at the Rust Sales Company near West 17th Avenue and Zuni Street, so compared to our first few months together, we were doing quite well.

I attended evening classes at the Denver extension of the University of Colorado, or UCLA, as I liked to call it (the University of Colorado between Lawrence and Arapahoe Streets), but I really wasn't ready for college and missed having my evenings free with my bride, and after a few short months, I dropped out of school.

Sandra and I moved to an apartment at 3001 West Colorado Avenue, then to another at 1428 West Mississippi Avenue, but when she went on maternity leave in December 1962, we were forced to move in with Mom and Dad.

On Sunday, January 6th, 1963 at 2:48 pm, my first daughter Kimberly Ann was born at St. Luke's Hospital . . . and just like her dad, had a protruding tooth in the front of her mouth. The following morning, I caught the city bus to work and strutted up and down the aisles showing pictures of my brand new baby to complete strangers. I was so proud!

Shortly after the assassination of President John F. Kennedy on Friday, November 22nd, 1963, Superior Oil Company closed their offices in Denver and returned to Houston. I found another job as a mail boy with the California Oil Company in the same building, and worked there until Dad made me an offer I couldn't refuse.

He offered to pay for all my expenses if I'd go back to school, including our housing and utilities. He bought a 10' x 42' two-bedroom trailer from my cousin Jim Oldson, and we lived in a mobile home park at 1050 South Pierce Street. (Most people preferred to call them mobile homes, but ours was so small it could only qualify as a trailer). In the spring of 1964, we moved into the trailer and I began my classes at "UCLA."

CHAPTER 13

"Sisters"

When I left home in November 1960, Darlene became the undisputed favorite Aumiller child on Bryant Street. She'd graduated from West High School just five months earlier, and immediately found a job at the U.S. National Bank at 817 17th Street. She never felt the oppression from Dad that June and I'd experienced, and as an eighteen-year-old responsible young adult, had much more freedom than either of us had. Living with Mom and Dad was easy for her, and to be honest, I think she enjoyed being the only child at home once we were gone.

She was uncommonly frugal with her earnings, and unlike the rest of us, actually saved her money. When our neighbors John and Marilyn Warren went through their unexpected divorce, she bought most of their furniture at a fraction of the cost of new furniture, and substantially added to the hope chest she was actually preparing for her future.

In the summer of 1961, Mom and Dad took Darlene and Grandma Oldson on another fantasy vacation . . . this time to the equally alluring and exotic state of Florida. A pattern was definitely emerging here, but I couldn't decide if these wonderful road trips were a reward for those of us who stayed at home, or a penalty for those of us who moved out.

By now, Darlene was deeply involved with a seventeen-year-old boy she'd met three years earlier at the Bowl-Mor bowling alley at 1441 Court Place in downtown Denver. She'd joined a bowling league with her best friend Judy Over, and during their weekly competitions, met Robert Arthur Brown, Jr., the (then) fourteen-year-old boy she'd eventually marry.

Bob was an athletic good looking young boy, who worked as a pinsetter at his parents' bowling alley. It didn't take long for them to feel the attraction for each other, and their meeting blossomed into an exciting four-year romance.

On Friday, November 9th, 1962, my twenty-year-old sister Darlene married her eighteen-year-old sweetheart at the Harvey Park Baptist Church at 2112 South Patton Court, with the Reverend D. Raymond Parry officiating. *"She wore a gown of white silk organza over white satin with embroidered rose's appliquéd. Her illusion veil was held by a crown of white roses, and she carried white roses on a Bible"*—Denver Post. It was a storybook wedding, highlighted by a beautiful rendition of The Hawaiian Wedding Song, sung by a very gifted and inexpensive singer . . . my oldest sister, June. There wasn't a dry eye in the house.

They moved into a little house on South Hazel Court near Jewell Avenue, and the furniture Darlene had stored at Bob (Senior) and Rose Brown's house at 2779 West Harvard Avenue, was finally put to use.

Two months earlier, Bob went to work at the Honeywell plant at 4800 E. Dry Creek Road, and Darlene continued to work at the bank. When she was eight months pregnant, she quit her job and began her brand new career as a stay-at-home mom. They had their son Robbie on Saturday, August 17th, 1963, and in September or October, they bought a rural little home on the east side of Parker Road, just north of the tiny town of Parker. With their very first mortgaged home and their way too cute new baby boy, they were ready for a long and full life together.

When Darlene got married and left home, Mom and Dad became the proverbial empty nesters . . . but their nest really wasn't all that empty. We may have been gone, but we were constantly coming back to visit, and by now, June and Tom had their three daughters: Crystal, who was born on Thursday,

December 12th, 1957 . . . Pam on Sunday, April 5th, 1959, and Becky on Wednesday, March 21st, 1962. Mom once told me becoming a grandmother for the first time was the most exciting day of her life, so having these grandchildren was an enormous blessing for her.

And over the next few years, we all did our very best to keep Mom happy.

Sandra and I had Kimberly on Sunday, January 6th, 1963, and Cynthia on Monday, February 28th, 1966; Darlene and Bob had their second child Connie on Thursday, January 20th, 1966, and June and Tom had their fourth child Tommy on Wednesday, November 11th, 1964. It was very hard work, but with a little sweat and effort, we all managed to get the job done.

In 1972, my twenty-eight-year-old brother-in-law Bob quit his job at Honeywell and began a new career as a building contractor. He'd always wanted to be his own boss, and this was the perfect choice for him. He worked on different projects in the Perry Park and Parker areas, but when the construction business slowed down in 1973, he and Darlene moved to Grand Junction, Colorado. Oil shale exploration was in full swing near the town of Parachute, and there was a huge construction boom to satisfy.

But the boom didn't last, and when the construction business started thinning out in 1976, Bob and Darlene decided to move to the west coast. They settled in Eugene, Oregon, and after a few years, moved north to the Portland area.

Bob eventually got out of the construction business and they opened four different .99 Cent Stores in Portland, Oregon and Longview, Washington, but never had more than two stores at the same time.

In March 1991, they finished building their beautiful new house and workshop (by themselves) on the hillside overlooking the Columbia River in Kalama, Washington. They'd been living in a small on-site trailer during the long construction process, so it was an especially good day for them when they finally moved in. They eventually closed their remaining store in Longview, and started their own furniture construction business at their home, which they still operate today.

•

In 1970, after suffering through thirteen long years of severe physical and mental abuse, June finally divorced Tom and was thrust into the role of a single mother with four young children to raise. She went to work at her local Safeway store, and struggled to make ends meet with her modest salary and the minimal child support she was getting from Tom. It was a tough journey for a thirty-one-year-old woman who'd never been on her own before, but she was far better off without him.

In 1971, June met a man we all thought would be her next husband. Leonard Thomas was much better looking than any of her other suitors, and according to June, was a real man in the truest sense of the word. He was quite a bit taller than June's Tinker Bell stature . . . both trim and fit, and had a full head of hair and thick brown mustache that made him look just like the Marlboro Man. He was a genuinely good and kind man with a great sense of humor (something June certainly deserved), and everyone in the family loved him . . . including our very discerning dad, who was usually overly critical about any man who showed any interest in his daughter.

By October 1973, June was tired of the constant conflict with Tom and decided a radical change was in order. Her solution was to move to Grand Junction, where she'd still have family ties, but without the constant grief from her ex-husband. Her company allowed her to transfer to a store in Grand Junction, where she continued to work for the Safeway family until her retirement in the summer of 2001.

By November 1974, June and Leonard had shared nearly four wonderful years together, but it all came to a tragic end when the brakes failed on the Western Air Drilling truck he was driving, and he was killed in the horrific accident that followed.

June was devastated!! She'd been through some very tough times in her life, but none of them compared to the grief and sorrow she now had to endure.

The next five months were excruciating. Loneliness gave way to even greater despair, then finally, on Friday, April 25th, 1975 (one day before her thirty-sixth birthday), the first glimmer of relief appeared when friends took her out to cheer her up with dinner and drinks at one of their favorite little bistros.

A much younger twenty-six-year-old Bill Studebaker came to her table and asked her to dance. June was a beautiful woman who never had any problems enticing good-looking men (if she wanted to), but she had absolutely no interest in being with a man that night, and curtly told him no. But instead of giving up like any normal man would, he asked if he could at least sit down with her. She gave him a look that was far less than friendly, then reluctantly said, *"Sure, but don't expect me to talk with you."* She ignored him as much as she could, but apparently this only made him more eager to know her. His perseverance seemed to pay off, because that night was the beginning of their twenty-two year relationship that led to their marriage in Las Vegas on Wednesday, May 3rd, 1978.

Bill's family owned pig farms in the Grand Junction area, but regrettably he didn't share in their wealth. He was selling pig heaters for a Swedish based company when June first met him, but his real passion in life was making custom jewelry. Unfortunately for him, it didn't pay well enough to make a decent living, and he was forced to keep the day job he preferred to do without. He gave up his job in sales and became a purchasing agent for several different companies in the Grand Junction area, and sometime around 1985, he and June built a beautiful new custom home at 2176 I-Road, where they lived until they separated in 1997.

This nineteen-year marriage wasn't abusive like her first one, and because it ended so amicably with their divorce in 1998, they remained close friends until he (too) was killed in a roll-over accident on Friday, May 1st, 2009.

He'd been out drinking with one of his friends somewhere near his home in Crawford, Colorado, and at the end of the night, his designated driver took the wheel of Bill's car and headed for his home. When they were just a mile or two away from his house, the friend lost control of the car, and Bill became the sole victim of this tragic one-car accident.

●

And now a little insight into the character of my two sisters . . .

As you already know, June is five years older than me. That really doesn't mean anything today, but when we were both little kids, there was an enormous difference between our size and level of maturity, and because June's maternal instincts have always been so strong, she thought it was her sworn duty to punish me whenever I did anything wrong. But just like my dad, I didn't need a different mother to keep me in line, and resented those fly-swatter whippings she'd give me when I was still a little boy. (Oh, yeah. I was the victim of sister abuse!)

And to retaliate for this horrible injustice, I tried my very best to be a pain in her side every time I had the chance. If you'd ask her, she'd probably tell you I was pretty successful . . . especially when she started dating. I was always peeking around the corner of the refrigerator to spy on her whenever she and her boyfriend "du jour" snuck to the back of the kitchen to smooch, and never hesitated to tell Mom if they looked like they were having too much fun. (Of course, this only happened on the nights Dad was at the Fire Station).

But my attitude toward her dramatically changed when I grew up. It didn't take long to see that she had an absolute heart of gold and would do anything she could to make your life just a little better.

She's never smoked, but definitely enjoyed a drink or two when she was a younger woman, and partied just as hard as most single people her age seemed to do. But that all changed during her marriage to Bill when she rediscovered her deep faith in the Lord and devoted her life to Christ. It wasn't a big change in character, since she's always been such a good and caring person, and if religion is something that gives her the joy and relief she needs, it's absolutely the right thing for her to pursue.

I'm also a Born Again Christian, but my devotion to the church was severely shaken when I recognized the hypocrisy of the *far* too many *Good Christians* I'd met in life, and soon discovered it was much easier for me to justify my self-serving actions when I wasn't encumbered by the strict doctrines of organized religion. But I certainly respect June for her devotion.

When her youngest daughter Becky gave birth to Cheyenne on Monday, September 17th, 2001, June brought her new grand-daughter home from the hospital, and for the past ten years has raised her as her own while Becky has chosen a different life.

Only a person with the soul of a Saint would make that kind of life commitment . . . the kind of commitment that deserves far more recognition than June's ever received.

She's had far more trouble and grief in her life than any one person could possibly deserve, and if nothing else is gleaned from reading this book, the beauty and purity of her very soul should be recognized and applauded.

I've made several seemingly disparaging remarks about June throughout this book, but they've all been made in goodhearted fun . . . the kind of fun June understands, and even more importantly, fully appreciates. Even today when she calls and says, *"Billy, it's your favorite sister,"* she knows when I laugh and say, *"Hi, Darlene,"* what I really mean is *"I love you and I'm so happy to hear from you."* That's the kind of relationship we have.

Now, Darlene's another story altogether. She's **always** been the sweetheart I've described, and because we're so close to the same age, there was a much closer bond between the two of us while we were growing up.

She was blessed to inherit Mom's gentle disposition, and you'll never find another person as kind or caring or mellow and genuinely good as my sister Darlene!

She's never smoked or had hard liquor touch her lips (at least that I've ever seen), and her idea of cussing is to say, *"Well, that's just ugly."* And if you have any doubts about how sweet and innocent she is, just call her sometime. When she answers the phone with her sweet childlike *"Hewwo,"* I'm pretty sure you'll ask to speak to her mother.

But always being the best person you can possibly be doesn't come without life's unjust penalties. Darlene suffered through a life-threatening bout of **extreme** postpartum depression following the birth of her daughter in 1966, and endured far more than her fair share of parental grief while her teenage children were discovering who they were. And now as a three-time cancer survivor, maintains a positive and optimistic attitude toward her future. If God is truly a just God, she'll outlive us all.

We don't say it often, but each of us knows we're loved by our siblings—a love that's always made our family the close-knit family that it is.

CHAPTER 14

"Colorado Springs Police"

By the Fall of 1964, Sandra and I started having fights. Nothing too serious in the beginning really; minor spats at best. But as the weeks turned into months, the arguing only got worse. This wasn't the same loving woman I'd known for the past four years . . . she'd always been so happy before, giggly even, someone who rarely argued with anything I said. But she was upset by the relative freedom I had with school and resented being the breadwinner in the family, so I knew if I ever wanted to see her happy again, I'd have to do something significant, and I'd have to do it now.

The timing couldn't have been better, I thought. It was February now, and the Denver Police Department had just announced their intent to test for new recruits. I was so excited when I heard the news, but the excitement soon turned to disappointment when I learned they'd be giving their exam two weeks before my twenty-first birthday, and wouldn't even let me apply. But when I learned the Colorado Springs Police Department would be testing two days before my birthday (and would let me to take the exam), I jumped at the opportunity.

On February 20th, 1965, on my twenty-first birthday, Sandra and I rode with Mom and Dad to the Big O bar at 3031 West Florida Avenue so Dad could buy his boy his first legal drink and celebrate the promise of my fulfilling a childhood dream.

It was a Saturday night, and inside this busy little "Cheers" kind of bar "where everybody slurs your name," people were laughing and joking and eager to break in another new drunk. Dad ordered me a mug of beer and the party began.

I drank as fast as I could, but before I could take my last swallow, another beer would magically appear before me. I had two or three more drinks, and was completely unaware that Sandy, the owner/bartender, was spiking my beer with shots of whiskey. It didn't take long before I understood why Dad liked his beer so much. My cheeks were numb, my teeth were numb, and apparently my brain wasn't that far behind. I was getting drunk much faster than I should have, and Dad absolutely loved it!

We left the bar a little before closing time and went to finish our party at my cousins Pudge and Bud Bullock's home at 1511 South Perry Street. (Pudge was Mom's sister's daughter). By now, I was learning a valuable lesson about limits, but not before I started getting sick. Dad took me to the backyard for some fresh air, and, thankfully, the bite of the crisp winter's breeze made me feel a little better. But I knew it wasn't going to last. While Dad stood beside me and laughed, I dropped to my hands and knees. Overwhelmed by a sense of nausea I'd never experienced before, I grabbed big clumps of grass with each hand and tried in vain to stop the world from spinning so fast. I told Dad I'd be alright, and asked him to go back inside. This was going to turn ugly at any moment, and I didn't want him there watching.

"Okay," he said, *"But don't lay on the grass, the dog "poops" out here."* (Not his word). *"No problem,"* I said, but when he came to check on me ten minutes later, I was completely sprawled out in the middle of the lawn with an imaginary chalk-outline drawn around my twisted and mangled body. But I didn't care if I was lying in dog waste . . . I was sick. And as undignified as it was, I'd survived this rite of passage, and in the eyes of my dad, was now a man.

A whole new world opened up for me when I turned twenty-one, and I savored every new and exciting moment. I could now drink at any bar of my choosing (even though I chose not to); enter into legal and binding contracts, and vote for the next great leaders of our country. But most importantly, I was finally old enough to be a policeman.

When I took the test in Colorado Springs on Thursday, February 18th, we were told only the top seven candidates would be hired. I'd never been in the top seven of anything in my life, and couldn't imagine how I could possibly compete with this full auditorium of much smarter and more qualified looking men than me . . . but once again, fate intervened, and this time for the better. To my absolute amazement, I passed fifth on the exam.

Dad hired someone to move our trailer to a mobile home park at 1209 South Nevada Avenue (just inside the southern limits of the city), and on Thursday, April 1st, 1965, I began my career at the alleged Police Academy in the Police Headquarters Building on the corner of East Kiowa and North Weber Streets. Sandra stayed behind with Mom and Dad while she honored the two-week notice she'd given at work, then she and my two-year-old daughter Kim joined me just as soon as they could.

There were 142 sworn officers on the Department when I started. Our badges weren't numbered in those days, but my serial number was 106-P (which meant I was the 106th least senior officer in the Patrol Division's force of 108 men). My $383 per month starting salary was a huge increase over anything I'd ever made before, and with gasoline at 25-cents a gallon and a sit down dinner and drive-in movie for under eight dollars, it was more than enough to support my family of three, and for the first time in her adult life, Sandra didn't have to work; at least for someone else.

The department operated with a lunar calendar of thirteen 28-day work periods per year, with twenty-one consecutive days on duty, and seven consecutive days off in each period. That was a little harsh I thought, but when my days off finally came around, it was really nice to have that full weeks' vacation. With absolutely no seniority, I was at the mercy of my Sergeant when new schedules were made. Most times I was able to work a normal rotation, but every now and again I'd have to take the first seven days off in a period, work twenty-one straight days in a row, then work the first twenty-one days of the following period before my next set of days off. A normal schedule was hard enough to handle, but when I had to work forty-two days (six weeks) in a row, it was just brutal.

After completing my less than extensive three week rookie school, I was on the mean streets of Colorado Springs where I'd spend the next six months being trained by a variety of veteran officers. It was **SO** exciting to be in that uniform (and yes, to be carrying that gun) . . . driving that police car . . . and finally doing the work I'd dreamed about since I was a little boy. But it didn't take long before I learned just how gut wrenching this job could really be.

During my first month on the street, my partner and I were dispatched to an ambulance call at a restaurant parking lot on East Pikes Peak Avenue, just east of Nevada Avenue (the main north-south street through the city). We'd soon learn that what started out as a very special evening for an ordinary young family of five, turned into a night of unfathomable horror.

It was a birthday celebration for one of their small children, and they'd gone to one of the more upscale restaurants in town to enjoy a treat they could rarely afford. Their four-month-old baby was asleep when they arrived, so they decided to leave him in the car while they went inside to eat. The mother checked on her baby several times during the course of their meal and found that he was always safe and sleeping soundly, and after returning to the restaurant one final time, the family decided to splurge just a bit more and ordered dessert for everyone.

As they left the restaurant, the two little kids giggled and danced gleefully around their laughing parents, but when they reached their car, they were horrified to see their baby violently gasping for air as he laid trapped on his back in the snugness of his bassinet. He'd simply spit up; something babies do a hundred times, but with no one there to clear his mouth, he choked on his own vomit.

We were only two minutes from the scene when we got the call, but by the time we arrived, the fire department was already there. By now this tiny, *tiny* little baby was on the ground outside the car and the firemen were frantically working to resuscitate him. But nothing they did seemed to help. As I helplessly stood there, I saw the baby turn a deadly shade of blue and watched in horror as his life quickly slipped away.

The ambulance crew whisked him into their ambulance and raced from the scene, and the family followed us in their own car as we escorted them the four short blocks to Memorial Hospital.

The doctors did everything they could, but soon came into the hallway and told the parents their baby was gone. The family was already in tears, but when the mother learned her baby was dead, she became hysterical and screamed, *"If we didn't have dessert, he'd still be alive!"* It was at that moment I first realized the difference between life and death could sometimes be determined by the *mere passage of seconds* . . . seconds we all take for granted during ordinary times.

I could hardly contain the grief I felt for them and had to walk away from the crowd. I found my way to the men's room, and there, behind the security of a locked bathroom door, I stood alone . . . and I cried.

When I was finally able to compose myself, I came back into the hallway and acted as strong as I knew I should, but I had serious doubts as to whether or not I'd be able to handle this job. Fortunately (or unfortunately) it got easier with each new death.

I saw several other deaths while I was with Colorado Springs, but they were all from natural causes or traffic accidents. The only homicide that occurred on my shift was the late night shooting of a service station attendant, but because of the petty territorial posturing of this small department, no patrolmen were allowed at the scene. This was strictly the domain of the Detective Bureau, and uniformed patrolmen weren't worthy enough to be nearer than a one-block perimeter around the crime scene.

But death wasn't the only thing I had to get used to. Seeing the terrible injuries people received from traffic accidents and aggravated assaults was something else that was entirely new to me, and something that would take a long time to adjust to.

The first aggravated assault I saw was the result of a fight in one of the rowdy cowboy bars on Colorado Avenue in the Old Town western section of the city. The victim's throat had been slashed with a beer can opener, and the deep gash literally extended from one ear to the other. I followed the ambulance to the hospital to continue my investigation and was allowed to wait in the emergency room while the doctor tended to his wound. Watching him being sewn up was something I knew I had to do if I was ever going to toughen up and be a real cop, so I stood in the room and watched as the doctor sutured the gaping wound.

Before I'd become a policeman I was deathly afraid of needles, so watching the doctor sewing this man's throat shut was a pretty hard thing for me to do. I was proud of how well I was handling the whole process, but when the doctor suddenly yanked the sutures tight, the raw flesh of his jagged wound puckered up around the taut bloody thread (not unlike a certain "puckering" part of my own anatomy) . . . and I really wasn't sure if the horrific scream that followed came from his mouth or my own. The room immediately started to spin and I (again) staggered to the safety of the nearby public restroom . . . sat on the toilet seat and put my head between my knees. When I was sure I wasn't going to pass out or throw up, I returned to the emergency room and took the victim's statement. I don't think anyone knew what I'd been through, and that was the last time I ever had to walk away from the blood, gore, and pain I'd see on the job.

The problems Sandra and I'd experienced had long since disappeared, and by the end of 1965, we bought our first house at 78 McBurney Boulevard in the little town of Widefield, a suburb just southeast of Colorado Springs.

We loved this house, a four-bedroom bi-level with a single car garage, but it cost far more than we could really afford. We assumed a VA loan of $15,200, with a monthly payment of $112, which was nearly half of my monthly check. We got most of our furniture from Mom and Dad, and even though our home was sparsely furnished, we couldn't have been happier.

On Monday, February 28th, 1966, our second daughter Cynthia Marie was born at Penrose Hospital, and our perfect little family was finally complete . . . the only thing missing from our family photo was a floppy eared little dog.

Working in Colorado Springs was a great learning experience, but it really wasn't what I'd hoped for. Denver had the biggest, busiest, and in my opinion, the best police department in the state, and I ached for the excitement they had to offer. After my first year on the job, I came to Denver for a Saturday night ride-along in the District One section of downtown Denver with Officers Bill Brannan and Dick Welch, and on that incredibly busy night, learned what real police work was really like. I couldn't believe the difference between the two police departments, and made up my mind that very night that I just *had* to be a Denver policeman.

I went to Denver's Civil Service Commission on my next set of days off, but was told I was too short to be on the Denver Police Department. They told me I had to be 5'9" (the same requirement as Colorado Springs), but I was only 5'8" and 5/8's inches tall. I was so disappointed . . . but still very much determined.

For the next six months, I did everything I could think of to stretch my body, and when I returned to the Commission, I arrived in the early morning hours instead of the late afternoon. I'd been told we're taller in the mornings, and could only hope this was true. They measured me again, and were surprised to see that I'd grown three eighths of an inch taller. They were skeptical of this growth spurt, but allowed me to apply for the testing process, then warned me that even if I got the job, I'd be fired at the end of my one-year probationary period if I didn't measure up to their height requirement. I was willing to take that chance.

Darlene, Sandra, Me & Bob

Who's more nervous?

Darlene on her
Wedding Day

This is me as a 21-year-old
Colorado Springs policeman

My precious daughters, Cynthia Marie
and Kimberly Ann

My "tough guy" daughter Kim
sitting on Dad's lap

CHAPTER 15

"The Denver Police Department—The First Year"

When I took Denver's next test, I was surrounded by three to four times more men than I'd competed with in Colorado Springs, but this time I passed third on the exam and would soon join the ranks with more than 1,200 other members of Denver's Finest. I don't know who was more proud . . . me or my dad.

My badge number was 67-3 (67 to show the year I was hired, and 3 because I was the third officer hired that year), however, when the department changed their uniform reporting practices in the 1970s, everyone had to have a five digit badge number, and mine was amended to 67003.

My starting salary was $475 per month, which was $5 less than I was making in Colorado Springs when I left. But that was okay. It wasn't a big loss in income, and the substantial pay raises I received over the next four years far exceeded the amount I would have received if I'd stayed in Colorado Springs, and only added to the benefits of this move.

We sold our house; packed everything we owned into a U-Haul truck and moved into a little two-bedroom house at 2315 South King Street in southwest Denver. We lived there until I got out of the Academy, then tried our hand at managing an apartment building at 6095 South Sterne Parkway. But because of my late night hours on the 7pm-3am shift, this didn't work at all for me. Someone was always coming to our door in the middle of **my** night, and I just wasn't getting the sleep I needed. By September, Sandra went back to work at Rust Sales, and we bought a small two-bedroom house at 995 South Pecos Way.

•

On Thursday morning, March 16th, 1967, the first twelve members of my academy class met in the Personnel Bureau at the Police Headquarters building at 1245 Champa Street, then walked the six long blocks to the City and County Building to be sworn in. Following this ceremony, we were instructed to report for duty at the Police Academy in the basement of the new District Four substation at West 22nd Avenue and Decatur Street. We were given thirty minutes to get back to our cars and make the drive to the academy, but when I quick-stepped it back to the parking lot, I discovered my car had been blocked in by several other cars, and the parking lot attendant was nowhere to be found. Truman Leuthauser, a fellow classmate, was in the same predicament as me, and as precious seconds ticked away, we decided to call for a cab. Luckily, the attendant returned before we made the call, and we rushed off to our new assignment.

But our luck turned sour when we arrived three minutes late. Our two new bosses, Lieutenant Art Dill and Sergeant Paul O'Hayre, had little sympathy for our plight and made examples of us to show the other recruits that insolent behavior would not be tolerated. Truman and I received demerits on our first day of the academy, and were ordered to turn in a five-hundred word essay on the importance of punctuality; due the following day.

Friday, Day Two:

Before we began our first day of lectures, we were each given minor housekeeping duties for the duration of our three-month academy class. I was given the task of turning the lights on for our class the first thing each morning and turning them off at the end of each shift. Simple enough, I thought, but when we returned from our very first lunch break, I received my second demerit for leaving the lights on while we were gone. I *very* respectfully argued that I didn't know the lights had to be turned off when we were on our breaks . . . but they didn't care.

The penalty? A five-hundred word essay on the importance of understanding and following orders; due the following day.

Monday, Day Three:

We'd been given instructions to stand at attention and address our instructors with the word sir anytime we had any questions. It was a sign of respect, and certainly wasn't something any of us had a problem with, but during one of our afternoon lectures, a civilian instructor who was uncomfortable with that much formality, asked us to just raise our hand if we had a question. That was okay with us, but, unfortunately, the lieutenant and sergeant were out of the room when he relaxed our classroom decorum, and I was the first to ask a question after they returned to the room. And **BAM!!** . . . demerit number three. One more five-hundred word essay on the importance of respect; due the following day.

Tuesday, Day Four:

At the end of each day, we'd be told which material we'd need for the following day's sessions, and on Monday, Sergeant O'Hayre specifically told us we wouldn't need a certain handout for today's lecture. But as soon as our class began, he told us to turn to a particular page in this brochure. Several of us didn't have the brochure, but I was the one who stood at attention and said, *"Sir, I didn't bring that handout because you told us we wouldn't need it."* He gave me his cocky little George W. Bush grin, and said, *"It doesn't matter what I said. It's your responsibility to be prepared for class."* You guessed it . . . demerit number four and another five-hundred word essay on the importance of being prepared.

Thursday, Day Six:

That's right folks. ***Demerit Number Five***, and another five-hundred word essay. I don't even remember what this demerit was for, but I do know it was for something extremely trivial, and I was becoming increasingly frustrated with the whole outrageous process. I was trying so hard to do the very best that I could, but the burden of writing these essays, typing my daily classroom notes on an old manual typewriter and studying for our exams till midnight each night was becoming over-whelming. By now my mind was numb with the arbitrary pettiness of this job, and I thought to myself, *"What have I done? I had a perfectly good job in Colorado Springs . . . and I gave it up for this??"*

What I didn't know at the time was that Dad and Art Dill were friends, and before I was hired, Dad told him to give me hell whenever he got the chance. And that's exactly what he did!

It was the last demerit I received, but I still ended up with the dubious honor of receiving more than anyone else in my class.

About two weeks into our class, we were all assigned to street duty throughout the five police districts while the second group of thirteen new recruits began their academy classes. When they reached the level of instruction we'd already received, our group would return to the academy and we'd all graduate together in mid-June.

I was assigned to work with Jimmie Hartford and Ed "Doc" O'Dea in the District One section of downtown Denver, and I couldn't have worked with two better men. They both had several years on the job, but had the energy and dedication of brand new officers. The difference, of course, was that they already had a wealth of knowledge and practical experience under their belts, and were truly outstanding policemen.

We'd begin each shift by trying to arrest someone new from our Daily Police Bulletin. We were usually successful, but even if we weren't, the momentum had already begun and we'd stay busy for the entire shift. We'd go from call to call, and during ordinary patrol time, we'd routine all the hot spots in our precinct. There were plenty of bars and strip clubs and seamy hangouts downtown, including the Continental Trailways Bus Station at 1669 Broadway, so we always had plenty of liquor code violations and shady looking people to check on.

Yes, something was always going on in downtown Denver, and one of the first great things I learned about the department was just how much freedom and authority the patrolmen had. Everyone was assigned to the boundaries of a specific precinct, but whenever a serious call came out from anywhere in the district, we just told the dispatcher we were covering the call. No questions . . . no comments . . . we went wherever we were needed, and everybody was happy. This was so great, because we always got the cover we needed, but it was completely contrary to the procedures I'd known in Colorado Springs.

There were only seven cars in the entire city of Colorado Springs, and we couldn't leave our precinct (they called them districts) unless the dispatcher specifically told us to. We couldn't even cover another officer without first being dispatched, and if we had the audacity to ask to cover a call, we were often denied permission. Denver was so much better!

Every night was a good night in District One, but my favorite shift began when we were stopped by an attractive blond at the curb in front of the Trinity Methodist Church at 18th and Broadway. She'd been beaten by her boyfriend, and to exact her revenge, told us where he had a stash of marijuana hidden in the apartment they shared. In the 1960s, the mere possession of *any* amount of marijuana was a very serious felony offense, so she knew the punishment he'd receive from that arrest would be far more severe than that from the assault charge.

We called for assistance from the Intelligence Bureau (who handled all narcotics cases in those days) and Detectives Steve Metros and Mike Dowd met with us near the victim's apartment building at 22nd Street and Glenarm Place.

She took us into their apartment, signed an assault complaint, and just as she was signing a search waiver, two women and her abusive burly middle-aged black boyfriend walked through the front door. Yelling *"Get Out of My Apartment,"* he barreled into us when we told him he was under arrest. We all grabbed for him, but only three of us could hang onto him at the same time. He bulldozed us across the living room floor, and as we slammed into the big second story picture window, I could feel my back straining against the fragile sheet of glass as the weight of our bodies urged us on . . . and knew at once it was going to be a **very** nasty fall! With an extra surge of adrenaline, we were able to move him back into the room, then all five of us found a body part and pinned him to the floor.

While we struggled to put him in handcuffs, one of the women suddenly emerged from the kitchen, screaming as she ran toward us with a 10-inch butcher knife raised high above her head. In that next split second, I heard the terrifying shrieks from the shower scene in the movie *Psycho* and watched as Doc jumped from the pile, pulled his gun and ordered her to drop the knife. This stopped her from coming closer, but she didn't change her posture, and the threat was still very near and still very deadly. Doc quickly holstered his gun; pulled his nightstick and yelled, *"Drop the knife, bitch."* When she refused, he hit her **hard** across her left shoulder. The knife flew from her hand, and those of us who weren't still struggling with the boyfriend wrestled her to the floor and put her in handcuffs.

This certainly wasn't the first resistance I'd had during an arrest, but it was definitely the first that could have ended with someone being stabbed or shot. *It was a very fun night!*

When our two weeks were up, we returned to the academy and joined the new members of our class. We were already spoiled by the experiences we'd had on the street and realized life in the academy was far different than what we'd encounter once we graduated. It made it all worthwhile.

Officers Hartford and O'Dea wrote me a letter of commendation for the way I handled myself during the arrest on Glenarm, and Lieutenant Dill read it aloud to the class. I was a little confused by the letter, since what I'd done was what every policeman is expected to do, but they were impressed that a rookie could react so quickly and behave like an ordinary policeman. I guess they'd forgotten I'd already been a policeman for two years before I came to Denver.

Lieutenant Dill announced that I was the first recruit who'd ever received a commendation while in the academy, and from that moment on, I stopped being the center of their disciplinary attention.

As we approached our final days in the academy, they announced that Tony Ryan and I were tied for first place in our class of twenty-five, and our final test score would determine who'd receive that high honor. When the results were in from our last exam, we were told that for one of the very few times in the Department's history, there'd be two Outstanding Police Recruits from a single class. We both received plaques from Mayor Currigan at our graduation ceremony, but it was a bittersweet award for me. I'd worked so hard to be the top gun in my class, and had a tough time accepting a tie. I rationalized I'd really won the top honor because I'd typed each of the 418 pages of my classroom notebook myself (which I'm proud to say was the best in our class), and knew Tony had done none of his own. And since his wife typed all of his notes for him, I, by the sheer volume of effort, should have been number one. (I don't know . . . too much ego?)

As a reward for graduating from the top of our class, the Department scheduled Tony and I to work for two months in each of the five police districts. This was a great opportunity for both of us, because it gave us the chance to see the dynamics of each area of the city and to work with a far greater number of seasoned officers. My first assignment was on the 7pm-3am night shift in District One.

Just like every other new rookie on the job, I was assigned as a relief officer and worked wherever I was needed. These were the years before the glut of special units depleted the ranks of the street cops (the Airport Police Bureau, Gang Unit, SSU/SWAT, SCAT, ESCORT, CRO's, et al), so there was always a full crew on duty, especially on weekend nights.

On my very first Saturday night shift, I was assigned as a Cruiser Driver with Sergeant Les Gebhardt (if I remember correctly), one of the few sergeants we had on the street. (Cruiser was the radio call code designation for a sergeant's assignment; Car, (i.e., Car 23, etc.) was the designation for a patrolman's assignment, and Command Car was the designation for a lieutenant or captain's assignment).

We'd just finished dinner at Trader Vic's at 1756 Broadway, when we were dispatched to a homicide at an apartment building at East 22nd Avenue and Clarkson Street.

When we arrived and entered the building, I was surprised to see two uniformed officers actually inside the apartment, and even more surprised to see that one of them was writing the offense report. The Homicide Bureau Detectives and Baker-4 Crime Lab Technicians were on their way, but these patrolmen were entrusted with preserving the crime scene and making all the initial reports. I continued to revel in the amount of authority and responsibility the first-line officers had on this department.

A young black woman was lying on her back in the center of the bed; her legs bent at the knees and her feet lying flat on the floor. Her eyes were wide open as she stared vacuously at the ceiling above her, and the pain and horror of her last breath at the hands of the man who'd strangled her were clearly evident in her expression. There was no blood, but a torrent of gelled mucus from each of her nostrils consumed the greater part of her lower face, giving her an almost mummified and gruesome appearance—an image, coupled with the overwhelming stench of decomposing flesh, nearly triggered my already severely compromised gag reflex; something no policeman wants to admit. If you've never experienced the unmistakable rancid smell of a three or four day old decaying body before, you have no idea how unbelievably vile it is; an odor so putrid and dense that it hangs in the air like a cool morning mist and clings to your skin like burning napalm. It was a grotesque sight; the kind that nightmares are made of, but everyone there, including myself, acted as though nothing was out of the ordinary. This was the way policemen were supposed to handle this type of situation and would be the standard for the dozens of other homicides I would cover during my career.

This was my first homicide . . . you never forget your first!

The sweltering days of summer were in full swing by now, and we all hoped the race riots that had become so commonplace since the Watts riots in 1965 wouldn't return to our city. But that was just wishful thinking.

Shortly after dark on a hot July evening, Bobby Suer, one of our motorcycle traffic officers, wrote a ticket to a young black man who'd jaywalked in front of traffic in front of the YWCA at 1545 Glenarm Place. The man refused to take the ticket and his outrage over this trivial violation only fueled the tempers of the angry mob that soon came to his aid. It was a simple ticket, punishable by a ten-dollar fine, but he and the ensuing crowd apparently saw it as just another racially motivated act of police harassment, and they were mad as hell. I don't know if they were right or not, but I was certain the color of a person's skin had never stopped Bobby from writing a ticket before. Black white or brown, it didn't matter. If you broke the law, he owned you. That was his job.

When Bobby realized just how serious the situation was becoming, he called for help. Within minutes there were thirty to forty officers at the scene, and in the very few minutes that it took for my partner and I to arrive, the crowd had swollen to a sea of about three hundred people. I couldn't imagine how so many people could get there so fast, especially since all of the city's previous race riots occurred in the predominantly black areas of town. Following the sound of screaming sirens and the flood of flashing red and white police lights, even more non-police supporters arrived, and the crowd soon doubled in size. We tried to push them back, but soon found ourselves being pelted with beer cans, bottles and even broken pieces of brick.

As I moved toward the crowd, an enormous overly obese black man yelled, *"This is the reason we riot! It's that look on your face."* I'm sure I had a look of anger and frustration, because, to be honest, riots were the only part of police work I didn't like, and I truly hated being there. But whatever look I had on my face was tame compared to the hatred and violence I saw in this mob, and contrary to what this man believed, my expression would have been the same for any other riotous mob, no matter who was involved.

The crowd eventually dispersed into smaller groups and moved to the Five Points and Park Hill areas of northeast Denver, and the violence slowly subsided when the rioters finally needed their sleep. But the riots of the long hot summer had begun, and wouldn't end again until the cold nights of winter returned.

On Tuesday, August 1st, I transferred to the District Six substation at West Florida Avenue and Eliot Street; just five blocks west of Mom and Dad's home. I liked the idea of working my old neighborhood as a cop, and had already made plans to terrorize my old friends on traffic stops, just like Buster Snyder had done when he was the number one ticket writer on the Department. The difference was that I'd only pull them over as a joke. But, unfortunately, most of my friends had already moved away from the district and never had the "pleasure" of experiencing my warped sense of humor.

Except for traffic enforcement, I'd never seen the police in my neighborhood before, so I wasn't quite sure just how busy the district would be. I soon found there were always family disturbances and such, but it seemed like our biggest problems came from erratic teenage drivers and the routine fights we'd handle at the 3.2 bars that were frequented by the beer-drinking eighteen to twenty-year-old crowds. It was much quieter than District One, but I enjoyed the reprieve from the mob violence that was still occurring across town.

High-speed chases were a common occurrence for the police in both Colorado Springs and Denver, and one of the most exciting things we did. But none of the previous chases I'd been in could even begin to compare with the slow-speed pursuit I was involved with during my two-month stint in District Six.

I was home asleep after working a 7pm-3am shift when I received an urgent call from Truman Leuthauser. He told me a robbery at the King Soopers store in the Dahlia Shopping Center had gone awry this morning, and Sergeant Larry Morahan and three or four store employees had been taken hostage and were slowly being pursued by the police south-bound on Interstate 25. He said several police cars and off duty officers in their own personal cars were following the robbers, and asked if I wanted to go. I threw my clothes and gun belt on; grabbed my .30 caliber carbine and a 12-gauge shotgun for Truman, and met with him at the District Six station. He jumped into my white 1961 Chevy and we headed for the highway.

By the time we reached Monument near Colorado Springs, I had to stop for gas. While I was hurriedly filling my tank, a Denver police cruiser pulled in beside us. Sergeant Hank Newell got out to fill his tank, and when he recognized the cross-draw holsters on our uniform belts, asked if we wanted to join him. We grabbed our rifles and ammo, and within three or four short minutes, we were speeding south on the highway to catch up with the caravan of heavily armed policemen. Because we were in a marked Sergeant's cruiser, we were able to pass the mile-long string of police and civilian cars, and soon fell in behind two other police cars . . . just behind the robber's van.

Before we'd arrived at the scene, the police had already made one attempt to a stop the van, but when the captors shot one of the hostages and threatened to shoot the others, they were left with no other choice but to pull back. The wounded hostage was thrown from the van so he could be treated, and all the police could do now was follow the van and wait for the inevitable conclusion.

We continued the slow speed pursuit into Colorado Springs, then east on U.S. 24. We drove through several rural towns; ending in Limon, then drove west on Interstate 70 toward Denver. I think Channel 4 News had a helicopter following the chase, so every time we drove through the smaller towns, people who'd been following the story on their TVs were lined up on the side of the road to watch as this *Sugarland Express* unfolded before their very own eyes.

As we approached the outskirts of Denver, the van turned onto U.S. 40 (which would eventually become East Colfax Avenue), and as we continued toward the business section of Aurora, we were able to reestablish radio contact with our dispatcher. We learned the Aurora police were setting up a road block just a few blocks ahead of us, and by the time the suspects reached the gridlock of Aurora police cars, they'd run out of gas and had no place else to go. As I leapt from the car, I saw the roof tops lined with men with rifles, and was nearly trampled by a hoard of policemen running toward the van. The first two people out of the van were hostages, followed by the two suspects . . . and everyone was forced to the ground until they could be sorted out. By now, dozens of other off duty Denver officers had left their cars and were running to the scene, but by the time most of them got there, it was already over. I'd never seen so many guns in my life, and I'm certain if just one shot had been fired from that van, there would have been some *very serious wounds* from all the crossfire.

We'd covered over two hundred miles during this pursuit and our adrenalin raced the entire time. We knew it could end at any moment, and the actions we took could mean the difference between life and death for the hostages, or even for ourselves. But when it was finally over, I thought to myself, *"What a great job this is!"* I definitely made the right choice in coming to Denver.

On Sunday, October 1st, I transferred to the old District Two substation at East 17th Avenue and Gaylord Street.

It was one of the busiest Districts in the city, and working the 7pm-3am night shift was an unbelievable experience. Between the constant conflicts with the ultra-radical and militant Black Panthers, the chaotic race riots, and the Fuck the Establishment lawlessness of the hippie movement, we were busy all the time. We didn't have the gang-bangers that are so prevalent today, but the mean streets of Denver were filled with ordinary bad ass thugs, and violent crimes were common and abundant in this district.

But District Two was far more than just a busy place to work. The Sexual Revolution had already begun and was alive and thriving in Denver, and one of its largest battlegrounds played out on East Colfax Avenue.

East Colfax bustled with restaurants, bars, Go-Go dance clubs and strip joints, and the streets teemed with young people out looking for a good time. I soon learned there were groupies who actively sought us out; looking to vicariously share the adventure and excitement of our job, and still others who were just drawn to the lure of our uniform. It often felt like we were a fleet of sailors who'd just anchored at the friendliest of ports, and in later years I'd compare the job to the lyrics from Dire Straits hit single . . . money for nothing and chicks for free.

I envied those few single officers in the District who had such great opportunities with these women, and had no idea that any of the rest of us who were so inclined could also be enjoying that same kind of rapture. The constant string of idling cars at the curb beside our station at the end of each shift should have been a hint of what was happening, but to me, only suggested the officer's wives were there to pick up their husbands. Made sense to me, but when I told my partner how great I thought it was that so many wives came out in the middle of the night for their husbands, he laughed at my naïvety and said, *"Those aren't wives . . . they're chippies."* I asked what a chippy was, and learned for the first time what could make this job so great. These were the women they'd met during the course of their shifts who were there for some after midnight delight.

On Thursday, November 14th, just two days after Sandra and I celebrated our seventh wedding anniversary, I was assigned to work with one of the growing legends of the Department.

Don Rask had only been on the job three years, but at the mature age of thirty-one, already had the mind of a well-seasoned officer, and his professional bearing and crisp uniformed appearance made him the role model I only wished I could be. He was a bull of a man, with a cold steely stare, a gruff sounding voice, and the aggressive demeanor of someone you definitely tried to avoid if you were breaking the law.

(The following summer, I watched him in action when part of a motorcycle gang stormed the station to free one of their buddies who'd just been arrested. It wasn't a very well thought out plan, because they came in just before 7pm when nearly every officer from the day shift, and double that number from the night shift was in the building. In the ensuing chaos, I saw Don grab the biggest and meanest looking biker from the group and throw him completely across the garage at the rear of our station; slamming his body into the hard brick wall. It was a great way to start the shift . . . eight arrests before we ever left the station, and it proved to me what I already knew; that Don was probably the toughest man on the entire Denver Police Department).

As I stood in the crowded roll call room and looked down the two rows of standing policemen, I saw spit shined black leather shoes, weapon charged holsters and night sticks hanging from the black Sam Browne belts of the men dressed in their dark blue and impressive, almost "SS" looking uniforms . . . and saw that Rask stood out from all the rest. He was taller than most everyone there, and his trim waist and enormous barrel chest made him a giant among men. I had the greatest admiration and respect for Don (even to this day), but I was more than just a little intimidated to be working with a man of his great stature.

Our evening started out like most others—writing tickets and handling routine calls, but just after 9pm, we received a Code 17, at 1717 E. 17th Avenue. (Code 17 meant an ambulance had already been dispatched to the scene and one of the few calls we actually used our red lights and sirens for).

We arrived before the ambulance, and as we ran to the front door of the apartment building, we were met by two young hippies. They told us one of their friends was upstairs and wasn't breathing, so Don and I ran to the top of the stairs to see if we could help. A deathly pale shirtless eighteen-year-old boy was lying on his back on the floor of the bathroom, and it was pretty clear that he was dead. I checked for a pulse, and briefly considered giving him mouth to mouth resuscitation, but in his death throes, he'd vomited all over his face and I just couldn't bring myself to put my mouth on all that vomit, especially since it was so clear that he was already dead.

Don went back downstairs with the others and learned the three of them had made a suicide pact, then formed a circle in the center of the large bathroom while they finished preparing their deadly potion. They poured potassium cyanide into their teacups, filled them with water, then contemplated their next move. When the first one drank his poison, he immediately went into convulsions and began to vomit. When the others saw how violent his death was, they jumped up and ran to call for an ambulance.

I stood in the bathroom until the paramedics arrived, then looked around the adjoining bedroom for any possible suicide notes they may have written. The fire department arrived at about the same time as the ambulance, and as soon as the fire captain learned what had happened, yelled for everyone to get out of the building.

As Don and I were standing on the sidewalk in front of the apartment building, he asked how I was feeling. I told him I was feeling a little strange, but thought I was okay. He said he felt the same way and thought we should go to Denver General Hospital to be checked out. I started driving, but was already disoriented from the poisonous gas my body had absorbed, and was mistakenly driving away from the direction of the hospital. Don had me pull to the curb and we switched places with one another, then sped Code 10 west bound on Colfax Avenue. He told the dispatcher we were en route to the hospital, and by the time we pulled into the dock outside the emergency room, I was nearly unconscious, and every muscle in my body was in spasms as I thrashed uncontrollably about in my seat.

There were three or four doctors waiting outside when we arrived, and as they pulled me from the car and threw me onto a gurney, they stuck two monstrous hypodermic needles into my arms; fed some kind of inhalant into my nostrils, and stuffed oxygen tubes deep into my nose. They wheeled me into the Intensive Care Unit, but there was nothing more they could do now but monitor my condition and wait to see if I'd survive.

By now I knew I was in serious trouble, and all I could think about was the tour my academy class had taken at the State Penitentiary in Cañon City. Part of our tour included visiting Death Row, where those of us who were willing to could actually sit inside the gas chamber. Of course, I wanted to, and as I sat on the perforated metal chair in the center of this cold green glass enclosed metal chamber, I contemplated the deaths of those who'd been here before, including John Gilbert Graham. The guard then told us when condemned prisoners were executed, they'd hold their breath for as long as they could, hoping, I guess, that this would extend their lives. But that didn't matter. He explained breathing had nothing to do with the effects of cyanide, because the poison was absorbed through their pores, which in turn collapsed their blood vessels, and just before the inmates died, they'd go into convulsions. And here I was, just twenty-three-years-old, with a wife and two little kids . . . already in convulsions . . . *and I was dying!!*

Sandra and I were both aware of the emergency procedures of the Department, and she knew if the police ever came to our door in the middle of my shift, it either meant I was in serious condition or already dead. So when I was told Officer Al

VanderVelde and his partner were picking her up from our home and bringing her to the hospital, I expected her to be consumed with panic, with tears of grief pouring down her cheeks.

As I laid there, images of the dead young man kept flashing through my mind, and I thought of all the things I still wanted to do in life. I didn't know if I should breathe deeply or take shallow breaths to keep myself alive, and with each new breath, wondered if it would be my very last.

A priest was with me when Sandra was brought into the Intensive Care Unit, but to my amazement, she acted like nothing was wrong. I was stunned by how cold and aloof she was, and half expected her to sit down at any moment and file her nails. It wasn't what I'd expected, and definitely wasn't what I needed . . . I thought I was dying, and needed the love and comfort from the woman I loved. (Eleven years later, VanderVelde recounted that night with me, and told me how bad he felt for me over my wife's lack of emotion).

As I laid on my death bed, demoralized over the callousness of my wife, I promised God if he'd let me live, I'd get the love and attention I needed from as many other women as I could, and within a week after returning to duty, I had my own idling car waiting for me at the curb. I'm sure it really wasn't God's will, but I was still willing to uphold my end of the bargain.

In retrospect, I probably shouldn't have been so quick to judge Sandra, since I'd never seen her in crises before . . . and for all I knew, this was the way she handled trauma. But if I was truly honest with myself, I'd have to admit I was probably just looking for an excuse to join the revolution.

But the damage was already done, and the rest would become history.

On Friday, December 1st, I transferred to the District Three station on South University Boulevard and East Iowa Avenue. I teamed up with Tom Coogan (a Robert Stack lookalike who'd become our chief in 1983), and even though we worked in one of the busiest precincts in the district, it was a pretty quiet assignment.

The only memorable thing that happened here was on New Year's Eve when we stopped for a routine check at the 404 Club at 404 Broadway. The place was full of revelers, and everyone was having a great time. We were welcomed into their festivities, and as the clock struck twelve, the place went absolutely crazy. Everyone was kissing everyone else, when a sultry dark haired cocktail waitress oozed up beside us. As the crowd cheered her on, she kissed Tom on the lips, then turned to me. I stammered and backed away as I mumbled I wouldn't even kiss my own wife in public while I was in uniform. But she didn't care. She grabbed me and kissed me like I'd never been kissed before, and I thought she was going to swallow my face . . . and the crowd just roared!! When she'd finished taking advantage of this babe in the woods, she tilted her head, smiled provocatively, and casually walked away. I yelled, *"I love you,"* but the woman who could have been the mother of my next twelve children never looked back.

I was supposed to transfer to District Four in northwest Denver to complete my rotation, but was asked to return to District Two, instead. I jumped at the opportunity, and on Thursday, February 1st, 1968, I began my first permanent duty alongside the best officers in the best District in the city.

CHAPTER 16

"The Street"

Things were much different in the olden days when I first came on the job. We didn't have the hand held transistor radios the police have today, and there were no cell phones, pagers or Internet text messaging services to make our jobs easier. The only communication we had with the rest of the Department was through our vacuum tube Motorola radios that were permanently mounted in our cruisers. When we were away from our cars and needed help, we had to run back to our cars, start the engine, and wait the painful twenty to thirty seconds for our radios to warm up before we could call for help. When we needed an ambulance or immediate cover, it was an excruciating delay.

We didn't have sophisticated onboard computers, and even lacked the simple luxury of the National Crime Information Center (NCIC) for our clearances. When we ran a records check on someone, a manual search was made of our files by clerks in the Identification Bureau, but the search was generally limited to local warrants. If our suspect was wanted anywhere else in the country, there was a very good chance we wouldn't know about it.

There were no strobe lights, takedown or alley lights on our cars; no stun guns, tasers or mace; no bulletproof vests, and no shotguns. Everyone carried a Colt or Smith & Wesson .38 Special revolver with a six round capacity, and twelve extra rounds in our ammo pouches. Today our officers carry 15-round semi-automatic pistols with two extra magazines.

Our time honored nightsticks and saps were our only non-lethal weapons and were used whenever they were needed. The criminals understood the rules of cops and robbers, and anyone who resisted arrest could count on the inevitable thumping that was sure to follow. Sometimes it was excessive; most times it was not . . . but it was always immediate and always memorable. Yes, things were much different in those days . . . ships were made of wood, and men were made of steel, and we were ready for anything that came our way.

District Two was rich with extremely dedicated policemen, and for the next several months I was fortunate enough to work with most of them on the 7pm-3am night shift. They all taught me something new, but some of them were more competent and street wise than the others, and the things I learned from them helped mold me into the policeman I would eventually become.

One of these men was an unusually urbane thirty-five-year-old policeman named Larry Peters. His badge number was 60-3, (which was just one more reason to like him), and he was absolutely the best street cop I've ever known. He was an inch or two taller than me . . . a little broader in the chest and shoulders, and was definitely a lot tougher than me. He had an air of confidence that made him stand out from everyone else, and he looked just like all of those *"real"* Denver policemen I'd admired and feared so much when I was just a boy. His imposing stature, superior intellect, extremely cool demeanor and low masculine voice reminded me of the character played by Richard Burton in the movie Where Eagles Dare . . . and I wanted to be just like him when I grew up.

Larry was baptized by fire early in his career, when, on Monday, April 24th, 1961, he and Sergeant Wally Horan covered an 8:25 pm Denver Burglar Alarm call on a narcotics drawer alarm at the Glendale Pharmacy at 3660 Tejon Street.

As they eased their way through the front door of the neigh-borhood's favorite little malt shop, they were met with total silence. There were no clerks or customers anywhere in sight... the place was completely empty. Sergeant Horan whispered to Larry, *"It's too quiet, kid,"* and they both drew their guns and split up to search the store. Larry quietly stepped into a back room and saw three teenage boys, a teenage girl, and the store's pharmacist lying face down on the floor, with a swarthy twenty-two-year-old Hispanic man huddled just over him; fumbling for the keys in his pocket that would unlock the store's double-padlocked back door. (A getaway driver was waiting in a car in the alley immediately outside the door).

As Larry moved toward the two struggling men, Sergeant Horan rounded an end of the soda fountain in the main section of the store and was immediately shot by a gunman who was standing just behind the counter. The bullet ripped into his upper left thigh, and as he collapsed to the floor in pain, he fired two quick shots, hitting his assailant once in the neck. When the gunman fell to the floor, he saw a sixteen-year-old employee cowering there in fear, and callously shot him in the stomach for reasons no one has ever understood. When the man in the back room heard the barrage of gunshots, he turned away from the pharmacist, and seeing Larry standing immediately behind him, stuck a gun in his face and pulled the trigger. In the agonizingly slow motion of that last split-second that separates life from death, Larry heard the loudest **"CLICK"** he'd ever heard . . . grabbed the man around his neck . . . "screwed" his gun barrel into his mouth, and pulled the trigger. Blood flew everywhere as the bullet ripped through the back of his head, and as he fell to the floor, he defiantly turned toward Larry and tried to fire again. Larry shot him a second time, hitting him in his side; this time rendering him harmless.

Suddenly, the wounded man who'd shot Sergeant Horan just a few seconds earlier, ran across the room. He pointed his gun at Larry as he ran, but when he stumbled over one of the teen-agers on the floor, Larry brought him down with a single shot that slammed through both of his legs. A third man jumped up from behind the soda fountain in the main room, and a startled

237

Sergeant Horan (fearing he'd be shot again), fired another round, hitting him hard in the stomach. Three up; three down; it was a very good day . . . until they learned the third man was just another customer who'd panicked at the sound of gunshots in the back room.

Most policemen have no qualms about shooting someone who threatens their lives, but shooting an innocent bystander is the worst nightmare they can imagine . . . and this was a nightmare Sergeant Horan would anguish over for the remaining years of his life.

It was a big story in the papers and nightly news, and the Sons of Italy and the city's Safeway and King Soopers stores soon started a fund raising drive to pay for the customer's hospital and doctor bills. But, as Larry remembers, when he announced his intent to sue the police department, all three groups were so outraged by his actions, they withdrew their offer to help and started returning the money to the donors. When he saw the incredible support the public had for the police department, he dropped his lawsuit and took the donations instead.

The Department was still reeling from the effects of the police burglary scandal that had recently rocked the city, and in an editorial in the Rocky Mountain News on Wednesday, April 26th, 1961, the author described how the actions of these two officers helped rekindle the trust and respect Denver's police-men rightfully deserved:

Dedication to a Responsibility

"The bark of pistols in North Denver Monday night spoke in tragic eloquence of the hazard and dedication in the job of a police officer.

A task force of policemen answered an alarm at a drugstore in the midst of a holdup. Before the incident was ended a police sergeant, two customers and two holdup suspects were wound-

ed. One policeman was spared death because a gun held at his temple misfired.

The drugstore robbery became another notation on the long police blotter of crime in the Denver area. But more than a statistic, it became a dramatic exhibit of the hazardous occupation carried out 24 hours a day by the police in protecting Denver from the cancerous inroads of the lawless.

The robbery incident was less a role of heroism than the carrying out of sworn duties. It is a role the people expect and one which policemen knowingly undertake.

The abortive drugstore robbery accomplished many things. It served a warning to the lawless and an assurance to honest citizens that we still have an alert and dedicated department. It answers sharply the jibes brought by a handful of dishonest men. It should lift the morale of the department—which in recent months was torn by the degradation of a few dishonest policemen.

It seems a bit awkward to draw satisfaction from something as unwarranted and as tragic as an attempted holdup with gunfire. But the incident shored up a lot of shattered confidence— for us and for the police."

This was the experience we all anticipate when we respond to this type of call, but very few of us actually see. Larry had stared death in the face and survived, and for the remainder of his thirty-one year career, was fearless in his pursuit for justice.

He was one of the few officers in the District who was allowed to work exclusively on the night shift, while everyone else worked a rotation schedule with one month on the night shift (7pm-3am), followed by a month on the day shift (11am-7pm), followed by a month on the morning shift (3am-11am); over and over again.

Because the night shift was so much busier and more dangerous than the others, it was staffed with two-man cars, and the day and morning shifts were handled with solo assignments. Since I had to work with a partner during my probationary period (there were no Training Officers in those days), I was forced to stay on the night shift for the first year of my career, and it wasn't long before I had my first opportunity to work with one of the few true legends of the Denver Police Department.

Larry and I hit it off right away. Apparently he was impressed by my eagerness and desire to learn, and soon agreed to have me as his partner as often as the schedule would allow. And I couldn't have had a better mentor. No one on the department had a better command of the law or understanding of the primal nature of the criminals we dealt with, and his cold killer instincts all men feared, and bad boy persona most women couldn't resist, made him the policeman we all wished we could be. There was no call he couldn't handle, and the hotter the situation became, the cooler he remained. I was constantly amazed by his ability.

Side Note: *Following the annual Denver Police Memorial Ceremony on Friday, May 14th, 2010, a very proud seventy-seven-year-old retired Sergeant Larry Peters and an equally proud eighty-seven-year-old retired Lieutenant Wally Horan received the Medal of Honor (the highest honor the Department can bestow) for their heroic actions during that shootout some forty-nine years and twenty days before. Wally was also honored with a Purple Heart for the bullet he'd taken . . . an award Larry was happy to do without.*

I'd love to be the one who could take credit for this long overdue award ceremony (since I'd written this story two years before Larry and Wally finally received their medals), but the truth is, the recognition of their bravery was the sole and direct result of the constant recommendations by retired Captain Larry Britton; the gracious concurrence and in-depth investi-

240

gation by Deputy Chief John Lamb, and the even more gracious acceptance by Chief Gerry Whitman.

I'd worn a right-handed Jordan holster while I was in Colorado Springs, and could outdraw Gunsmoke's Matt Dillon every time he was on television. But the cross-draw holsters the department issued to us were worn on our left side, and were extremely cumbersome to use. Most officers manipulated the leather on their holster straps until the holster would lay diagonally across the front of their belt and place their gun within reach, but even in this position, I was never comfortable with the access to my gun . . . until it was put to the ultimate test.

I'd just celebrated my first year on the job, and after finishing my 7pm-3am shift in District Two, I headed for home in my personal car. The city was fast asleep by now and I was completely alone on the street as I drove westbound on East 16th Avenue. As I reached Ogden Street, the traffic light turned red and I stopped in the right hand lane. A single car was stopped at the west curb in front of St. Paul's Church on Ogden Street, a few degrees to my right, and I watched as a woman got out of the car. As the car drove away south bound on Ogden, a man stepped from the darkness of the bushes . . . ran to the woman and knocked her to the sidewalk. I ran the light and pulled to the curb; jumped from my car and threw him against the church wall. As I wrestled to put him in handcuffs he yelled, *"It's okay. She's my wife."*

The woman had been cheating on her husband, and when her lover dropped her off near her home, her husband was there to confront her. As I listened to him talk, I heard the deadly sound of a gun cocking behind me. I felt the painful blunt trauma of the bullet that was about to rip through my back, and jerked around to see a man standing just three feet behind me. I pointed my hand at his chest, and to my amazement, I'd already drawn my gun and was ready to fire. It all happened so quickly, I didn't have time to think about what I was doing, and was very impressed with the speed of my draw.

The man's eyes nearly popped out of his head as he stared down the barrel of my revolver, and he screamed he was a friend of the family. When I finished searching him, I learned the sound of a cocking gun was only the sound of a broken twig he'd stepped on, and the split second decision I'd made to hold my fire when I thought I was about to be shot, turned out to be the right one.

The woman got up from the ground and told me she was alright, and just wanted to go home. Current domestic violence procedures demand that we arrest the aggressor in a family fight, but at that time we were powerless to arrest someone without a signed complaint. When I was certain she knew what she was doing, I released her husband, and the three of them walked peacefully away. And from that moment on, I never worried about the inadequacies of my holster.

On Wednesday, May 1st, 1968, I worked my first solo assignment on the day shift and experienced a brand new kind of policing. By now the creatures of the night were tucked away in their beds, trying to shake off their drunkenness and debauchery of the previous evening, while ordinary people went on with the business of their day. The majority of our calls were on routine traffic accidents, neighborhood disputes, car thefts, burglary or malicious mischief reports, but most of the really dangerous calls took place on the night shift. We still had other violent calls to cover, but without the blanket of darkness to limit the scope of our vision, the crime scenes took on an entirely different flavor, and everything just felt safer.

On my very first shift, I met an officer who'd be my best friend for the next thirty-eight years.

As he walked into the roll call room, Darrell Bolton smiled as he extended his hand and introduced himself, and I immediately knew he was no ordinary man. He looked like a Roman Centurion . . . handsome, noble and proud; his head held high; oozing with the confidence of someone clearly headed for much greater things. He had a soft olive complexion, pale green eyes, straight dark hair and the pronounced chin dimple of Kirk Douglas. We were both the same size (although we always argued over who was taller), and even though he was eight years older than me, his lack of any discernible facial hair made him look much younger. His badge number was 66-3 (what are the odds?), but he'd been a Jefferson County Sheriff's Deputy for ten years before coming to Denver, so he was already a well-seasoned officer. We were lucky enough to work adjoining precincts, and soon found ourselves covering each other on calls and sharing our lunch breaks together. It didn't take long before we realized we shared the same philosophy on how police work should be done. We were both extremely dedicated and aggressive in our duties, but always treated people with respect and compassion, even if they were being arrested. We had an immediate liking for each other, and with our sergeant's permission, would work the same car assignment when we rotated to the night shift in July.

On Monday, July 1st, 1968, Darrell and I became partners. We worked Car 23, which included everything from Downing Street east to Colorado Boulevard, and from Colfax north to East 23rd Avenue. We drove an unmarked light green 1966 Plymouth with no overhead light, and the only things that distinguished us as policemen were our two spotlights and siren, and our menacing squinty-eyed *"Schwarzenegger"* stare.

Darrell worked five shifts a week; went to college during the day, and helped his wife Nancy raise their four little children at home . . . and the stress of trying to budget his time between them all was taking its toll. It was painfully apparent when he came to work, and the man I admired so much when we were just covering each other's calls, became completely intolerable when we were confined to the same car.

It took the first half of our shift before he could shake off the burdens of his mind, and if he wasn't bitching about one thing or another, we drove around in complete silence. It took about two weeks before I couldn't take it anymore, and as I was driving east on Colfax at Vine, Darrell grumbled at me one last time. I slammed on the brakes; stopped in the middle of heavy traffic and yelled, *"I'm sick and tired of all your whining . . . Shut The Fuck Up!"*

Well, that got his attention.

We jumped from our seats and ran to the front of the car. Darrell threw his clipboard to the ground and we raised our fists; each fully prepared to embarrass ourselves in a battle that neither of us really wanted, while astonished motorists drove quizzically by; stunned by the realization that they were about to see two policemen fighting. We stopped for a second, looked each other square in the eye, and busted out laughing. It was probably one of the most ridiculous things either of us had ever seen or done before, and from that moment on, we were best friends and devoted partners for life . . . until it ended with his heartbreaking death on Wednesday, December 27th, 2006, when he succumbed to respiratory/lung complications.

I had a lot of friends on the job over the span of my career, but when any of us transferred to another assignment, we'd rarely see each other again. It wasn't that we weren't friends any-more; it was just an out of sight, out of mind phenomenon where we tended to socialize more with those we currently worked with. But Darrell was the exception to that rule. We'd see each other on a regular basis, no matter where we worked, and the great times we had together began in that summer of 1968 when he invited Sandra and me to a party at his home in Golden, where I met his wife and four children for the very first time.

Nancy was a stunningly attractive woman (who reminded me of Suzanne Pleshette, the actress who played the wife on the old Bob Newhart Show), and was by far the most sophisticated woman I'd ever met. She graciously welcomed us into their home for the first of an endless number of parties I would enjoy there, and Darrell immediately introduced me to one of his oldest and dearest friends, Jack Daniels.

Scott was the oldest of the three boys and was an absolute handful for his parents. He was as rowdy as any boy I'd ever seen, and with his devilish little boy grin, always looked like he was about to do something completely outrageous (which he usually did). But his younger brother Sean was just the opposite. Sean was always this perfect little boy (who grew up to look and sound like Nicolas Cage) . . . always quiet and very soft spoken, and always on his absolute best behavior. I loved them all as if they were my very own, but to be honest, their youngest boy Sam was my favorite of all the boys. He wasn't quite as rowdy as Scott, but shared the same impish smile, and was just about as cute as any little boy could be. He always made a point to greet me when we'd visit, and hang by my side throughout most of the evening and listen to every word I said. But he was especially likable because he was so easy to embarrass.

During a later visit in December 1970, my second wife Cheri and I were there tipping a toddy or two to celebrate the yuletide season, and as everyone grabbed a seat around their elegantly decorated Christmas tree, Sam darted around the living room trying his best to keep us entertained with his exuberant six-year-old charm. He may deny it now, but it was pretty clear that he liked Cheri . . . **A LOT!** . . . and was doing everything he could think of to keep her attention. I soon slipped into the kitchen to fix another drink I really didn't need, and while returning to the living room, I noticed the next great thing I could tease him about. Chuckling to myself I said, *"Sam your fly's open."* He stopped in his tracks, looked down at his zipper and yelled, ***"Oh, My God!"*** He'd never been more embarrassed in his entire life and ran from the room screaming in shame; horrified that Cheri might have actually seen all of his manly stuff. We laughed and laughed over his reaction, but within minutes he returned to the room and joined us in the laughter, and completely at his expense. Now that's a real trooper!

But the real jewel of the family was their daughter Stephani. At eleven-years-old, she was the oldest of her siblings, and was just as precious as she could be. Like Sean, she was very shy, but over the next few months gradually warmed up to me, and during the course of our parties would come sit by my feet while we all sat in the living room and talked. I thought that was just about the cutest thing I'd ever seen, and because I believed she had a little crush on me, I'd tease her by saying, *"Oh, Stephani, you're getting so pretty,"* then to mortify her even more, I'd say, *"I'll meet you out back in ten minutes."* She'd turn bright red and giggle like the little girl that she was, and we'd all have a big laugh at her response . . . but as embarrassed as she was, she always came back for more.

I continued to tease her like this for the next several years, and by the time she was seventeen or eighteen, she'd grown into the most beautiful girl I'd ever seen! When Cheri and I came over for another of my favorite drink 'till you drop parties, she was all dressed up and ready to leave for the evening with some unworthy young jock. I was clearly stunned by how beautiful she looked, and she took full advantage of my reaction. As she started out the door, she stopped, turned to me . . . smiled mischievously and said, *"Bill . . . I'll meet you out back in ten minutes."* She laughed as I turned the brightest shade of red she'd ever seen before (relishing in the knowledge that she'd finally gotten even with me), and laughed even harder when I stammered and stuttered, completely unable to speak. Yes, payback is truly a bitch.

Civil unrest and rioting were commonplace in the summer of 1968, and the Black Panther's propaganda machine was hard at work. We'd be given the latest intelligence at roll call each evening, and were often told some of us may not survive the night. The chant burn baby, burn wasn't a joke, and there were those out there who were bent on creating as much chaos and destruction as they could. The Molotov Cocktail was the weapon of choice for rioters, and burning and looting was always a very real threat.

The first riot of the summer began at 27th and Welton Street, and nearly every car from District One and Two responded. The Department had finally issued gas masks to all the troops, and as we forged our way through the crowd, we geared up for the dispersal of tear gas. Our masks slipped over our heads and covered our faces, but they weren't anything like the compact models they have today. Ours were tethered by a breathing tube to a large bulky red T-shaped filtration canister that cover-ed our chests, and as it turned out, that was actually a pretty good feature. With our heads protected by helmets and our chests protected by the canister, we felt much safer facing the onslaught of bottles and cans.

As we moved through the sidewalks and streets, someone opened fire from one of the rooftops, and the sound of bullets whizzed by our heads. The men I was with took cover behind the Rossonian Hotel and peeked from the corner of the wall, hoping to see where the fire was coming from. Rioters scram-bled in all directions while the shots were being fired, but within seconds it was over. We never saw who was firing at us, and luckily, no one was hit by the sniper's fire, but the psychology of rioting had changed in my mind, and this new level of danger made me hate them even more.

But it wasn't all doom and gloom. Normal police business kept us just as busy, and I enjoyed the diversity of these calls. Stick-ups, shootings, fights, high-speed chases, murders . . . all so much nicer than riots.

July 28th, 1968 started out just like every other Sunday night. Not much going on really, the liquor stores were all closed and the bars would close early . . . it was usually our quietest night.

Darrell and I began our shift by cruising East Colfax Avenue. We knew it would be another two hours before sunset and we'd have time to unwind before any real action would begin. As we slithered our way through traffic searching for our next ticket, we talked about things that were going on in our lives and shared the latest jokes we'd heard. When I started telling a patently offensive joke, I heard a very bizarre sound coming from the front of our car. I stopped mid-sentence and yelled, *"What The Hell Is That?"* and heard the echo of my words bouncing off the nearby buildings. People driving by looked at us and laughed, and Darrell was beside himself with laughter over my embarrassment. While I was emphasizing the crude-ness of my joke, he'd keyed the P.A. system microphone with his knee and broadcast my vile words to everyone on the street. Yeah, it was gonna be a good night.

As Darrell drove east on Colfax, I looked to my right and saw two girls in a black '63 Chevy Corvair convertible in the lane just next to me. The driver briefly glanced over at me, then did a quick double-take when she realized who we were. I laughed at how shocked she looked, and she rewarded me with a smile. What I didn't know was that she'd just taken a big swig of beer and was afraid she'd been busted by the cops. We turned left onto Colorado Boulevard and they continued east on Colfax. As we made our turn, they honked and waved.

A short time later we saw them again on Colfax at Adams Street (they were west bound; we were east bound), and as we passed each other, we all honked and waved.

We went about our business and soon fell in behind a speeding car, north bound on Colorado Boulevard, just east of City Park. As the car passed the little black Corvair, the girls screamed "COPS!" and the driver slowed down before we could get an accurate clock on his speed. Believe me, that didn't set well.

About twenty minutes later, we eased our way in behind the Corvair as it was heading east on Colfax again. It couldn't have been better . . . their left taillight was burned out and gave us the perfect excuse to pull them over. I told Darrell to stop the car, and as they turned left onto Harrison Street, Darrell tapped the siren for a short burst or two, then we both hit them with our spotlights. We usually handled minor violations like this with a verbal warning, but they'd interfered with the long arm of the law and needed to be taught a lesson.

I walked sternly to their car; ticket book in hand and fully prepared to write the ticket they'd just deprived us of. *"License and registration,"* I said in my firmest voice. The driver looked up at me with the wide-eyed innocence of a three-year-old child and said, *"But Officer, what did I do?"*

"You pissed us off!" is what I wanted to say, but instead settled with *"Your left taillight's out."* I had her get out of the car so she could see the violation for herself, but when she stepped from the car and I saw the petite and ravishing figure of this wonderful nineteen-year-old girl, getting even with them no longer seemed important.

She looked like a cross between Nancy Sinatra and Carol Burnett, and was wearing a pair of yellowish cream colored culottes, with button down straps that came over her shoulders, ending at a low cut bib that revealed the tanned flesh of her abundant breasts. When Darrell saw the stunning beauty of her figure, he got out of the car and joined us.

I was completely professional during this entire encounter, but the moment I told her I wasn't going to write her a ticket, the entire mood switched from matter-of-fact business to absolute pleasure. She smiled and said, *"Oh, thank you . . . Thank You,"* and Darrell, recognizing the obvious attraction we both felt for each other said, *"Well, he didn't write you a ticket. The least you could do is have him over for a cup of coffee."* She looked at her roommate with a puzzled expression, then looked back at me and said, *"We don't have any coffee . . . but we've got beer."* She gave me her address, and when I finished my shift at 3am, I went to collect my reward.

Cheri Gruben met me at her door on the fifth floor of the Viking Apartments at 1260 York Street and invited me in. I stayed just long enough to have a beer with her and her roommate Candy Hays, but immediately knew we were **absolutely** meant to be together. She gave me her phone number as I was leaving, and as we stood smiling at each other at the door, I leaned down and kissed her goodbye. Yup, I definitely wanted to see her again.

I don't know how I did it, but by the next day, I'd lost her number, and for the life of me, I couldn't remember which apartment she lived in. I watched for her every evening while we were on patrol, but that elusive little black convertible had all but disappeared from the face of the earth, and I was afraid I'd never see her again.

A few weeks later, Candy ran up to me as Darrell and I'd just walked into the International House of Pancakes at 2001 East Colfax, and yelled, *"What's the matter with you . . . why haven't you called Cheri?"* Taken aback by this unexpected berating, I stumbled through with my pathetic excuse. She rolled her eyes (like only Candy could) then gave me her all too expressive *"you're such an idiot"* look I'd soon become very accustomed to, then just as vigorously, wrote her phone number on a napkin and told me to call her ***"Right Now!!"*** Always willing to do whatever I was told (by just about any woman I've ever known), I made the call, and within minutes Cheri joined us for dinner . . . and our fourteen-year love affair officially began.

Dick McNamee was an investigator with the Denver District Attorney's Office, and a close personal friend of Darrell's. He rode with us on numerous occasions during the summer, and on one particularly busy weekend night, he got to see what working the street was really about.

It was approaching 11pm, and we'd already handled a few minor calls and written two or three tickets, but we knew the night was still young and we'd have plenty more to do before it was over. Our radio buzzed with the chatter of police calls, and as we cruised the arteries of our precinct, an endless stream of cars moved back and forth between the vast array of night spots that permeated East Colfax Avenue; the street Playboy magazine once called the longest, wickedest street in America.

As we drove west on Colfax, we saw a small group of excited people standing in front of the entrance to Sid King's Crazy Horse Bar at 1211 East Colfax Avenue. We turned north into the alley, immediately east of the bar, and saw a man lying on the sidewalk in the center of the crowd. We jumped from our car to investigate and soon learned he wasn't the typical losing combatant in a barroom brawl, but the victim of a shooting who'd been shot five times in the chest and stomach. It didn't look good.

I was reasonably certain I'd seen this much blood at some other crime scene during my short career, but to be honest, I couldn't remember when or where. We radioed for an ambulance and comforted him as best as we could, but there were far too many wounds for us to treat with the limited first-aid training we'd received while we were in the Academy, and all we could do was wait for the ambulance to arrive. Fortunately for him, ambulances in Denver were never that far away.

While we were questioning the witnesses, a cab driver ran over and told us he'd followed the suspect across East Colfax Avenue and saw him hiding under one of the cars in the hotel parking lot. We drew our guns as we ran, and fought our way through the onslaught of heavy traffic. Actually, "fought" probably isn't the most appropriate word to describe that moment, since everyone either stopped or got out our way when they saw the serious and determined looks on our faces, and the even more serious and deadly guns in our hands.

When we reached the parking lot, we saw a man lying face down beneath a car, fumbling with loose bullets, desperately trying to reload the magazine for his well-worn .32 automatic pistol. As we grabbed his legs and fought to pull him from his hiding place, he fumbled to cram the magazine back into the butt of his pistol. Darrell straddled his back, buried both knees into his upper back, then forced his head to the ground to keep him from moving. I grabbed the gun from his left hand and stuffed it into my back pocket, then helped Darrell force his arms around to put him in handcuffs. It took every last ounce of our combined strength to control his contortions before we were able to restrain him. He was a very tough guy!

While we were in the middle of our struggle, a well dressed society looking middle aged couple walked quickly to our side. Already barking unintelligible orders as she approached us, the irate woman grabbed Darrell's right arm and screamed, *"How dare you treat this man that way! Let him go!!"* With no restraint or consideration for her blatant stupidity, Darrell brusquely shoved her aside and yelled, *"Back off, lady, or you're going to jail, too."* She stepped away, but was still very upset with us . . . that is until we told her he'd just shot someone five times. Her jaw dropped and her eyes twitched as she digested what we'd just said, then stepped back as if to say, *"Oh, yeah . . . now I see,"* and she and her escort walked silently away.

With our suspect handcuffed and finally under control, we walked him back to our car. By this time, the ambulance and several other police cars had arrived, and we learned what had happened.

The suspect and victim had been in the strip club at the same time, but apparently neither of them knew each other. According to witnesses, there'd been no altercations in the bar or any hint of trouble between either of the men, and for no apparent reason, the suspect followed his victim from the bar, and without saying a word, opened fire. The gunshots were critical, but amazingly, the victim survived.

A week later, Dick rode with us again. We were having a great time reminiscing about the fun we'd had the previous week, when we received a call on a disturbance at a house in the 1800 block of Race Street. As we pulled to the west curb, just two or three houses north of East 18th Avenue, we heard the sound of angry voices coming from inside the home directly across the street. When we walked to the front door, we were met by a room full of screaming people; most of whom were ranting and raving about a man who'd threatened them with a gun. The suspect left just after they called the police, but they were still extremely upset, and it was nearly impossible to get them to stop yelling long enough to tell us what had happened. After several futile minutes of trying to deal with their hysterics, we finally took one of the victims to our car where we could write the offense report in relative peace and quiet.

The victim sat in the back with Dick; Darrell sat in the front passenger seat and I sat behind the wheel. The sun had just gone down and the neighborhood soon eased into darkness. Darrell turned the ceiling light on so he could see to write his report, and we listened to the man describe the assault.

I was watching the street looking for any sign of the suspect, when a white 1963 Chevrolet turned the corner a full block behind us and stopped in the middle of the street. I watched in the side view mirror as the bright dual headlights glared at us for a few seconds, then heard the explosive **BANG** of a gunshot. We jumped from our car and heard an even louder **BANG,** then the sound of a bullet bouncing off the pavement in front of us. The Chevrolet screamed down the road and headed straight for us. We drew our guns and aimed at the charging car, but just before it reached us, it swerved to its left, jumped over the high concrete curb and slammed head-on into a large oak tree. Steam spewed from the broken radiator and the engine raced as though the driver was trying to get away.

We ran to the car, desperately shining our flashlights to see through the windows, and fully expected to be shot by whoever was inside. When we got to the wrecked car, we saw a lone woman sitting behind the wheel; her chin resting on her chest, with blood gushing from a bullet wound to the right side of her head. The engine kept racing . . . vroom, vroom, vroom . . . and we could see her foot pushing up and down against the accelerator as her body viciously jerked and kicked with each grizzly spasm of her horrible death.

Everyone in the block came out to see what had happened, and the woman's husband became hysterical when he saw his dead wife slumped over the steering wheel. Filled with absolute rage, he ran back and forth in front of the car, flailing his arms in the air and screaming we'd just killed his wife. I was certain we were about to be in the middle of another race riot, but fortunately, he calmed down when we convinced him we weren't the one's who'd fired the fatal shot. The angry crowd that had gathered around us suddenly became subdued as they realized a friend had been killed; but not at the hands of the police—*hmmm*, just think about that for a second or two—*it only mattered if the police pulled the trigger.*

The dead woman was a part of the original disturbance and had gone to look for the suspect by herself. When she found him at the end of the block, she stopped and rolled her right side window down to have words with him. He walked to the side of her car, leaned through the open window, and after a brief exchange of profanities, fired his fatal round. Her foot stomped against the accelerator, and as her reflexes propelled her down the street, he fired his second round at us.

Several other officers covered the call, and the Homicide Detectives and Crime Lab Technicians soon arrived. While the others secured the crime scene, we drove to the nearby International House of Pancakes and enjoyed our favorite meal while we finished our reports.

When we were finished, we took the reports back to the detectives. By now they had a copy of our suspect's mug shot and the last address he was known to have, so we headed to east Park Hill and called for cover. Two other officers and Sergeant Glen Pierson met with us near the suspect's home, and the six of us went to make the arrest. The two officers covered the back while the sergeant, Darrell, Dick, and I went to the front. We stood to the sides of the door (in case he shot through the door—a procedure every policeman is familiar with, but few television writers seem to understand), knocked four times, and within seconds, the suspect opened the door. We jammed our guns into his face and charged into the room. We arrested him without incident, and the gun battle we were fully prepared for never occurred.

This was typical of how we operated in those days. There were no SWAT teams to make entries during dangerous arrests . . . every policeman was properly trained for any circumstance, no matter what it was, and in the end, critical situations were usually handled much faster . . . and probably just as well. Yes, we truly were men of steel.

Halloween always seemed like the perfect night for trouble . . . teenagers smashing pumpkins; stealing candy from little kids and vandalizing everything they could get their hands on. But that wasn't the case on the Halloween of 1968 . . . this Halloween was unusually quiet. Summer had long past slipped away, and every time we stepped from our car on this cold Thursday evening, the chill of the deep autumn air filled our lungs. The trick-or-treaters had already collected their booty and returned to their homes. Tomorrow was a school day and most everyone had settled down for the evening; watching their favorite television shows or doing their homework before an early night's sleep.

Darrell and I were in our second month as partners on the night shift. Our unmarked Plymouth was being used in a different part of the District, so we were driving a fully marked white 1967 Ford, with two spotlights, an overhead bubblegum machine, and two large gold colored Denver Police badge decals appropriately placed on each of the front doors. We couldn't have been more conspicuous if we tried, and should have been visible and identifiable to anyone in our path.

As we cruised randomly down the side streets and alleys, we complained about how boring the night had been, and just before 2am, we decided to head for Presbyterian Hospital at East 19th Avenue and Gilpin Street to grab a cup of coffee. We needed a break from all of the monotony and thought if we were lucky enough, we might even find a nurse or two to flirt with while we were there. As we made our way west on East 24th Avenue, we received a call to the 2300 block of Downing Street on a report of a man holding people at bay with a gun inside one of the apartments. This wasn't a Code 10 run, so we sped silently down 24th and turned left onto Downing Street. Downing was a one-way street for northbound traffic, but with no other cars on the street, we raced the half block south to the apartment building.

When we pulled to a stop at the west curb line, I saw two men standing in front of the building; facing each other just fifteen feet to my right. Apparently neither of them noticed our dazzling new police car, and when I reached down to undo my seat belt, I heard the sharp **POP** of a small caliber pistol just outside my window. I drew my gun as I jumped from the car and saw one of the men turn and run northbound on the sidewalk as the other raised his arm and aimed at the now terrified man. *"Hold It"* I yelled, and watched in disbelief as he fired his second round. I yelled again, *"Police . . . Hold It!"* and he turned and pointed his gun directly at my face. The tiny bore of his .25 automatic looked more like 12-gauge shotgun as it glared at my forehead, and as the world stood still for a second or two, I leveled my gun at the center of his chest and fired. A huge ball of flames burst from the end of my barrel as the loud **BOOM** echoed off the buildings. He turned and ran toward the north edge of the building, and I fired again. I waited for him to fall, but he just kept running. I couldn't believe I didn't hit him . . . *we were so close!*

He ran to the narrow gap between the apartment building and the building to its north, and disappeared from my view. When I got to the edge of the building, I realized I didn't have my flashlight (everything happened so fast, I didn't have time to grab it), and immediately regretted the horrible mistake I'd just made. I peeked down the pathway, desperately trying not to reveal any more of my head as a target than I absolutely had to, but it was so dark I couldn't see anything ahead of me.

Darrell radioed that shots had been fired and we were in pursuit of a suspect on foot, then ran down the south side of the apartment building toward the alley, hoping to capture the suspect himself.

The welcome sound of sirens screamed from every direction of the District, and within seconds I heard the screeching of tires as our cover arrived. I slowly ventured down the coal-black pathway, and was startled when my body hit the three-foot chain-link fence between the two buildings. As my hand touched the crossbar, I saw a man lying face down on the ground on the other side. My eyes had slowly acclimated to the darkness by now, and seeing the gun still in his hand, I yelled, *"Don't Move! Don't Move Or I'll Blow Your Fucking Head Off!!"* He had the advantage up until this moment, and with four bullets still left in his gun, could have easily shot me as I stumbled into that fence. But he didn't fire, and at the moment of truth, chose to surrender. I guess he believed me.

I scrambled over the fence and took the gun from his hand, then put him in handcuffs and hauled him back over the fence. By now the neighborhood was swarming with police cars, and everyone was extremely relieved when I walked out safely with the suspect in custody.

The next afternoon, I drove back to the scene to see where my bullets had gone (detectives didn't respond to police shootings in those days unless someone was hit—but I had to write a letter—different times). I was fully prepared to kill the man who was so willing to shoot another man (and take aim at me), but, as it turned out, the only things I killed that night were an old oak tree and a relatively innocent basement window.

It was a very exciting night and I loved every second of it, but it taught me a valuable lesson I would never forget: no matter how dull or routine my shifts would become, I would never be lulled into complacency again . . . and was always ready for the fight of my life!

Friday, February 14th, 1969 was Valentine's Day. Husbands and lovers were giving their sweethearts heart shaped boxes of chocolates or bouquets of red roses; making plans to take them out for a romantic dinner and wine, and maybe even to a movie. Everyone seemed to be celebrating this day with love and gentleness, except for a bitter old Park Hill couple who lived in a modest little blond brick home on Ivanhoe Street. There was no love at this house, and their fighting was so loud and vicious, their neighbors called for the police.

When I pulled to the east curb just south of their home, three very excited neighbors ran to my car. They told me they'd heard screaming and yelling coming from the house, then heard a gunshot . . . and whoever did the shooting was still in the house. Another officer was covering the call, but with the possibility that someone was seriously injured inside, I couldn't wait for him to arrive. I pulled my gun and ran to the front door. It was slightly ajar, so I kicked it hard, slamming it against the wall. Now that I knew no one was hiding on the other side, I stepped inside and slid my back against the wall to my left, just to make sure I wouldn't be ambushed from behind. It was bright outside, but with the drapes all drawn, I had trouble seeing anything in the darkness beyond that rectangular sliver of light that beamed through the front door. The house was completely silent, and the only sound I could hear was the rapid thump, thump, thump from the beat of my own heart. When my eyes finally adjusted to the darkness, I inched my way across the living room floor and came to a hallway on my right. A woman was lying face down in the hallway, and every ounce of her blood had drained from the huge bullet hole in the left side of her head. I was certain she was already dead and knew there was nothing I could do to help her, especially since I still had her killer hiding somewhere in the house just waiting to kill me.

The hallway led to a bedroom on the left; a bathroom in the middle, and another bedroom on the right. I crept to the bedroom on my left and began my search. My heart was pounding even louder now, and for the first time in my life, I learned my nose would run when I was sure of my imminent death. I stood to the side of the closet and jerked the door open, and just prayed I could get the first round off before I was shot.

There was no one in the closet.

I wiped my nose with my arm and walked to the bed. *(You don't think about it much, but there's really no safe way to look under a bed when you're looking for a man with a gun).* I carefully lifted the edge of the bedspread and slowly leaned down to take what I thought would be my very last look.

God, the anticipation was excruciating!! One peek; one shot . . . and that would be that. Another horrendous headshot and the most gruesome crime scene photos I could imagine.

When I saw that he wasn't there, I went into the second bed-room and repeated my exact same moves . . . one more closet of horror; one more terrifying bed. My heart was pounding, my nose was running, and my bowels were giving it a great deal of thought.

Second bedroom . . . clear!

I stepped over the dead woman's body and walked back to the living room. I glanced out the front door and saw another police car stopped at the curb, but Bill Goodard, the policeman who'd been sent to cover me, was still sitting inside his car. I ran to the door and yelled, *"Hurry up! The man killed his wife and he's still in here."* He didn't move . . . he just sat there and looked at me. I turned and eased my way back across the living room floor and searched the small kitchen. It was empty, but the door to the basement was standing wide open and led to the only place left for the suspect to hide.

Goodard still hadn't come to the house, and by now I was really pissed!! I ran to the front door to yell at him to get his cowardly ass in here because we still had a basement to search. He was still sitting behind the steering wheel, and as my blood started to boil, I saw a handcuffed man sitting in the back seat. I ran to the car to find out what was going on, and learned why he'd failed to cover me. His initial hesitation and blank stare was focused on the husband who was walking down the north side of the house, with a gun dangling from one of his fingers, and his hands raised high in the air. He'd gone out the back door while I was still searching the bedrooms, and walked to the police car to surrender. While I was frantically searching for the killer, Bill was taking him into custody all by himself. You can't imagine the relief I felt as I wiped my nose one last time and called for an ambulance and the Homicide Detectives.

In 1969, Darrell was promoted to the rank of Technician and transferred to the Video Training Bureau at our new Police Academy at 550 East Iliff Avenue. I cried real tears when he left the District and sank into an abyss of depression and self-pity (well, almost). I bounced around from one car to another, mournfully trying to find someone new I could call partner, but for the time being, it just wasn't meant to be.

While working with a probationary officer one Darrelless night, we received a call to a family fight at a house in the 2400 block of Humboldt Street. A frightened young woman answered the door when I knocked, and I was stunned by what I saw. Her face and blouse were covered in blood, her eyes were nearly completely swollen shut, and her lips were so swollen, she could barely speak. As she described the beating she'd just taken, her husband stood silently in the background. He'd been through this same scenario several times before, and knew if he remained calm in our presence, we couldn't arrest him unless she was willing to sign a complaint. I was thrilled when she nodded that she would, but his attitude immediately changed, and it was now very clear to us that he wasn't going to make our job any easier.

I sent my partner to get an arrest slip from our car and waited alone with this monster for the next several minutes; protecting his wife from further abuse and trying to keep him as calm as I could. When my partner returned and said he couldn't find the arrest slips, I sent him back out for an offense report (either of these would have worked), but after another excruciatingly long four or five minutes, he returned and said he couldn't find the offense reports. (For the record, the arrest slips were in the glove compartment and the offense reports were on our clip-board . . . I don't know where his glasses were).

Time was working against me as the husband became more and more aggressive with each new delay, so I sent my rookie partner back out a third time and told him to call for another car to bring us an arrest slip. He made the call, but instead of coming back inside to assist me in what was turning into an increasingly volatile situation, he waited in our car until the officers arrived. By the time he and the two cover officers finally walked through the door, the husband had worked him-self into a state of rage and was ready to fight.

As his wife was signing the complaint, he looked me straight in the eyes and said, *"You wouldn't be so tough if you didn't have that gun and Billy club."* I drew my gun from my holster and nightstick from its sheath and handed them to my partner as I said, *"I don't need them for you,"* then shoved him into a nearby bedroom where I could deal with him in private.

I've always had sort of a little man complex, and rarely saw men as bigger than me, but when I closed the door behind us, I suddenly realized just how big he really was. He only weighed about 190 pounds, but was at least 6'8" with arms half a room long, and now trying to subdue him alone sounded like a pretty absurd idea. My mind flashed back to those boxing lessons I'd had with my dad in the projects when I was still a little boy, and I realized this match up wasn't really that much different... except this guy's arms wouldn't be tied down to his sides, and I was pretty sure he wasn't going to get down on his knees just so I could punch him in the nose. And, oh, yeah . . . this time I was going to get my ass kicked!

At that point, I just hoped he was impressed enough by how gutsy I was and would just let me arrest him without making me embarrass myself by having to scream for help. That sounded like a much, much, better plan to me, but he made it pretty clear his giving up was just never going to happen.

He glared fiercely into my eyes and said, *"Okay, mother fucker, let's see what you got."* And now, backed into a corner by my own stupidity and ego, I was forced to fight with some-body way out of my class. I knew the only way I could pos-sibly win this fight was to bring him down to my own level, so I lunged at him with the Kung Fu agility of a young Chuck Norris and side-kicked him hard in the groin. But instead of bending over or collapsing to the floor like any other normal man would, he just stood there and looked at me. *"Oh, shit,"* I thought to myself, then kicked him again. My foot ached from this second powerful kick, but apparently I was the only one who felt the pain. He put his knees together; leaned forward just the tiniest bit, and said, *"Don't do that."*

Well, I was done.

I opened the door and told the other guys, *"Uh, you can come in now,"* and it took the four of us the next ten minutes to wrestle him to the floor and put him in handcuffs. Turns out he was right . . . I wasn't nearly as tough without my gun and nightstick, and was never baited into making that mistake again.

By mid-summer 1969, I found a new partner to work with on the night shift. John Schnittgrund and I came on the job together and became close friends while we were still in the Academy. We were told we'd get to walk the beat on East Colfax, and were anxious to work one of the last foot beats left on the Department. At 6'9' and 240 pounds, John towered over my diminutive frame, and knowing I'd soon be walking shoulder-to-waist beside this incredible hulk, I felt the need to enhance my physical stature. I bought a new pair of Acme boots (with two-inch heels), and at our next roll call, bragged about how much taller I was. John was impressed; thought I looked great, but by our next shift, had his own new pair of Acme boots, with the same two-inch heels. I guess he was intimidated by my new and formidable appearance, and just needed to maintain that twelve-inch gap. By the time we started the night shift, they cancelled the foot beat, and we were assigned to a car in the eastern part of the District. Our precinct covered everything from Colorado Boulevard east to Monaco Street Parkway, and East Colfax Avenue north to East 23rd Avenue.

It was a good assignment, especially since John was so big. Answering a Code 9 to see if an ambulance was needed, John said, *"If that's Carl again he's going to jail!"* This was John's car; he knew the trouble spots, so this was a heads-up for what may lie ahead.

It wasn't Carl this time, but his sister who'd swallowed a button. *Oh, the horror!* Everyone was screaming — sisters, mother and Carl (no father) barking, *"Where's the ambulance?"* There was no danger; the button was small and wasn't lodged in her throat, but safely in her belly. Screaming like she was dying, John finally yelled, *"Shut up, Dorothy. You'll poop it out."* She calmed down, but Carl was livid! He ran to the rear of the house, maybe to get a gun, I didn't know, but knew it happened with others. I was hot on his trail until he raced out the back, presumably to cool off and avoid the arrest he knew John was hoping for. I returned to the living room, and seconds later, Carl was in the front yard, screaming and drawing a crowd. I stepped out to confront him and he grabbed my shirt and tried to throw me to the ground. There were no punches, but the fight was on! Wrestling across the yard, lots of cussing (mostly on his part), one of his sisters watching from the window yelled:

"CARL'S FIGHTING THE POH-LEESEMAN!"

John walked out the door, Cheshire cat grin and chuckling, he pulled Carl from my back. On the way to jail, John laughed and said, *"Carl's blind in one eye and can't see much out of the other... all you had to do was stand to his left and he couldn't see you."* Lesson learned; you never wrestle a blind guy — they never let go!

During my next rotation to a solo assignment on the day shift, the dispatcher sent me to a single story apartment complex at East 37th Avenue and Columbine Street to see if I could help a woman with some kind of problem with her car. Well, I'd handled just about every other kind of call I could think of, but checking the mechanical condition of someone's car was a new one to me.

The woman met me at her door and told me she'd gone to the store a little earlier, and could hear something dragging underneath her car. She apologized for bothering me, but said when she looked under her car, she saw something suspicious looking, and thought I should take a look.

She walked me to the parking area behind her apartment and directed me to her car. I hated doing anything that got my uniform dirty, because it distracted from my well groomed All

American Boy image, but I made the supreme sacrifice and got down on my hands and knees on that filthy dirt lot and peeked under her car.

"Suspicious looking?" That was the understatement of the year! A cold shudder ran up and down my spine when I saw fourteen sweating and unstable sticks of dynamite hanging to the ground. They were bound together with duct tape, with an electrical wire leading from a blasting cap, up into the engine area. I stood up, wiped my running nose, and told her to go back to her apartment. I knew keying our radios could detonate certain types of bombs, so I drove to the north end of the block and called for the Bomb Squad.

My sergeant and two cover officers arrived right away, but it took another twenty minutes before the detectives showed up with the bomb disposal trailer. We evacuated the homes that were closest to her car, and watched from what we hoped was a safe distance while the detectives carefully removed the bomb.

One of her neighbors told me he'd seen a man crawling out from underneath her car earlier that morning, and his description matched that of a man she'd been having problems with. The neighbor later identified the suspect through a photo line-up, and he was arrested by the detectives. Four days later, while he was still in our jail, an explosion blew off the front part of her apartment. The suspect was released from jail, and the woman entered her own self-imposed witness protection program and moved out of the state.

I *always* thought I'd get shot on the job, but generally believed I wouldn't be killed, and up until that day, I never considered the risk of being blown into small pieces by a bomb. If I was going to be killed on the job, I wanted to look as good as I could in my coffin, and explosions just didn't fit in with my plans. *I hated bombs!*

As Dragnet's Sergeant Joe Friday would say, *"It was the day after Thanksgiving; Friday, November 28th, 1969. I was working the Day Watch out of the old Curtis Park area, when the dispatcher asked me to call a detective in the Assault Bureau."*

He was buried in paperwork and asked if I'd bring one of his witnesses to Headquarters for a written statement. I told him it would be my pleasure (you always helped a detective whenever you could), then picked him up at his home in the projects and headed down Champa Street.

By the time I reached 24th Street, a newly promoted Sergeant Steve Metros came on the air and said he and his partner Detective Mike Dowd had fallen in behind a car filled with three robbery suspects and an escaped murderer in front of the Denver Post Building at 15th and California Streets. Several officers said they were covering the call, and within seconds, the dreaded *"Officer Down . . . Shots Fired"* call rang out. I pulled to the curb and kicked my passenger out, then screamed red light and siren through the onslaught of heavy downtown traffic.

When I screeched to a stop in the middle of traffic on California Street, people were running in every direction. Some were trying to get away from the hail of bullets while others rushed to get as close as they could to see the kind of horror they'd never seen before.

Detective Dowd was lying on the sidewalk and was writhing in pain as blood poured from his serious but non-fatal gunshot wounds, and his assailant was lying on his back just a few feet away. As several officers attended to Detective Dowd and still others helped Sergeant Metros with his three robbery suspects, I walked over to the body of James Sherbondy and stared into the cold brown eyes of one of the meanest looking men I'd ever seen. Even in death he was a scary looking man—street ugly, if you know what I mean—a rock-hard middle-aged man whose Mexican bandito mustache only accentuated the ruggedness of his ogre-like face—a man you never wanted to meet alone in a dark alley.

His left arm laid parallel to his side and his right arm stretched away from his body, just inches from the stolen .38 revolver he'd fired six times at Detective Dowd; the gun Bill Carter (my next partner) kicked out of his reach. His lightweight jacket draped open and revealed an empty shoulder holster hanging along his side. I was more than a little surprised when I saw it, because I'd never seen a holster on anyone but a policeman before, and would only see one other throughout the remainder of my career. An empty holster is a dead giveaway that a gun is nearby, and most criminals carry their guns in their waistbands or pockets so they can ditch them whenever they see the police. But Sherbondy didn't care if the police saw his holster. He carried it for only one reason, and that was to have his gun secure and accessible, and he welcomed the chance to shoot anyone who got in his way.

When the excitement finally died down and Detective Dowd was safely in the hospital, the District One officers took over. My witness was still waiting for me at the curb where I'd dumped him, and couldn't wait to hear what had happened. He'd witnessed a pretty good fight himself, but had to admit my story was far more exciting than his own.

By the summer of 1970, I had the opportunity to work with another of my academy classmates. All the cars on the day and morning shifts were staffed with solo officers, with the exception of Car 27 (I believe), a single two-man assignment in the northern warehouse section of the District. Since Schnittgrund was still happy working his Colfax car, Bill Carter and I jumped at the opportunity to work this car as permanent partners on the 3am-11am morning shift.

Bill and I sat next to each other in the Academy and became immediate friends. He was one of the happiest men I'd ever known, and his little boy smile and incredible sense of humor made him a very easy man to like. He was just a few months older than me, five or six inches taller, probably better looking and smarter (depending on who you asked), but in spite of my obvious shortcomings, he chose me to be his friend and Academy study partner. On weekend nights, he and his pretty young wife Jan would welcome Sandra and me to their apartment at 598 South Lincoln Street, where we'd study for our Monday morning exams. We always managed to get some studying done, but spent most of our evenings just laughing and enjoying each other's company.

In December, I was pulled off my car and worked with Mike O'Neill on a special plain-clothes assignment. (Years later, Mike would follow in his father's footsteps and become one of our most respected Division Chiefs). Our main objective was to fight the rising tide of burglaries, and with the freedom to go anywhere in the District, we were pretty successful in our venture.

We were also available to cover any hot calls that came out, and covered Detective Larry Smith at E. 31st Avenue and Jackson Street when he stopped a car with three robbery suspects who were wanted for beating and robbing several elderly people.

We drove the suspects to Headquarters and took them to separate interrogation rooms on the third floor of the new Detective Bureau Annex. I took my seventeen-year-old suspect to a room by myself; removed his handcuffs, stepped back three or four steps, then reached behind my back to hang them from my belt. Without saying a word, that arrogant little bastard picked up one of those heavy old wooden chairs and raised it above his head. *"Don't even go there,"* I managed to squeak out just before I was hit, then crashed to the floor, thinking to myself, *"I've seen this in a hundred cowboy movies, but never believed it could happen in real life."*

I ducked at just the right moment, and the brunt of its force fell across my shoulders and back; not really painful, but absolutely incapacitating for the first four or five seconds. He jumped in the middle of my back and brutally beat me . . . four, five, six punches; one after another before I was able to regain my balance and defend myself. I grabbed him around his neck and hit him as hard as I could; one ineffective punch after the other; barely fazing his impervious boxer-like jaw; all the while desperately moving my body around to keep my exposed gun out of his reach. Being murdered with your own gun was the ultimate insult on the job, and I wasn't about to let it happen to me.

Brain Moran came in to see what all the noise was about, and when he saw I was losing the battle, knocked my suspect unconscious with his sap. As I staggered to my feet, I could feel my lips and eyes swelling and felt blood flowing down my face. I went to the bathroom to see how badly I'd been beaten, but when I looked at my reflection in the mirror, the imagined swelling and blood had disappeared, and the only damage I sustained (other than to my ego) was a single tiny pink spot in the center of my forehead.

I thought to myself, *"That's it? That's all you could do?"* It wasn't much, but it was far more damage than my prisoner received . . . that is until Brian came into the room.

CHAPTER 17

"The Detective Bureau"

On Monday, February 1st, 1971, I was sent to the Detective Bureau for a three-month training session with Walt Radovich and Paul Riggs, who with nearly twenty-three years apiece on the job, were two of the best and most colorful detectives in the District Four Burglary Detail. (In 1970, the original five Districts were condensed to four, and the area previously designated as District Six (southwest Denver) was now District Four).

Walt was a big man. And when I say big, I don't mean tall, I mean he was just big . . . and tough, and strong; so big he could actually conceal his snub nose .38 revolver in the palm of his hand. He looked like a broader version of Wilford Brimley (star of the movie, Cocoon), but in spite of his imposing stature, he was truly a gentle giant, and as soft spoken and mellow as any man I'd ever known.

But Paul was just his opposite. He was a wiry dark haired little guy, who looked like his namesake Paulie from the HBO series The Sopranos . . . and with just one look at his battered prizefighter face, you knew he wasn't someone you wanted to mess with. I liked Paul (actually quite a bit), but even with his keen sense of humor, he was easily angered by the most trivial things, and was more than a little intimidating to me.

They came on the job together in 1948 when policemen were generally hired more for their brawn than their brains, and at a time when most of them were known to be quick with their sticks and fast on the draw. For the most part, they worked their beats alone, and with very little cover from other officers, used whatever force they deemed necessary to resolve any problems that came their way. And believe me, the force they used was severe (at least by today's standards), but the crim-

271

inals who were thumped by the beat cop in those days, just considered it to be part of their punishment for being arrested and rarely whined to the press or hired an attorney whenever their fragile little egos were bruised. Those were different times.

They were both as tough as nails, and seemed to embrace the belief that Psalm 23:4 actually read, *"Yea, though I walk through the valley of death, I shall fear no evil, for I am the meanest son-of-a-bitch in the valley."* They were what my generation reverently called, ***Real Cops.***

They were a part of that privileged group who'd been policemen before the Supreme Court severely handcuffed law enforcement with two of the most debilitating court decisions America has ever seen . . . the 1961 Mapp v. Ohio decision that ruled evidence obtained in violation of the Fourth Amendment (which protects against unreasonable searches and seizures) could ***no longer*** be used in criminal prosecutions (as the state courts had approved of before), and the 1966 Miranda v. Arizona decision that required the police to advise a suspect in specific detail of his rights prior to being questioned. But until that time, they were still free to conduct their probable cause searches and interrogate their prisoners with near impunity for any abuses, just as they'd done since the ratification of our Constitution in 1787. (It kind of makes you wonder why something that worked so well for the past hundred and seventy-some years was no longer acceptable?)

Paul died on Saturday, November 3rd, 2007, and Walt just forty-nine days later, on Saturday, December 22nd . . . and in an article in the Rocky Mountain News, Gary Massaro wrote a tribute to Paul that was one of the best I've ever seen:

Saturday, December 15, 2007
By Gary Massaro, Rocky Mountain News

Paul Riggs fought the good fight. In fact, he fought a lot. That's what made him one of the toughest cops in Denver.

"You should have seen the marks on his gun from hitting people," said his wife, Vi. *"He'd rather fight them than shoot them."*

Don't think he was just a tough guy.

He worked hard. He supported his family. He was faithful to his friends. If they needed something and he had it, it was theirs.

He'd get a sly grin on his face when he'd tell a joke to his pals.

Despite a ferocious temper, he loved to laugh.

He died Nov. 3. He was 86.

He was born Sept. 2, 1921, in Albany N.Y, to James and Maria Palumbo Riggs. The last name used to be Riggio. But his father couldn't get a job with that last name because of anti-Italian prejudice so he changed it to Riggs.

The family moved to north Denver when Paulie—that's what his friends and family called him—was a little squirt. That's where he became tough. He had to be.

"He was sick all the time when he was little," Vi said. *"He got picked on a lot when he was a kid, like until he was 16."*

Then he started fighting back. And the bullies left him alone.

He joined the Navy in World War II. The submarine he was on got shot up and sank. Paulie was in the water, wounded, for six days until he was rescued.

He came home to Denver, still banged up and unable to work a full shift.

"He tried to walk into his sister's house and fell flat on his face," Vi said.

He began working at the old Gates Rubber Co., moving up to night foreman. His brother encouraged him to become a police officer—sort of. *(This wasn't in the article, but his brother, Joe, was also a Denver Policeman).*

"He told him, "You're too dumb to be a cop," Vi said.

He took an agility test and failed because of his injured leg. He went over a jump and landed on his good leg. The instructor said he had to land on both feet.

"He worked out for a whole year on that leg," Vi said. *"The next year, he passed the test, doing a flip at the end."*

Vi recalled a story about Paulie's first shift on the job. He showed up with a pressed uniform and spit-shine on his shoes. Some older, wiseacre cop said Paulie must be the new guy and walked up to him—and stepped on his shoes, scuffing them. Paulie hauled off and clipped the guy a good one, knocking him down.

Just then, he saw his boss, a lieutenant. Paulie took off his gun belt and badge, handed them to the lieutenant and said *"I guess I'm fired."*

Not so.

"You're my driver tonight," the lieutenant said.

He met Vi while she was a hostess at the Old South Restaurant near Zuni and West Alameda.

"He worked a car lot there," Vi said. *"He always worked two, three jobs all his life. Anyplace they needed help, he worked."*

They were married April 1, 1966, in Boulder. *"He wasn't just my husband. We were best friends,"* Vi said.

He liked to fish on the Western Slope and bird hunt in Kansas and northern Colorado. *"I fished right beside him"* Vi said. *"I hunted right beside him."*

She said his feisty nature kept him going.

A month before he died, someone pulled into a parking spot he had been waiting on. So he got out of his vehicle to tell the guy he'd stolen his spot.

"Yeah?" the guy responded.

"You see who's parking here."

So Paulie dragged the guy out of his car and thumped him. Then he drove home. He told Vi he was having chest pains.

"You got them for fighting," she said, *"Then you just keep them."*

At the end of my training period, I was sent back to District Two with the promise that I'd be considered for promotion sometime in the near future, and on Thursday, July 1st, 1971, with just over four years on the job, I was promoted to the rank of Detective. I worked the District Two Burglary Detail out of the old police headquarters building at 1245 Champa Street.

Exams weren't required to be promoted to the rank of Detective. New detectives were selected by the quality of offense reports and follow up investigations submitted by patrolmen on the street, so this was strictly a promotion of merit. I was pretty proud of my accomplishment.

Being a detective was a radical change from working the street. The thrill of rushing to so many exciting calls immediately disappeared, and our lackluster involvement with burglaries generally began after the initial investigations and arrests had already been made. Unless you worked homicides, narcotics or vice, being a detective had none of the glamour that's portrayed on the silver screen, but there were still plenty of other perks for us to enjoy. We got to wear fancy suits; drive around in unmarked cars . . . eat lunch whenever we felt like it (and took as long as we wanted), and weren't tied down to our radios like the District officers were. And even though we were assigned cases within specific areas of the District, we had the freedom to go anywhere we needed in order to pursue our investigations.

But the workload could be staggering. Each of the ten District Two Burglary Detectives were assigned five or six burglary cases a day, and often received as many as ten. There weren't enough hours in the day to give each of them the attention they deserved, and much of my off duty time was spent just trying to keep up with my reports.

Hours were consumed with the interrogation of suspects who were either in jail or the Gilliam Juvenile Detention Center, writing and executing search warrants, inventorying evidence and other recovered property, typing supplementary reports for each of the cases we'd investigated, and typing case filings for the District Attorney's Office when a suspect was actually charged with a crime. The largest part of our job was consumed with paper work.

We still covered any serious calls we happened to be near, but for the most part, we were only there as backup firepower, and weren't involved in any of the follow-up investigations or paperwork.

But in the early afternoon of Friday, March 16th, 1973, I covered a call that was especially noteworthy to me, because it was at 1717 E. 17th Avenue. Sound familiar to you? *It did to me!!*

I was three or four blocks west of the apartment building when a call of a shooting came out, and a shudder ran up my spine as I remembered my first experience there. This was a very serious and dangerous call, and I wondered if returning to the scene of my first near death experience was an omen of my impending doom. I arrived before anyone else and cautiously walked up the steps to the open front door. As I entered the apartment, I saw a man standing in the room immediately to my right, with the body of a woman lying directly at his feet. I had my gun at my side and asked what had happened. He meekly looked up and mumbled quietly that he'd shot his apartment manager over a simple argument they'd had, and the remorse he now felt was clearly evident on his face. I asked where the gun was, and as he reached for the .38 revolver on a table behind him, I aimed at his chest/side and yelled for him to back away from the gun . . . but in spite of the fact that he'd just killed someone, there was never any real threat to me. As I was putting him in handcuffs, the uniform officers arrived and took him into custody and I returned to my car to write my statement for the Homicide Bureau Detectives.

What could have easily been a life or death gun battle with an unstable murderer ended calmly enough (and I was thankful for that), but when I finished my paperwork, I vowed to myself that I'd never cover another call at that address.

For the first year, I worked as a temporary partner with Rob Steely, Bob Steen and John Thompson, but by 1972, I teamed up with my old friend Bill Carter when he was promoted to the rank of Detective.

Bill and I were great together! We handled our cases with the same level of competency and energy, and together with our wives, spent a lot of our off duty time partying together.

After seeing the latest Dirty Harry movie, we decided we were under gunned and went to Gart Brothers to buy the appropriate guns to fit our new perceived image. Dirty Harry carried a .44 Magnum (the most powerful handgun known to man), but we were limited by the Department's strict weapon's policy, and couldn't carry anything larger than a .357 Magnum. Bill bought a chrome-plated Colt Python and I bought a Smith & Wesson Combat Magnum. They weren't quite as big as the .44 Magnum, but their large frames and 6" barrels made them the biggest guns in the Bureau. Bill was tall enough to accommodate his new weapon, but at my height, my six inch barrel hung down to my knees.

And unlike me, Bill worked some very exciting assignments during the remainder of his career—Miami Vice or French Connection adventures—lots of action and gunfights. I called him a shit magnet; one of the few cops who was always at the right place at the right time. His wife Jan probably hated getting calls in the middle of the night about his latest near death experience, but Bill thrived on that kind of danger. He DID need a bigger gun!

CHAPTER 18

"Sergeant"

In 1970, a civil suit was filed against the Civil Service Commission that prevented the Department from promoting any new sergeants, but by August 1974, the case was resolved and a new test was given. It was the first test I'd been eligible to take, and I was lucky enough to pass on my first attempt.

On Wednesday, January 1st, 1975, with just under eight years on the job, I was promoted to the rank of Sergeant, and returned to uniform duty on the 3am-11am morning shift at the new District Two station at East 35th Avenue and Colorado Boulevard.

I loved being a Sergeant! It was a very prestigious position on the police department in the 1970s, and District Sergeants were still important enough to have patrolmen as their personal cruiser drivers, and were even picked up at their homes at the beginning of their shifts, and returned at the end of their working day. Of course, this practice ended the very day I was promoted, and now sergeants were the only officers in the entire city who worked solo assignments on the night shift.

But there was still a lot of status in being a sergeant, and my rank was recognized and welcomed wherever I went. Few people ever addressed me as Officer or Detective in my earlier years (it was usually just pig), but now when I'd meet someone new on the street, they were quick to say things like, *"Hey, Sarge, how's it going,"* or *"Yo, Sergeant, you got a minute?"* just like we'd been friends for years. The three stripes on my sleeves were banners of authority to most civilians (including the press), and when I was in the company of lieutenants or captains, they'd bypass the gold bars and badges and come directly to me with their questions. I thought it was great.

District Two included everything within the city limits from Broadway east, and Colfax Avenue north. It was divided into nineteen precincts (patrol car assignments), and the precincts were split into three sectors. Sector One included all the precincts from Broadway east to Downing Street; Sector Two had all the precincts from Downing Street east to Colorado Boulevard, and Sector Three had the remaining precincts from Colorado Boulevard east to the city limits. A sergeant was assigned as the first-line supervisor for each of the sectors, and there were two relief sergeants who assumed their duties on their days off.

I was responsible for covering the major calls in my sector to make sure the officers were doing their jobs properly, but I could also pick and choose from any of the other calls that just sounded like fun. As a supervisor, I could cross most police lines at any crime scene in the district and share in the thrills and excitement of every call, but without the anti-climactic, time consuming and buzz killing burden of writing reports. That kind of access is probably what drew me to law enforcement more than anything else.

I grew up watching old newsreels and television accounts about horrific crimes and disasters; political rallies and celebrity galas, and recognized very early on that all of these events had one thing in common: that no matter what the situation, or where it occurred, the police were on the scene, and in charge, and were usually there to restrict access to the general public. The police got to see all the good stuff up close and personal most people could only read about or see in limited versions on their local news, and that was something I wanted to be a part of. And now, as a sergeant, I was even more privileged to be involved in the innermost details of those situations. I loved that part of my job.

Darrell Bolton and I were promoted on the same day and sent back to District Two. It was great to be back in my favorite District with my old partner, but since he worked the night shift and I worked mornings, I'd only see him for a few minutes at the end of his shifts. But by the summer of 1976, I was able to transfer to the night shift, and two of the founding members of the group Darrell liked to call The Wild Bunch were finally back in action again.

The Department had a provision that gave responsible adults the opportunity to ride with officers for a full tour of duty, as long as they were willing to sign a liability waiver and risk life and limb to see what police work was really like. Darrell thought this was something our wives needed to do, and with a little coaxing, Cheri (my wife of seven years now) and Nancy joined us for what we hoped would be a night they would never forget.

The first hour of the shift was pretty boring for them. They waited patiently while we held our roll call and nightly briefings, and chatted with one another in the Sergeant's Office while we approved the previous night's log sheets. When we were finished with our paperwork, we hit the streets, confident it would be another typical busy Saturday night.

Unfortunately it was not. Apparently all the criminals were on holiday that night and there wasn't a bad guy to be found.

When we met for dinner at the Blue Onion Restaurant at 8675 East Colfax around 10pm, Darrell and I tried to convince our wives that this wasn't normal, that we usually went from call to call all night long. But they didn't buy into our story and weren't at all hesitant in telling us they thought we were grossly overpaid for what we did. But that all changed when we left the restaurant. The city finally woke up and we definitely earned our pay!

We each had our own sectors to cover, so I'm not quite sure how Nancy fared out on her big adventure, but Cheri was nervous the entire time. I'd let her come in with me on the calls that weren't out of control, but made her wait in the locked cruiser if it was too dangerous. She was afraid every time I cruised through the Five Points area, especially when I stopped in front of a rowdy black biker's hangout on Welton Street, and was terrified when I waded into a gang fight at the Esplanade Street entrance to City Park. I covered as many calls as I could, but my last call of the night was by far the most exciting.

A call came out on a report of a man with a gun at an apartment building at East 24th Avenue and Williams Street, and several officers came on the air and said they were covering. We were less than a minute away when the call came out, and as we approached the intersection, I turned my headlights off and quietly pulled to the east curb, just across the street and south of the apartment (given the opportunity, you always assess the situation before you approach a dangerous call). There were four men on the large full-length front porch, and when they saw me walking toward them from my car, they frantically waved for me to come over. I walked to the porch and asked what was going on. As the men were telling me about the man who'd threatened them with a gun, the front door of the apartment building burst open and an angry young man stepped to the porch. The men all yelled, *"That's Him!"* and I pulled my gun and told him to stay where he was.

If he had a gun, I couldn't see it, but that didn't mean it wasn't in one of his pockets or down the back of his pants, and finding it was absolutely my first priority. I put my 3-cell Maglite in my sap pocket so I'd have at least one free hand to work with, then shoved him against the building to pat him down. I buried my gun barrel in the center of his back, just to remind him I was in control, and when I was certain he wasn't armed, I holstered my weapon. I grabbed his wrists to put him in hand-cuffs, but the second he realized I didn't have a gun in my hand, he jerked around and split my lip with a punch that rattled my knees and knocked my hat nearly ten feet away.

Now he did it . . . you never, *ever* knock a policeman's hat off!

I charged at him and we fought all the way to the south end of the long porch; each of us punching and cussing, and telling the other he was a mother lover (but not in those words). The men were all screaming and cheering me on, but, as usual, none of them offered a helping hand. The bad guy was every bit as strong as me, and since my Maglite flew out of my sap pocket during our scuffle (the substitute for my nightstick), it became real clear, real fast, that this battle would only end when one of us threw the best punch. Then suddenly, I heard the crashing sound of broken timber as Sergeant Doug White ripped the guard rail from the wooden porch as he climbed up to help me. Doug was 6'6" and weighed 260 pounds, so the rail (and my suspect) didn't stand a chance. This was a much better ending than when he broke my toe while stepping between me and another man during a later fight at Smitty's Bar at 3940 York Street. *DAMN HE WAS BIG!!*

With our prisoner in cuffs and on his way to jail, I walked back to my car. Cheri was nearly hysterical! From her vantage point, it looked like I was fighting with all five of those men, and if that wasn't frightening enough, she thought she'd seen a man with a rifle in the second floor window of the apartment building immediately to her right, and was certain he was going to shoot us all. It was all more than she could handle, and she never rode with me again.

But it didn't take long before I found a new rider, and this one loved the thrill of police work just as much as I did.

Gary Mandelbaum was one of those wealthy childhood friends of Cheri's I allude to later on in this book, and after hearing about him for the past seven years, I finally met him at a small party at our house. He was just a few years younger than me, about six feet tall, with a rather slender build; had brown eyes, dark brown hair (that was considerably longer than I was used to) and a full bushy mustache. He was much more conservative than I expected, and didn't fit into the image I'd already formed in my mind of a pampered and privileged rich kid I'd have nothing in common with. His father owned the Karman Manufacturing Company (a western clothing manufacturer, now known as Karman Inc., manufacturer of Roper Apparel and Footwear), but Gary didn't rest on his father's laurels . . . he earned his own keep in the family business, and worked harder and longer than anyone I knew. And unlike so many young men of his generation, he didn't smoke or drink (at least to excess), and even more importantly, he didn't do drugs. Smoking and drinking would have been okay with me (I'm not a hypocrite), but smoking dope and taking drugs were felony offenses, and their use was a real deal breaker for me when I was making new friends.

The next time Gary came to one of our little family functions, I discovered he had an interest in police work and was genuinely interested in riding with me. I was thrilled when he met with me on a Saturday night for our very first of many ride-alongs in District Two.

The night shift was always busy in our district, and to make our evenings as exciting as I could, I'd cover every hot call that came out, even if it wasn't in my sector. Shootings and stickups were his favorite calls, but he was almost as excited every time I made a simple arrest or wrote a ticket, and was especially thrilled when we covered calls where dead bodies were involved.

Most of the calls were pretty routine for me, so I really don't have any specific memories that come to mind . . . except for the burning car we found in the dirt triangle lot across the street from Zona's pig-ear stand on the corner of 27th and Welton

Streets. I called for the fire department and we watched help-lessly as the flames consumed the car and soared forty-feet into the dark summer sky. This was the hub of Five Points, and the sidewalks were teeming with rowdy people; some cheering the "bonfire" as if they were at a college football rally, while others casually mingled around the area; eating their pig-ear sandwiches and slurping their drinks, completely indifferent to the horrible scene as they watched J.B. Mingo (one of their friends) burn to a ghastly charred skeleton in the back seat of the car. To me, that spoke volumes about the character of many of the street people who frequented the Five Points area during the 1970s, and it was a coldhearted attitude I never really got used to.

It wasn't long before Gary asked if one of his best friends could ride with us. Steve Balkin was about Gary's size; prob-ably the same age, and with his dark brown eyes, long brown hair, horseshoe mustache and stubble growth beard, looked more like a hippy than he really was. His father was a surgeon, and his sister Diane later became a Deputy D.A. with the Denver District Attorney's Office, but even with the I.Q. of a genius, he never had a desire to be a doctor or lawyer, and bounced around quite a bit between odd jobs. I know he drove a cab for awhile, said he had a waterbed store he wanted to name Wet Dreams (but didn't), and I think he was working for Gary at Karman's when I first met him.

He always had a gleam in his eye and a mischievous smile that made you appreciate his great sense of humor even more, and he never missed an opportunity to prove his quick wit. On a rare night when just the two of us were riding together, he grabbed my hat from the seat, squared it off in proper police fashion across his brow and said, *"Well, whad'ya think?"* I yelled, *"Take that off! I don't want people to think you're a policeman with all that damned hair."* He gave me his roguish little boy grin, and said, *"If I wanted people to think I was a policeman, I'd do this,"* then turned the hat sideways and stuck his finger up his nose. You had to love him.

On the nights they both rode with me, they'd argue over who'd get to sit in the coveted front passenger seat, but the natural pecking order usually prevailed and Gary was the one who most often got to operate our emergency lights . . . clear the traffic in front of us with his spotlight, and play with the siren as we raced to our next call. Not at all happy with his position in the food chain, Steve would pout for a few minutes before remembering even the back seat of a police car was a very good place to be if you were looking for an exciting night in the city.

I miss those days!

In the fall of 1976, I was asked to join a small but important sting operation to investigate allegations that one of our District Two officers was fencing stolen property. Our team consisted of a lieutenant and five sergeants, and we worked under the immediate direction of Chief Arthur Dill and pro-cedural scrutiny of District Attorney Dale Tooley. To avoid the inevitable grapevine rumors that were common when unusual requests for special equipment were made, we went outside the department for assistance. Radios, vehicle tracking devices, undercover vehicles, night vision telescopes, and audio and video recording devices were provided by the DEA, and decoy personnel by the Wyoming Attorney General's Office and the Colorado Springs Police Department.

At the end of our three-month investigation, we arrested three people . . . the police officer, a prominent real estate broker, and a manager from one of the Denver area King Soopers grocery stores. At his trial, the police officer admitted under oath that he was guilty, and even described how he spent the illicit money, but his attorney convinced the jury he was the victim of entrapment. He was acquitted and escaped a certain prison sentence, but was immediately fired from the depart-ment. The other two men who'd been arrested with identical sting operational procedures were convicted of their felony charges.

When it was time for me to return to normal duty, Chief Dill and Division Chief Robert Jevnager called me into the Chief's Office. Because so many officers have a problem with policemen who investigate other policemen, they thought it would be uncomfortable for me to return to the district where I'd arrested one of their own and offered me the choice of going to any Division on the department, including the Detective Bureau. I thanked them for their generous offer, but I still loved the street and told them I preferred to continue with my assignment in District Two. They honored my wish and rewarded me with a transfer from the night shift to the 11am-7pm day shift.

I didn't have any problems with the officers who worked for me (or from my fellow sergeants), but I had two lieutenants in the station who made no secret of their disdain for what I'd done, and did everything they could to make my life as miserable as possible. Both lieutenants were black (as was the arrested officer), and they thought the investigation was nothing more than a blatant racially motivated witch hunt. Apparently they chose to ignore the fact that the source of the original allegation was a black civilian, and the police officer a confessed criminal.

It was good to be back to my usual routine, but I was soon drawn into another internal complaint of police corruption . . . the second and last I would see during my entire thirty-four year career.

In the late summer of 1977, two sergeants on the night shift put together a team of officers and raided the Los Dos Amigos in the northern section of the district for alleged liquor code violations. The following morning while I was approving log sheets in the Sergeant's Office, an officer came in and asked if I'd heard about the raid the previous night. I told him I'd heard it was a big success, and he said, *"Yeah, but I heard that not all of the evidence made it to the Property Bureau. I heard they took a bunch of booze for choir practice when they were done."* It was hard to imagine anyone would do something that stupid, but I promised that I'd investigate.

At the end of my shift, one of the sergeants who'd conducted the raid came into the office. I asked, *"How'd your raid go last night,"* and he answered, *"It was great! We cleaned everything out of that place, even the bar."* I listened as he continued to rave about the arrests they'd made, then said, *"I heard a rumor that not all of the evidence made it to the Property Bureau."* Smiling broadly, obviously very pleased with himself, he said, *"Yeah, that's a rumor that's true. The guys did such a great job, Dennis (the senior sergeant) decided they needed a break, so we took some beer and had a big party when we were done."* I just looked at him; stunned that he was so cavalier in admitting they'd committed what was probably a felony theft, misappropriated evidence, and committed such a deliberate act of malfeasance.

The next morning I went to our District Commander, Captain Wayne Pennel, and told him about the crime. He thanked me for bringing it to his attention and said he'd turn it over to his night shift lieutenant to investigate, then added, *"It took real balls to report this, Bill, but even though it's the right thing to do, you know there'll probably be consequences."* I told him I didn't mind, but since I didn't have much faith in his lieutenant (one of the two who'd castigated me for the witch hunt), I asked for his permission to take it to the Chief. He approved my request.

As a sergeant, Chief Dill had been a major investigator in the burglary scandal that rocked our department in 1960-61 with the arrest of fifty-three and subsequent conviction of forty-three police officers, so I was confident that he'd follow up on this complaint. I drove to Headquarters to meet with him, but was disappointed to learn he was out of town for the week. I was asked if it was something I could discuss with the Acting

Chief, and believing he would pass the information on to the Chief when he returned, I naïvely said yes. He, too, thanked me for the information, but as I later learned, never mentioned it to Chief Dill.

A week went by and nothing was done. The night lieutenant didn't come to me with any questions, and there were no rumors floating around the station. This was extremely rare. There were always rumors about one thing or another . . . but not about this. I went to my lieutenant (the other witch hunt accuser) and asked if he knew if anything was being done, and was met with a terse *"It's being looked into."* I waited another two weeks, and asked again how the investigation was going. He said the two sergeants received oral reprimands (even though they were later lauded for their actions in their Annual Performance Evaluations), then he asked, *"Who are you, Sergeant Aumiller, that you have to be the watchdog for the entire police department?"*. . . he always called me *"Sergeant Aumiller"* when he was talking down to me. *"I'm a policeman, just doing my job,"* I said, then added, *"I was told that most of the policemen who were arrested during the burglary scandal weren't arrested for committing the crimes, but for failing to report the others who were, and that's what I'm doing now."* He didn't like my answer and his open contempt for me only increased as the months passed by. Apparently, it didn't matter that this time the bad cops were white . . . in his eyes, going after any policeman was a witch hunt, no matter what their race.

In October 1977, the Denver Police Department established a Bureau at Stapleton International Airport, and Captain Don McKelvy was put in charge. I'd served under him when I was in the Detective Bureau and there was no other commander that I trusted, respected, or admired more. I met with him at my first available opportunity, and after explaining my dilemma, asked if he had an opening for me at the airport.

On Saturday night, New Year's Eve 1977, I transferred to the airport. I thought this assignment would seem pretty boring compared to the action I'd seen in District Two, but when I walked into the terminal and saw hundreds of people scurrying in every direction, I immediately knew I was wrong. Our office was in the basement baggage claim area, just inside Door #7, and directly across from Continental Airline's Baggage Carrousel #9 (and their Lost and Found Office). A mass of anxious and unruly passengers scrambled to retrieve their luggage just outside our office, and the ensuing chaos wasn't at all what I expected.

I was briefed by the sergeant from the previous shift, then held my first 10pm roll call. I had six officers working that night, but soon found it wasn't nearly enough. We only had one car assignment, and it wasn't even a real police car. This officer was forced to drive a yellow Department of Public Works Chevrolet Suburban (which was formally known as Airport 59), and was responsible for all traffic related calls on airport property and with inspecting the twenty-six mile chain-link perimeter fence that secured the AOA (Air Operations Area) from the public. Three of the six officers were confined to permanent stationary duty at the concourse screening areas, and under a mandate by FAA regulations, couldn't leave their posts. A fifth officer was assigned to relieve these officers for bathroom, coffee and lunch breaks, and was rarely available to cover other calls. The sixth officer and myself were responsible for handling any calls inside the terminal and all four con-courses.

We ran from call to call, defusing arguments and arresting rowdy drunks, and by midnight, the pilot of a Continental Airlines 727 called the Control Tower to report one of his passengers had been overheard bragging he was carrying a .44 Magnum on board. The plane was being diverted to Denver and I had half an hour to prepare for its arrival.

I called for the SSU (Special Services Unit, now called Metro/ Swat), and talked with Lieutenant Roger Kaspersen. Roger told me his unit was attending a New Year's Eve party just west of town, and he was the only one available to help. It wasn't much, but it was more than I had, and I was happy to see him when he arrived. The two of us drove to the rear of the jet as it taxied to the Penalty Box (a staging area just east of C Concourse), and watched as the flight crew lowered the tail stairwell. We ran up the stairs and met a flight attendant who told us where our suspect was sitting. Everyone on the plane was facing forward, so he was surprised when we walked up from behind him and snatched him from his seat. We hand-cuffed him, patted him down; grabbed his carry-on bag and took him to our office. He was cooperative the entire time, and embarrassingly admitted he was only trying to impress the girl sitting beside him (you know how much girls like to hear there's a deranged killer sitting next to them) . . . and there was no gun.

By 2am, the ugly airport mobs turned a whole lot prettier, and I was finally able to catch my breath. This, too, had been a baptism of fire, and helped to prepare me for the best assign-ment I'd have during my entire career.

With over 100,000 people passing through the airport each day, we were busy most of the time. Most calls were non-violent and easy to resolve, but many days were as chaotic as my very first shift.

By the summer of 1979, I was working the busier 2pm-10pm afternoon shift. Our dispatcher Marilyn Bruffet called and asked me to phone her right away. Since bomb threats were never broadcast over our radios, I correctly assumed this was the case and wasn't surprised when she told me a Continental Airlines 727 had been diverted to Denver and would be arriving at C Concourse within minutes. Fortunately the afternoon shift had twice as many officers as the night shift, so I called for three or four officers to assist me at the boarding gate. I had Marilyn notify the Bomb Squad and call for our FAA certified bomb dog, then requested that Airport Operations bring a portable x-ray machine to the ramp at the base of the jetway. When the plane arrived at the gate, I initiated our protocol to have the passengers deplane with their carry-on luggage and had them line their bags on the floor inside the boarding area, then sequestered the passengers in a vacant boarding area away from the bags. The canine officer arrived within minutes and had his dog sniff the bags for explosives while baggage handlers removed the check-in baggage from the airplane's cargo area and had each piece x-rayed by airport screening personnel. When the carry-on bags were cleared by the canine officer, he had his dog search the empty plane's passenger section. The search was a very time consuming process that involved nearly every available officer I had.

As we were in the middle of our search, Marilyn asked me to call her again. She said, *"You're not going to believe this, Sarge . . . we've got another bomb threat."* A much larger United Airlines 707 had also been diverted to Denver and was taxiing to a gate on B Concourse. I had her call for another bomb dog and had two more officers meet me at that gate.

Airport Operations only had one portable x-ray machine, so we had to wait until they finished on C Concourse before we could start our new search of the United plane's cargo bin. We'd just begun the same carry-on baggage process on B Concourse when our distressed dispatcher called and asked me to phone her again. She told me an anonymous caller reported he'd overheard two men with European sounding voices on C Concourse, talking about getting through the screening area with guns. I couldn't decide if this call was better or worse than another bomb threat, but knew I needed a lot more officers than I had. I called the SSU for assistance and had our overtime traffic officers come in from the lower level drive to help search for anyone suspicious looking who could possibly be carrying a firearm. The full SSU team was here within ten minutes and their officers saturated the concourse. I was working my way back and forth between the two concourses to monitor the progress of our searches when the dispatcher urgently called me again.

An approaching Continental Airlines pilot radioed the Air Traffic Controller that he was having problems with a passenger on his plane, then the Tower suddenly lost all radio communication with him. As the plane approached the runway, the pilot squawked his radio to a frequency that alerted the Tower he was being hijacked, then when he landed, taxied to his gate with his wing flaps completely down . . . another aviation signal of a hijacking in progress. I grabbed two of the officers I was with and raced to the gate as the plane pulled to the jetway. One of the ground crew members handed me a set of headphones and told me I could talk directly with the pilot. Anticipating the worst possible scenario, I identified myself and asked what his situation was. He laughed and said, *"Oh, everything's alright now. One of the passengers got violent, but was beat to the ground and hogtied with his own belt."* We rushed up the stairs and entered the plane, and to the cheers of everyone on board, physically dragged our screaming suspect away.

As we were loading him into a police car, the dispatcher came on the air and announced that a man had just run back to the terminal from the C Concourse screening area after a supervisor was called to inspect his bag in the x-ray machine. No one had ever run from the screening area before (or since) during my time at the airport, and it sounded like a real bomb had arrived. I ran to the screening area, expecting the absolute worst, but was relieved when I found the bag had already been opened and searched, even though it was against our standard protocol. The only bomb was the vibrating kind, and our suspect apparently ran from the embarrassment of having his sexual toys scrutinized by airport officials.

The two bomb threats turned out to be hoaxes and the planes were allowed to continue to their original destinations; the European suspects were never found, and our rowdy passenger was turned over to the FBI for the federal felony charge of Interfering With a Flight Crew.

By the time I returned to our office, every television news crew in town was there waiting for me. I waded through the crowd to meet with Captain McKelvy and was told I'd have the "honor" of giving them a statement. When I walked back out the door, I was mobbed by the press. As they moved in closer, pushing their cameras and microphones into my face, my butt was forced against a drinking fountain; my back and head bent backwards, nearly pressed against the wall. Responding to a barrage of questions, I described the real life events that could have easily been from Bruce Willis' movie, Die Hard 2 (which was filmed in part at Stapleton International Airport), and when I finished my fifteen minutes of fame, the crews rushed off to get their stories ready for the ten o'clock news.

As I walked through the terminal at the end of my shift, I stopped to watch the news with a small group of people in one of the seating areas. The people just sat there staring at the television; fixated by what had happened at the very airport they were in. The next moment was like watching synchronized swimmers as they turned my way . . . turned back to the screen . . . turned back to me . . . smiled broadly, and stood to applaud me when they realized I was the media's star of the day.

I had a lot of good officers who worked for me at the airport, but none of them were more personable or competent than Marty Hanley. Marty was one of those rare breeds who always had a smile on his face and a kind word to say to everyone he met, and was probably the best all-around policeman I've ever worked with.

He had silky blond hair, a neatly trimmed mustache; wore gold-framed glasses, and had a ruddy complexion that turned beet red every time I complemented his work. He was a little taller than me, a little thinner, a little younger, and a little smarter than me, but he was definitely not a little man. He'd been a Marine in Vietnam, and like most soldiers who'd seen far too much combat, rarely talked about the experiences and horrors he'd been through. He received five or six Purple Hearts for injuries he'd sustained in battle, including one for nearly getting his head cut off with a machete during a battle to the death with a Viet Cong soldier. It was a very dark period in his life, and because his memories of the war were still so vivid and intense, he had to walk out of the theater when he heard the intimidating drone of helicopters in Robert De Niro's 1978 movie, The Deer Hunter.

The day after my five-year-old son met Marty at a party at our house, I told him what a good policeman and friend Marty was, and when I mentioned all the medals he received (and why he'd received them), Kevin's eyes grew as big as silver dollars as he said, *"WOW! . . . no wonder he quit the army."* But of course, he didn't quit, and served our country with great pride and honor until he was honorably discharged shortly before he came on the Department in 1971.

Marty was more like a partner to me than a subordinate, and like any good partner, always had my back. He was a master of tact and diplomacy, and always knew what to say and just how to say it . . . and with his keen eye for detail, I knew I could depend on his sound advice whenever it was needed. When I'd finish doing everything I could think of at the end of an unusually prolonged or involved call, I'd ask if he could think of anything else I needed to do. *"No,"* he'd say, *"I think you've done everything that needs to be done . . . unless you think you might want to"* (do something else I'd clearly missed).

We spent most of our shifts on foot patrol together . . . always mindful of our surroundings and alert for any potential problems (even before 9/11, there were serious security issues at the airport). We'd greet the scores of friends we had who were working throughout the airport, and if we weren't busy just spreading good cheer, we covered nearly every call that came out.

When Paul Jernigan was sent to handle a disturbance at a boarding gate on C Concourse, we quickly volunteered to cover the call. We were probably a good five or six minutes away, but told Paul we'd be there as soon as we could. My legs are pretty short, so I had a little trouble keeping up with Marty's fast pace, but when we reached the screening area and couldn't get a response from Paul, we assumed he was in trouble and ran the rest of the way to the gate.

Our suspicions were confirmed when we were about two hundred feet away and saw Paul struggling with a very tough young man at the podium. My adrenaline finally kicked in and my legs stretched farther and moved faster than they'd ever done before, and we reached the podium in record time. Marty grabbed the bad guy's right arm and twisted it behind his back to put him in handcuffs, but I wasn't strong enough to pull his left arm back far enough to finish the job, and now, completely unrestrained by handcuffs, the battle really began.

We wrestled our way across the seating area until we literally hit a bank of empty chairs . . . knocking the entire row onto its back as we plummeted over the top. Once we were flat on the ground, we were able to cuff him, but sometime during the struggle, I kicked Marty's left shin so hard, it immediately drew blood. When we got to our feet and walked our prisoner to the office, we learned he was a professional hockey player, and one of the toughest men I'd ever fought. When Marty showed me his bloody leg, I apologized for kicking him, but he just laughed and said, *"You know, I didn't really mind the kick, but it kind of ticked me off when you giggled when you did it."*

Well, I guess I knew when I kicked him . . . I guess . . . but I wasn't giggling about kicking Marty, I was giggling about the great fight we were having.

A few days later, we covered another disturbance call on D Concourse. This was an older frail little man, who, in an advanced state of intoxication, threatened one of the airline agents with bodily harm. We didn't have much trouble getting him in handcuffs, but he was loud and obnoxious the entire time it took to walk him to Elevator #5 at the head of the concourse; passing kids, parents, and grandparents; all shocked by his vulgar language. While we were waiting for the elevator to reach our floor, I tried to muffle his mouth from all the obscenities he was shouting, when he suddenly kneed me in the groin. He missed all the good stuff (which was nearly impossible to do), and I instinctively punched out at him in self-defense. As I threw my punch, Marty reached across his head to restrain him, and the force of my blow hit his right hand instead of my assailant, and broke his index finger. And if that wasn't bad enough on its own, I had him write the arrest slip by (broken) hand and type all the reports when we got back to the office.

The next day his wife Rosalie called and said, *"Bill, do me a favor . . . if Marty ever handles a really dangerous call, **Please Don't Cover Him!**"* We both had a good laugh over that, and I never hurt Marty again.

In 1979, the Civil Service Commission announced the next lieutenant's test. Promotional exams were given every two or three years and eligible candidates were given a reading list of four or five books to study. The list was changed with each new test so it was impossible to prepare in advance for future tests, which I thought was a very good system, since it always put candidates on equal ground for the next exam.

I spent the next three months *completely* devoted to my studies, but just like my dad, failed by a fraction of a point. This was my first stumbling block in my career and was more than just a little disheartening.

I took the next test in 1981, but didn't score high enough to be promoted.

By March 1983, I decided to leave the airport. I was ready to take the next lieutenant's test and felt my time at the airport, away from the grind of regular police duties, was hindering my chances of promotion. I transferred to the Radio Room (Communications Center) in hopes of easing myself back into the mainstream of the Department, and in December, nine months later, I transferred to the District Four station at West Florida Avenue and Eliot Street in southwest Denver. I was back on the street again, and definitely in the midst of real police work, but I was never more bored. My peers couldn't understand how that was possible, since I'd spent nearly six years away from the street, but my time at the airport was far more interesting, and surprisingly, much busier.

CHAPTER 19

"Lieutenant"

In September 1984, I took my third lieutenant's test, and was finally lucky enough to pass. I was promoted on Thursday, November 1st, 1984 and assigned to the 2pm-10pm shift at the airport.

By March 1985, Darrell Bolton asked me to work for him in District Two. He had an opening on the 2am-10am shift, but promised I could work the day shift when his senior lieutenant retired in the next two months. I made the transfer, but the deal fell through when Lieutenant Satterburg decided against retiring, and I was stuck on the morning shift for the next nineteen months. It was okay, though . . . I was still working for the best Captain on the Department, in the best District in the city.

I returned to Stapleton International Airport on Thursday, October 16th, 1986, and worked there until I helped close its doors at 12:01 am on Tuesday, February 28th, 1995. With the old airport closed, I moved to my new assignment at Denver International Airport, and was there to greet the horde of television crews and thousands of curious onlookers as they swarmed inside to see their brand new airport for the very first time.

The young officers on the job always considered the airport to be a dumping ground for the cops who were too old, too lazy or too incompetent to still be effective on the street, and with an average seniority of twenty (plus) years, they weren't entirely wrong about the age part . . . the street really is the domain of the young. But I'd worked with some truly great officers at the airport, and anyone who's been on the job long enough will recognize that most of them (who I considered to be my personal friends) were some of the best officers on the Department.

To avoid any appearance of playing favorites, they're listed in alphabetical order: Renee Adams, Steve Allison, Frank Amitrano, Bob Atkinson, Bobby Bales, Marsha Ballard, Jim Bame, Phil Barenberg, Bob Bickhard, Bob Bilstein, Dennis Brenning, Jesse Brezzell, Eddie Brooks, Don Brown, Mike Buckley, Aaron Burroughs, Don Calvano, Dale Canino, Jack Cantley, Kelly Carpenter, Bruce Carvajal, Kenny Chavez, Bill Clayton, Paul Colaiano, Yvette Corella, Bob and Cindy Crago, Bill Craven, Jim "JJ" Daley, Dennis Degenhart, Don DeNovellis, Denny Dickman, Stan Flint, Doug Frodine, Don Gavito (our first helicopter pilot), Jack Gierhart, Gene Gold, Bobby Gomez, Phil Gotlin, Bob Grimm, Jimmy Gropp, Carl Gustofson, Bob Hammons, Marty Hanley, Dave Harris, Mark Hellenschmidt, Joe Hernandez, Steve Hobson, Beal Holland, Henry Hunter, Louie Jaramillo, Paul Jernigan, Paul Kaiser, John Keckter, Jerry Kennedy, Hayden Kenny, Frank Kerber, John Kilpatrick, Jim King, Wayne Krieger, Dave Lusk, Don Maddock, J.W. Martinez, Glen Mathew, Manny Mauri, Steve McCray, Tom McCutchen, Robbi McKay, Don McKelvy, Tom Metzler, Al Mitterer, Pat Montoya, Porfirio (Junior) Naranjo, Harold Oaks, Ray O'Connell, Jerry Parton, Linda Piedra, Tony Pierson, Rick Pilling, John Rames, Dick Rankin, Ralph Reeve, Guy Richardson, Jody Roblez, Carl Scavo, Don Sharshel, Sam Singleton, Dean Smith, John Smith, Ray Snell, Don "Digger" Snider, Jack Sparks, Dale Squier, Dave Staebell, Larry Subia, Bob Swanson, Bill Talbert, Steve Tokarski, Mark Treidel, Al VanderVelde, Tim Vanportfliet, Darrell Wagner, Forrest Wagner, Terry Walton, Jeff Ward, Pat Ward, John Weber, Larry Wells, Joe White, Bill Wiederspan, Hank Wilcox, Billy Wolfe, Tom Wood, Steve Wright, Don Zarlengo, and Vic Zimblis.

Each of these officers were capable of handling the very worst of situations, but in all of my years at the airport, there was only one homicide, and very few aggravated assaults or robberies to challenge their abilities. We found two murdered victims stuffed in the trunks of their cars, and the bodies of two other men who'd literally blown their brains out while they were parked in the public parking lots, but the routine carnage that was so prevalent on the streets, was missing at the airport. That was fine with me. I'd had more than my fair share of violence on the street, and didn't miss the pungent smell of blood or the grotesque visuals and overwhelming stench of death.

Most of our time was involved with the public relations aspect of community policing and the normal goal of preserving the peace. Bomb threats, car-prowls, stolen cars, thefts, rowdy crowds and disturbances were the most common infractions we handled, but weapon violations and out of control in-flight passengers were our major issues. Real medical emergencies and Amber Alerts (planes with mechanical problems in flight) were almost an everyday event, but Red Alerts (actual plane crashes) were rare. I handled five Red Alerts over the years, but none of them resulted in death.

I had a number of challenging duties as a lieutenant at the airport. Much of my time was spent as the Captain's Administrative Aide, but I also worked as the Shift Commander on each of our three Details, had command of our Detective and Highway Motorcycle Units, oversaw our officer training program, and was responsible for scheduling more than 200 off-duty officers to work our overtime traffic assignments.

I was responsible for writing 90% of our airport police procedures (District/Bureau Directives) . . . I wrote a comprehensive Red Alert and Highjacking Policy; an extensive Weapons Violation Policy (that included specific procedures for handling local, state and federal criminal and civil violations, all of which were unique to the airport), and worked very closely with the FBI, FAA and the Airport Operations Manager to coordinate our combined efforts. Dignitary protection was common at the airport, and coordination with the Secret Service and State Department was essential when the President of the United States or visiting royalty came to Denver. The Airport Police Bureau may have been the Country Club of the Denver Police Department, but it was still a very busy place to work.

The next promotional step was to the rank of Captain . . . the highest Civil Service position on the police department, and the highest rank I'd hoped to achieve. In those days, the only ranks above Captain were the five Division Chief positions and that of the Chief of Police. Division Chiefs were appointed by the Chief, and the Chief was appointed by the Mayor, and none of these positions were protected by the Civil Service Authority. These commanders served entirely at the pleasure of the Chief or Mayor, and I had no desire for either.

The Captain's tests were much different than the others. There were no reading lists to prepare from, and your grade was determined by your ability to role-play in a comprehensive Assessment Center format. Clearly I didn't have what they were looking for, and never scored higher than twelfth place in the tests I took in 1987, 1989 and 1991. That would have been high enough to be promoted to Lieutenant, but not for the rank of Captain. There were usually only three or four vacancies for the Captain's position, and if you weren't in that range, you had to wait another two years to try again. When I reached my retirement age in 1992, with twenty-five years on the job, I stopped taking the exams. I'd known of only one man who'd ever been promoted beyond his twenty-fifth year, and I wasn't willing to fight that uphill battle.

My original pension plan would allow me to retire at 50% of my salary after 25 years of service, but just before my 25th anniversary, the Department initiated a new retirement program that offered a 60% pension if I worked for 30 years. Kevin was just starting his classes at the University of Colorado, and since I was paying for half of his tuition, making the payments on his new Toyota Tercell, paying for his car insurance, and sending him $400 a month for child support, I really couldn't afford to leave the Department until he was through with school.

I wearily trudged along, counting the days until my retirement, then shortly before my 30th anniversary, the Department offered a 74% pension if I worked for 31 years. I really, *really* wanted to retire, but this was too great an offer to pass up. Kevin had already graduated from college so I didn't have that obligation anymore, and convinced myself I could tough it out for just one more year.

As I approached my 31st year, the Department adopted a three-year DROP program (Deferred Retirement Option Plan), which was an even bigger incentive to stay. In essence, this plan meant I retired on the day I signed the paperwork, but I continued to work as a contract laborer . . . with my existing rank, seniority and other employee benefits, and with the exact same salary. The City stopped making its matching 7% semi-monthly contributions into my retirement plan, and the pension I should have received, went into a deferred retirement savings account. This was a win-win situation for both me and the City because the Department was able to keep a veteran command officer for 7% less than it had already been paying, and I was putting an additional $50,000 (plus) a year into my savings account. This was a significant supplement to my existing savings regiment, and hopefully an amount, coupled with my generous pension that would see me through the remainder of my retirement years. It was a lot more than I expected to have at this stage of my life (especially after so many divorces), and for an Aumiller boy, it was pretty good money.

I have friends and family who probably look at this as chump-change, and with their incomes, I can understand why. But everything in life is relative. None of them have private jets or yachts . . . homes in the Hamptons or villas on the French Riviera, and in the eyes of the truly wealthy, they're probably considered to be just as common and ordinary as me. I take comfort in this point of view, and believe the only thing that really matters in life is whether or not you're happy with what you have. My life hasn't exactly been a rags to riches story either, but it's definitely been . . . well, you know. And with Linda at my side (my fourth and best wife), I don't think I could ask for anything more.

Before Tom Sanchez' reign of terror as our commander, I'd served under six Captains during my long tenure at the airport: Don McKelvy, Paul Kaiser, Jerry Kennedy, Bob Swanson, John Weber and Kelly Carpenter. They each had their own distinctive management style, but all six of them had three very important ideals in common: (1) To provide a professional liaison between the efficient and essential functions of our Police Department and the necessities of Airport Operations, (2) to provide a safe setting for the airport employees and the traveling public, and (3) to maintain a friendly work environment for the officers.

There was no place on the department more stress free and comfortable than the airport, but when Sanchez was fired as our Chief of Police and put in charge of our bureau, everything changed. I felt he'd brought the bitterness of his demotion and the political turmoil he seemed to thrive on from his days in the Ivory Tower, and, in my opinion, aggressively and systematically destroyed everything that made the airport such a great place to work.

I spent the last three years of my career working the extremely quiet but satisfying midnight shift at Denver International Airport, and retired on the last day of the work period on Sunday, January 28th, 2001, just 47 days before my 34th anniversary, and 23 days before my 57th birthday.

Leaving after all these years was a bittersweet moment for me. The officers I'd spent my last years with were more like family to me than co-workers, and every night was an absolute pleasure to share with them. Phil Gotlin and Steve McCray led the detail as two of my favorite Sergeants, followed by Officers Bruce Carvajal, Yvette Corella, Bob and Cindy Crago, Bill Craven, Dennis Degenhart, Henry Hunter, Glen Mathew, Pat Montoya, Porfirio (Junior) Naranjo, Dale Squier, Mark Treidel, Hank Wilcox, and our long-standing civilian dispatcher, Mary Crespin. The camaraderie and true friendship I had with most of them is the only thing I miss in retirement.

CHAPTER 20

"Defending the Badge"

George Burns once said, *"Too bad all the people who know how to run the country are busy driving taxicabs and cutting hair."* That quip was wise well beyond its simplicity and humor, and in my opinion, is the way far too many people view law enforcement. It seems like everybody knows how to do a policeman's job better than they do, and that's always been my biggest pet peeve.

I'm not quite sure where these people learned the proper way to do a policeman's job. TV, I guess . . . I know that's where I learned how to be a doctor. But the reality is they've never received the extensive training police officers receive, and have no idea what police work is really like.

In Denver, the training starts in the Police Academy, where for the first six months of a new recruit's career, they learn the text book basics and ethics of law enforcement, and are taught all of the relevant federal and state criminal statutes . . . municipal and traffic code ordinances, and hundreds of departmental procedural guidelines and rules and regulations that govern just about every move they make (that's more than 1,000 hours of intensive classroom instruction). Their education continues with another six months of on-the-job training with Field Training Officers on the street, where they learn to temper their newfound knowledge with the good common sense that's absolutely essential in this line of work. They receive an enormous amount of firearm training, and are taught never to fire their weapons unless it's absolutely necessary to save themselves or others from grievous bodily injury or death (which includes shooting dangerous and fleeing felons who might otherwise severely injure or kill someone else if they're not apprehended). They receive countless hours of conflict resolution experience, learn how to interrogate suspects and investigate criminal complaints, receive topical in-service training at each daily roll call once they've graduated from the Academy, and return to the Academy for special tactical training on a regular basis. They learn to be fair and impartial in the application of the law while dealing with people of every ethnicity and social class, and apply what they've learned to Serve and Protect the citizens of Denver for the entire span of their careers.

There will always be a few officers we're not proud to claim as our own, but they (and every other officer on the Department) are under constant scrutiny by their sergeants and command officers, and are subject to appropriate and sometimes severe penalties for their misbehavior. But for the most part, Denver's police officers (and all other officers in this country) are extremely dedicated to their profession, and deserve far more credit than they receive for the excellent work they do.

I wonder how those people who find it so easy to complain about the police would act if they were police officers themselves? Assuming they understood their primary role was to **enforce the law** with people who hated to be punished for their misdeeds (even a child hates to be spanked when they do something wrong) . . . and assuming they took pride in doing the very best job they could, just how many tickets would they write, and how many arrests would they make . . . and just how would they react to the ravings from those disgruntled traffic violators they'd cited, or from the criminals they'd just arrested? I don't think I've ever met anyone new outside of the police department who didn't complain about a ticket that he or she'd received (I'm not quite sure what they wanted me to do about it), and if you're one of those who feel you didn't deserve the ticket you received, the only question you really need to ask yourself is whether or not you actually broke the law. I think most of you already know the **true** answer to that question, so don't blame the police officers for doing their jobs.

I've received three tickets in my life . . . all three of them in Denver. One for an illegal left turn when I was seventeen; one for going 10 mph over the speed limit when I was off duty as a Lieutenant, and another for the exact same violation after I'd retired. No, I wasn't too happy either, but it wasn't because the policemen were doing their jobs, it was because I was stupid enough to break the law, and even more stupid to get caught. But I knew it was my own fault, and took full responsibility for my actions . . . and paid the tickets without complaint.

And as biased as you may think I am toward the police, I'm absolutely certain policemen aren't the problem. I'd worked with hundreds of policemen during my career, and I've never known of a single officer who's ever written a ticket or made an arrest without legal justification. Believe me, no policeman likes to hear your complaints of harassment. It would be *so much easier* for them if they just turned their heads and ignored your indiscretions. They'd still get paid the same, either way.

But if you're one of those people who fuels my pet peeve, just how would you deal with the violence you saw on a daily basis? It's easy to pass judgment from the comfort and safety of your own home, but just think about it for a moment or two . . . *seriously*. What would you do if you responded to one of those frequent calls of violence and came face to face with a man pointing a gun at your chest? If there'd already been two other police shootings that month, would you worry about how intensely you'd be scrutinized by the public and press, and hold your fire until you were killed . . . or would you prefer to go home at the end of your shift and hug your wife or husband and your little kids?

Imagine *you're* the one standing toe-to-toe with someone much bigger and tougher than you who's about to beat you senseless. Do you understand tact and diplomacy doesn't work with most of these people . . . that wrestling them to the ground or using your nightstick or mace is almost always the right thing to do?

If you're going to protect the masses from the violence of hardcore criminals, you have to stand your ground; fight the fight regardless of the danger. Superman's not coming . . . it's up to you. I think if you're truly honest with yourselves, you'd be a lot more empathetic in your opinions.

But complainers aside, I think most responsible and law abiding people would agree with what Vice President Spiro T. Agnew said during the violent anti-war demonstrations of the 1970s . . . that *"confronted with the choice, the American people would choose the policeman's truncheon over the anarchist's bomb."* As a private citizen today, I know that's what I'd prefer . . . each and every time.

No, a policeman's job is not always easy, and it's definitely not an easy job to get. There are thousands (if not tens of thousands) of men and women who try but fail to become police officers each and every year, including some very bright and well educated people you'd expect to be at the very top of any Department's list. Many are eliminated immediately because of their poor physical histories or through their extensive background checks (in 1967, you wouldn't even be considered for the job if you had too many traffic tickets, let alone *any* history of marijuana use or simple arrests) . . . and others are systematically eliminated by the stressful written, physical agility and polygraph exams, and the final, but incredibly intimidating oral interviews. Certainly there are some who've failed who may have become truly outstanding police officers if given the chance, but for the most part, those who've survived this rigorous screening process are those most suited for the responsibilities and real world demands of law enforcement.

Few people doubt that police work is dangerous, but most people, including several members of my own family, have no idea how dangerous it is.

There were ten Denver Police Officers murdered in the line of duty during my career (four who were my personal friends), and three who were killed in traffic accidents. Seventeen of my other friends and co-workers were shot, three were stabbed, one lost an arm, another was permanently blinded in a car bomb explosion, and literally scores of others were involved in shootouts with some incredibly dangerous people. (There were probably several others who were seriously injured, but these are the events I personally remember). This wasn't some Hollywood fantasy where the dead got to go home at the end of the shoot. This was real life . . . with real blood, real death, and real emotional trauma for families to bear for the remainder of their lives. To put this into perspective, count the number of people you know who've been shot, shot at, stabbed, lost limbs, or were killed by felons and compare it to this list. It's not your usual job, and the reason officers sometimes appear rude during events that you perceive to be benign encounters. It's called survival; watching your back.

Every person has an innate choice of fight or flight, and when threatened by a truly dangerous situation, most people will choose to flee. But that's not true with police officers. They're there for the battle, no matter how bad it is, and most of them are always ready and eager to rush into the face of extreme danger whenever they're needed. That's why you call the police instead of your neighbor when someone's breaking into your home in the middle of the night.

The average person rarely worries about their safety when they go to work, but when police officers leave their families for the day, they know in the course of their shift they may be called upon to jeopardize their own lives in order to protect the lives of complete strangers, and every homicide, shooting, stabbing or armed robbery they respond to reminds them that they could be forced to kill another human being that day, or even be killed themselves.

While the threat of being killed on the job is constant and very real, the biggest threat of personal injury comes with the normal day-to-day activities of police work. By the very nature of evil we're sworn to suppress, we know there's a very good chance we'll be involved in some form of physical confrontation with some of the worst predators society has to offer, and as I've noted before (and will note again), the results of these encounters usually aren't that pretty.

I'd arrested thousands of people during my career and was frequently met with resistance, but even though fighting was often a necessity of the job, I'm proud to say that in thirty-six years of law enforcement, I only used my nightstick once, and never used my mace. I loved my job, but suffered from far more than my fair share of bumps and bruises, and in the end, believe I'd fought with more men than George Foreman and Muhammad Ali combined.

CHAPTER 21

"Cheri"

Shortly after Cheri and I began seeing each other in 1968, she and Candy moved from the apartment they'd shared with Sherry Strathman and Linda Deiger on York Street, and moved to a smaller two-bedroom apartment at 1402 Race Street. She was working the night shift at the GEM discount store at 5200 Smith Road, so her late night hours and the close proximity of her apartment to my district station gave me plenty of opportunities to stop by for some very serious cuddling after nearly every night's work.

When her grandfather Clarence Leisenring died a few months later, she moved to 900 St. Paul Street, and lived with her Grandma Ida, Ida's son Burt, and Cheri's older brother Eddie.

Friday night dinners were a longstanding tradition in the Leisenring family, and I was soon invited to share in what I expected to be a very pleasant meal with Cheri, Grandma Ida, Dorie (Cheri's mother), Eddie, Burt and his ex-wife Ruthie, and their two daughters, Judy and Nancy. It started out well enough, but before the potatoes made it half way around the table, everyone was screaming at each other at the top of their lungs. I'd seen this kind of family fighting in certain Home For The Holiday types of movies, but I'd never been in the middle of this much friction before (at least away from the job), and I wasn't quite sure how to handle it. I finally got up from the table and walked outside to sit on the front porch; certain the police would come screeching to the curb at any moment. Cheri came out a few seconds later; sat beside me, and assured me everything would be alright. She said this usually only happened when Ruthie was there (she always seemed to know just which buttons to push), then explained this wasn't really a big deal to her family, it was just the way they handled their disagreements. If they had a problem with something someone

313

said, they didn't hold back their feelings of resentment . . . they just got it all out in the open . . . and when everyone had a chance to speak their piece, everything would return back to normal.

And she was right . . . by the time dinner was over, everyone settled down and acted like nothing had even happened. It took awhile to understand how it worked for them, but when I finally figured it out, I accepted it as just part of the family's charm. Over the years I'd grow to love Cheri's family just as much as my own, and in the dozens of times I'd laugh and retell this story to our friends, I'd remember just how special they were.

The family fights didn't happen that often, but the screaming they all seemed to be so comfortable with showed me the level of passion they were capable of, and should have been a hint of the same kind of passion I could expect to see from Cheri during our next fourteen years together.

●

Through no real fault of her own, Sandra and I separated on Tuesday, July 1st, 1969, and I moved into a two-bedroom apartment at 3150 West Louisiana Avenue with Terry Walton, another of my Academy classmates.

Terry and his wife split up a month or two earlier, and we both needed to room with someone we could share the rent with. Financially, it was the most sensible thing I could do, but because I've always been so guarded with my privacy, I was more than just a little apprehensive about living with another man. (If I was going to lie around the apartment in my under-wear, I preferred to do it in the company of women). As it turned out, this wasn't an issue. We both worked the same shift (me in District Two, he in District Six), but because he spent so much time at his girlfriend's house, we were rarely in the apartment at the same time. And on the few nights he'd actually stay at home, he'd drink himself into a stupor and pass out on the couch before I ever got home. The only problem we had together was when he yelled at me for filling the refrigerator with too many groceries and not leaving him enough room for his beer. I lived there until Wednesday, October 1st, then Cheri and I moved to the Keystone Apartments at 161 South Emerson Street.

By now Cheri had graduated from beauty school, quit her job at the GEM store and was working as a hairstylist at Jo Ardens, a trendy little salon in an apartment complex at East 11th Avenue and Pearl Street.

On Halloween, Friday, October 31st, 1969 at 2pm, Sandra and I were divorced, and at 7pm (Pacific Standard Time), at the age of twenty-five, I married the third love of my life, twenty-one-year-old Cheri Beth Gruben, at the Chapel of the Bells in Las Vegas, Nevada. I'd only been officially single for six hours, but it was long enough for me! We flew to San Diego the following morning so I could meet her sister Renee and brother-in-law Bert Levine. This was the first time as an adult that I'd traveled anywhere beyond Kansas, New Mexico or Texas (with an exciting side-trip to Juarez, Mexico), and because this was the first time I'd ever flown on a commercial jet, I was thrilled by the whole experience.

Staying with my new in-laws wasn't the European honeymoon I'd always wished I could have, but Bert and Renee were extremely gracious hosts and did everything they could to make sure we had a wonderful time while we were there. They generously gave us one of their cars to use, and we drove to Disneyland to enjoy the Magic Kingdom as only young newlyweds can. When we returned to San Diego, they took us on a harbor cruise, where, for the first time in my life, I saw actual World War II combat ships in the Navy's enormous Mothball Fleet . . . we toured the 1863 merchant ship, The Star of India, and ended our trip with my *very first* lobster dinner at the Rueben E. Lee restaurant on Harbor Island. I'd led a sheltered life.

Cheri's mother moved to Los Angeles just a few months earlier, and sometime during our visit, decided she wanted to move back to Denver. I guess you could say my honeymoon was officially over when my mother-in-law flew back with us on our return home.

Within days of my wedding, Sandra married my cousin Jim Oldson (the son of Mom's oldest brother Voyde), and they and my two daughters moved to Green Mountain Dam, where he worked for the Bureau of Reclamation. They soon moved to Phoenix; continued on to Yuma, Colorado, and finally settled in Loveland, Colorado. I'd rarely see my girls when they were young, and it was very difficult for us all. But I always felt they were in good and loving hands with Jim and Sandra (even if it did create another convoluted branch in our family tree), and it helped ease my enormous guilt.

•

In December, Cheri and I had our first fight, and the anger I'd seen at those family dinners was finally directed at me. I have no idea what we were fighting about, but she screamed at me like I'd never been screamed at before, and as she stormed out the front door, she yelled, *"Have A Good Life!"* I was stunned that she'd gone and wasn't exactly sure what to do next, but when she returned fifteen minutes later, I learned firsthand just how much fun making up could be. And that's the way our entire marriage would be. We fought *far* more often than we should have, but we loved just as passionately as we fought, and in the end, the love was always worth the battle.

•

Shortly before I was promoted to Detective on July 1st, 1971, we moved to a larger one-bedroom apartment at 1300 Monroe Street, then in 1972, we moved to a two-bedroom apartment at 3595 South Washington Street. Cheri quit her current job at Key Savings and Loan and went to work in the Revenue Accounting Office at Frontier Airlines. We took full advantage of her flight benefits and flew as often as we could. We took weekend trips to the newly opened Disneyworld in Orlando, and to New York City (where we saw the nearly completed twin towers of the World Trade Center from the 86th floor observation deck of the Empire State Building). We flew to Phoenix, Las Vegas, and San Francisco, and made two or three more trips to San Diego, but our biggest adventure began on Saturday, March 17th, 1973, when we left for our two-week trip to Europe. We rented a car in Frankfurt and drove to the German cities of Heidelberg, Munich, Dachau, and Garmisch, and visited Zurich, Switzerland and Innsbruck, Austria. It was an unbelievable trip for a boy of such humble roots, and set the stage for the incredible trips I would take over the next thirty-eight years.

Before we were married, we agreed to wait at least five years before we started a family. I'd become a father way too early in my first marriage, and wanted us to have enough time to enjoy our freedom before we were tied down with little kids. That was a good plan, I thought, but after only three and a half years, Cheri decided it was time to have a baby. Since we'd already done far more than I ever expected to do, I willingly agreed, and by the end of May she was pregnant. She worked until she started to outgrow her clothes, then quit her job and prepared for the birth of our only child.

In January or February 1974, we bought our first home at 1400 Newport Street, a thirty-eight-year-old, 900 square foot, two-bedroom, one bathroom brick home. It wasn't much, but better than an apartment, and in dire need of modern upgrades. We'd had several discussions about the condition of the house before we decided to buy it, and we both agreed that for $15,000, it would be the perfect starter house for us until we could afford something better. But as soon as we moved in, Cheri made it pretty clear that she absolutely hated it.

We painted the interior, installed new carpeting throughout the house, replaced the original purple flowered draperies with contemporary drapes, and removed the old non-working gas fireplace in the living room and replaced it with a faux-brick fireplace and dark wooden mantel. The place was definitely shaping up, and Cheri was a much happier camper.

•

Cheri had all the goofy cravings pregnant women have, and whenever hot and spicy food or sweet chocolate and dill pickles called her name, she was all too quick to respond. When she said, *"I feel like having a little Italian tonight"* on February 19th, 1974, I wasn't too surprised, and assumed (correctly, I think) that what she really wanted was a nice Italian dinner. I took her to one of our favorite little eateries in the Buckingham Square Mall, but spicy food this late in her pregnancy was definitely not something our baby appreciated! Shortly after we left the restaurant, it started kicking harder than it had ever kicked before, and without warning, Cheri's water broke and the first of her labor pains began (not a good thing to happen on a full stomach). She never admitted it, but I think she would have been a lot happier if she'd just hooked up with some little guy named Mario that night.

The short drive to General Rose Memorial Hospital took much longer than it should have, and every time we'd get stopped at a red light, the crying and screaming would begin. It was unbelievable, the wailing, the moaning, the *Oh, My God, Oh, My God,* **Oh, My God!!** breathless panting and shouting . . . it was completely out of control! When she couldn't take it any longer, Cheri turned to me and said, *"Bill . . . just try to relax; we're almost there."*

Okay, I made up that last part, but the anxiety really wasn't that far from the truth. I'd beg her to hold on for just a little longer, hoping against hope that we could make it to the hospital in time. I'd delivered a baby while I was still working the street, so I knew I could deliver my own if I had to, but I really didn't want to go through that kind of mess again, especially in my own car.

318

When we walked through the Emergency Room doors, the nurses met us with a wheelchair and rushed Cheri to her room. I kept telling her to hold out for as long as she could, and just prayed she could last until my birthday the following day. I know it's probably a chauvinistic thing to say, but I was really hoping for a boy this time, and having him on my 30th birthday would be a wish come true. Don't get me wrong . . . I loved my girls, but I think it's every man's dream to have a son.

Midnight came and went, and with a heavy sigh of relief, I stood smiling contently at Cheri's side, reveling in what would be the greatest birthday of my life! But Cheri wasn't smiling. The screaming and crying were very real this time, and the pain and nausea were overwhelming . . . and in no time at all, we both regretted that big plate of spaghetti she'd eaten just a few hours before. *Ugh!!*

Things were a little different than when my daughters were born. Instead of being relegated to the isolation of a distant waiting room, new fathers were now encouraged to share in the birth of their children, and in the dark early morning hours of Wednesday, February 20th, 1974, I watched as our son Kevin Edward Aumiller was born.

Watching my son come into this world was the most incredible thing I'd ever seen!! The doctor slapped his naked little butt and he let out a little yelp and cried . . . and in that amazing first breath of his life, we knew everything was alright. When the doctor held him up to show us his "little boy indicator," he immediately stopped crying and stared directly into the doctor's eyes. *"Oh, yeah,"* the doctor said, *"He's got a lot of questions. What day is this? Who's the President? Yeah, he's just fine!"*

He was a scrawny little guy, all red and wrinkly and wiggly, but the two (or four) things about him that stood out more than anything else were his saucer-sized eyes and his even bigger balls. I stared suspiciously at Cheri with a *"Lucy, you got a lot of 'splainin to do"* look on my face, but she just smiled a little smile, shrugged her tiny shoulders, and said, *"What can I say. He's his father's son."*

"YOU BET HE IS!!" I thought to myself (with a false sense of pride), but when the light bulb suddenly switched on inside my feeble little mind, I said, *"Hey, wait a minute. What's that supposed to mean?!?"*

The doctor and nurses had a good laugh over my response to Cheri's witty double-entendre, and that lighthearted moment became a running joke in our family that still exists today.

When the dust finally settled and Cheri laid down for a much deserved full night's sleep, I headed home for a nap. It was still dark outside, but the stars looked especially bright to me and seemed to help warm the cold morning air. But I really didn't notice the cold that much. I still had that warm fuzzy feeling from the best birthday present I'd ever received, and would be spoiled even more by the new electric sander I had waiting for me at home.

Having a new baby created an enormous change in our life-style, and doing what we wanted, when we wanted, became an abrupt thing of the past. But the tradeoff was more than worth it. Kevin was absolutely the best son we could have asked for, and was as well mannered and well behaved as any boy I've ever known. He was always a straight "A" student, and by the time he finished high school, he'd received more academic awards in algebra, geometry, trigonometry, calculus, physics, chemistry and biology than I could even count. He was one of the class valedictorians at his graduation from Smoky Hill High School, and graduated with distinction from the University of Colorado with a Bachelor of Science Degree in Chemical Engineering. He'd grown into an incredibly gifted and intelligent young man, and I couldn't be more proud of him if I tried! But with that kind of intelligence, the question just begs to be asked . . . *where did his genius come from?* I know he didn't get it from his mother, and he definitely didn't get it from me . . . so if he didn't get it from either of us, then . . . *Heeey, wait a minute!!!*

●

On January 1st, 1975, I was promoted to Sergeant, and by that spring, we decided it was time to buy a bigger house. We sold our house on Newport and bought a brand new $30,000 home at 16168 East Harvard Avenue. A three-bedroom tri-level with one bath and single car garage, it was twice the size of our old home . . . but with twice the mortgage payment.

My new salary as a sergeant helped a lot, but when Cheri returned to her original profession as a hairstylist at a neighborhood salon, our quality of life dramatically improved. I was happy that she was working again, but to be honest, the free haircuts I now received in a beauty parlor were a *very* poor substitute for the free airline tickets we'd once enjoyed!

We rarely left the house when Kevin was a baby, but by the end of the summer in 1975, we were ready for our first family trip. We took my daughters with us when we flew to visit Bert and Renee in San Diego, and took them all on the harbor cruise; went to Sea World and the Wild Animal Park, and ended our vacation with a trip to Disneyland and Universal Studios. This was the only trip I'd ever taken with Kim and Cynthia, and it was one of the best vacations I've ever had!

●

Raising a son and trying to keep Cheri supplied with new shoes turned out to be a very expensive proposition, so our major trips were soon relegated to the back burner. But whenever we needed a day or two to ourselves, Mom and Dad would take Kevin and we'd head for the mountains.

Estes Park had always been one of my favorite mountain towns, and the place we picked for an overnight stay on Friday, July 30th, 1976. Sandra and I would spend some time here when we'd go camping in the nearby Rocky Mountain National Park, but Cheri didn't share that same pioneer spirit, and her idea of roughing it was to stay at a Hilton Hotel. But since there were no Hilton's in this town, we drove to the next best thing; the (then) sixty-seven-year-old Stanley Hotel. Neither of us had ever been there before, but its stately white buildings on the hillside overlooking this quaint little town made it a very inviting place to stay.

The following year, Stephen King wrote about ghostly encounters and madness at the Stanley Hotel, but when we checked in that afternoon, being influenced by his still unwritten classic wasn't even an option. *THE SHINING* was arguably the best ghost story ever written, but it was fiction, and couldn't compare to the horror I'd soon experience in this same terrifying hotel.

We didn't think to make reservations before we left home and were lucky enough to get their very last room. I don't remember our room number, but vividly remember that it was on the second floor, in the northwest corner of the hotel.

It looked like a grand old hotel from the outside, but I was more than just a little disappointed when I saw how meagerly our room was furnished. The headboard on what looked like an oversized rollaway bed butted up against the north wall, with a bare wooden chair to its right, and a cheap little nightstand and lamp to its left. There was a window on the north wall (just west of the nightstand), and another on the west wall, with a small wooden table and two chairs sitting between the two windows.

The spacious bathroom at the southeast end of the room looked even worse than the bedroom. The fixtures looked like they'd been there since the 1940s (or before), including the frayed black cord that hung from the center of the high plaster ceiling, with a 100-watt drawstring light bulb at its end.

A single closet faced the bedroom from the south wall (immediately west of the bathroom), and when I opened the door to put our suitcase away, the overwhelming stench of a recent fire eased its way into the room. The damage wasn't evident, so I didn't give it a lot of thought, and just assumed it had been repaired and covered with a fresh coat of paint.

We drove into town for some window shopping, and after visiting every tourist trap on Elkhorn Avenue, we returned to the hotel for dinner. I admit to having a drink with dinner, but that single glass of Smith and Kearns certainly wasn't strong enough to impair my mental faculties, or create the horrible vision I'd soon have. When we finished, we returned to our room.

I crawled into bed and assumed my normal position on the right hand side, and patiently waited for Cheri to join me. When she finished her nightly cleansing routine, she turned the light off, and guided by the faint glow from a single lamppost just below our window, inched her way across the floor and gently slid in beside me. We ended our night as we always did, then cuddled closely together, and within minutes, we were both sound asleep.

Two or three hours later, I rolled over to my left side, and for some unknown reason, I opened my eyes. In the next terrifying moment, I saw the profile of a charred human corpse sitting in the chair immediately beside our bed, *just inches from my face.* His skeletal arms hung limp on both sides of his bare-boned ribcage . . . his black skinless legs stretched rigidly in front of him. His eyes and nose were missing, and his charred and shriveled skin drew his face into a horrifying death mask, showing two grotesque rows of grimacing teeth.

I screamed and jumped from the bed, and in just two bounding steps, made it all the way to the bathroom some twenty feet away. I yanked on the drawstring, and the bare light bulb jerked violently back and forth across the ceiling; casting ghostly shadows on the walls that even Alfred Hitchcock would fear. I looked back into the bedroom to see the horror I'd escaped from, but to my amazement, the chair was empty!

"Oh, God," I thought to myself. *"Where'd it go?"*

I stood there for several seconds, still gasping in terror; certain my heart would explode at any moment. I walked back to the bedroom and searched for the apparition that had nearly scared me to death, but it was gone . . . and I finally realized I must have been dreaming.

I'd had nightmares before while I was completely asleep, but this wasn't like any dream I'd ever had. I may not have been completely awake when I saw that horrible corpse, but my eyes were wide open, and what I saw in that room was as vivid as anything I'd ever seen; in my mind, a man who'd died in a fire that began in the coat closet.

Blood raced through my veins and every nerve and muscle in my body felt like it was on fire. I broke into a cold sweat and suddenly realized I needed fresh air. I walked to the west window; unlocked the turn lock on top of the wooden frame, then reached down to pull the window open. The window slid up for just a few inches, then **ripped** from my fingers and violently **slammed shut.** I tried again, but this time it wouldn't even budge. I looked for a spring or coil, or anything that could have forced it from my hands, but couldn't find anything wrong. I finally gave up and crawled back to bed; careful not to wake Cheri, who'd slept through the whole ordeal. I left the bathroom light on (just to make sure I wouldn't see more ghosts in the dark), and eventually managed to get back to sleep.

We slept late into the morning and had to rush to get out before our 10am checkout time. While Cheri was taking her shower, I paced around the room and decided to see why I'd had so much trouble with the window the evening before. I checked the top and sides, but still couldn't find anything that would have kept me from opening the window. I unlocked the window again, grabbed both handles and gently pulled up. A cold shudder gripped my spine as the window slid effortlessly to a fully opened position, and I suddenly realized *something* in our room didn't want me to open the window last night, but now in the relative safety of daylight, it no longer cared.

I'd been a policeman for eleven years when this happened, and like most cynical cops, I was skeptical about almost anything that couldn't be backed up by clear and hard evidence . . . especially if I hadn't seen it with my own two eyes. But I did see this "ghost," and even though I understood it was probably a part of some horrible dream I'd had (that made sense), I was completely awake and lucid when that window was ripped from my fingers, and I'm convinced that for the only time in my life, I experienced something truly paranormal.

As we drove out of town, black clouds began to form over the mountains as The Storm of the Century was just beginning to gain momentum . . . and by late that evening, the skies opened up and the ensuing flood that roared down the Big Thompson River destroyed homes and property and killed 144 people. I never equated that carnage with what I'd experienced in our hotel room that night, but the aura of death was definitely a part of that weekend in Estes Park.

•

In the spring of 1978, we moved into our dream home at 3591 South Yampa Way. We'd selected it from a model in the Carriage Place subdivision in southeast Aurora, and watched its progress from the exciting groundbreaking day until it was finished several months later. The two-story, three-bedroom, two and a half bath, two car garage house was far more home than I ever expected to have, and cost an incredible $64,450. Our $600 mortgage payment was almost more than we could afford, but living in such a luxurious home made me feel like the richest man alive!

It was a very good year in Aurora, but not so great in Loveland.

By the end of the summer, my fifteen-year-old daughter Kim had entered the rebellious stage of her teenage years; was hanging with a bad crowd, and had nearly flunked out of school. She and her mom were constantly fighting, and Sandra finally threatened to send her to live with me if she didn't straighten up. Things didn't improve, and finding herself backed into a corner, Sandra called and asked if Kim could move in with me. I was thrilled by the opportunity to have my daughter back, and to Cheri's credit, she also agreed to the move. My only regret is that Cynthia was too well behaved to deserve the same horrible punishment.

It started out well enough, but when school started in the fall, Kim migrated to an equally delinquent group of kids, and was soon in trouble with the law.

She called to get permission to go to the Aurora Mall with one of her girlfriends after school, and just after dark, I received a very disturbing call from the manager of the J.C. Penney store. She and her friend were caught stealing cosmetic jewelry, and the police were holding her there until we could arrive.

I was so mad at her! We were trying so hard to make a good life for her, and this was how she repaid our love and kindness.

When we walked into the manager's office, Kim was defiantly sitting erect in her chair, with just a hint of panic bleeding from her feigned bravado. As we all talked, her expression changed to remorse, and she soon convinced everyone that she was truly sorry for her misdeed. The manager accepted her apology and the police released her to my custody, with my promise that she'd be punished when we got home.

As we walked into the east parking lot, two drunk couples were walking several yards to our right; yelling and cursing, with absolutely no regard for the families around them. When one of

326

the men yelled, *"Fuck You,"* Cheri mumbled, *"Nice mouth."* After nine years of marriage, I knew this was a clue that she was offended and yelled, *"Hey, I've got my wife and kids here. Do you mind?"* He yelled back, *"Well, excuse me you potbellied son-of-a-bitch,"* and the worst fight of his life was about to begin. I took my glasses off and handed them to Cheri, and as I started walking toward the group, Cheri yelled, *"Bill, Look Out!!!"* I turned to my left and saw an eighteen-year-old boy rushing toward me with a tire iron raised high above his head . . . a split second away from slamming it into mine. I drew my gun from under my jacket and yelled, *"Drop It!"* When the tire iron hit the pavement, I grabbed his arm, shoved him into the side of his car, and immediately pulled my badge and identified myself as a policeman. When the two couples saw what was happening, they silently slithered away into the night; happy that they'd avoided contact with a crazed man with a gun. A mall security guard came out to check on a report of some unruly people, and when he saw me struggling with the boy, helped me take him back into Penneys, where the police were still finishing their paperwork. I signed a criminal complaint, typed them a statement, and they took him to jail.

The car was completely silent on our drive home.

When we arrived, we had a **very** serious talk . . . and from that moment on, Kim was the quintessential daughter. She turned into a cheerful and energetic young woman who willingly cleaned and vacuumed the house, babysat for us when Cheri and I needed a night out, and went on to graduate with honors from Smoky Hill High School.

She didn't say it at the time, but years later she confided that she was **SO** happy when I had that altercation in the parking lot, because all of my anger she was going to receive was channeled to the boy with the tire iron. I think she still sends him Christmas cards today.

A month or two after the incident, the District Attorney called to tell me my assailant had pled guilty to felony menacing. He never explained why he was going to hit me.

●

Elvis Presley was a big fan of the Denver Police Department in the 1960s and 70s, and was befriended by several members of our department. He was given a gold Police Captain's badge as a token of their esteem, and in return, bought Lincolns and Cadillacs for three or four of his favorite policemen. Those of us who didn't get new cars thought it was outrageous that they were allowed to accept these great gifts, but secretly envied their association with The King of Rock and Roll.

But Elvis was always generous with the Denver Police Department. Two or three years after the new District Two station was finished at East 35th Avenue and Colorado Boulevard in July 1970, he gave the Department $5,000 (a lot of money in those days) to furnish the basement with a complete set of weights. The gym was eventually named the Merle Nading Memorial Gym, in honor of the District Two officer who was murdered with his own gun in a fight on Sunday, October 3rd, 1971 beside Clark's Diner (formerly the White Spot) at 2201 East Colfax Avenue.

I started working out at District Two while I was still a detective, and by the summer of 1979, I was in pretty good shape and ready to introduce my five-year-old son to the wonderful world of exercise. I took him to the gym with me on one of my nights off and had him lift some light weights in between my sets. It didn't take long before he got tired and bored, and he spent the rest of his time playing on the machines while I continued with my workout.

I was bench-pressing 300 pounds by now, and with my boy there to watch his old man in action, I lifted better and heavier than I'd ever done before. It took an hour before I was finished, and when I went into the bathroom to wash up, Kevin stood in the adjoining recreation room and watched. The mirror gave me two thumbs up and I sighed and said, *"Wow, that was tough. I think your daddy just might have overdone it tonight."* Without hesitation, my judgmental little boy said… *"No balls."*

No Balls? What do you mean No Balls?? Astonished that he even knew what that meant, I jerked around to scold him for his impudence, and saw him looking across the empty pool table with wide eyed innocence as he said, *"There's no balls, Daddy, where's the balls?"* I laughed and thought, *"Yup, that's my boy!"* and couldn't wait to get home to tell the story to his mother.

●

My apologies to Charles Dickens for borrowing from his novel A Tale of Two Cities, but my marriage to Cheri can be summed up in just two of his opening lines: *"It was the best of times, it was the worst of times."*

She wasn't wealthy like so many of her childhood friends, but had the bearing of someone far beyond her station in life and lived life to its fullest. She introduced me to a lifestyle I probably never would have known without her, and now, instead of staying at Best Western Motels and eating at greasy spoon diners on my limited road trips, I was jetting off to faraway places, staying in four-star hotels and dining at the finest restaurants we could find. *Let the snobbery begin!*

She was a woman of elegant style and grace who always looked like she'd just stepped from the pages of Vogue magazine. Her impeccable attire was matched by her beautifully styled hair, delicately manicured nails, and the exquisite essence of her expensively perfumed soft silky skin. If I'd been an older rich man, people would have considered this beautiful and extremely sexy woman to be my trophy wife, but since I was a grossly underpaid policeman, most of them just assumed I was well endowed.

We had an incredibly passionate, loving and nurturing relationship for most of our marriage, but were burdened with far more than our share of rough patches that usually ended in horrific screaming matches, especially during our final years together. But even in battle we never crossed the line by saying something we couldn't take back . . . that is until our worst fight ever on Sunday, April 20th, 1980.

I have no idea what we were fighting about, but for the first time in our marriage, Cheri told me she hated me and was going to take our son and move to San Diego to live with her sister. Hate and divorce were never mentioned in any of our previous fights, and this new revelation scared me to death. I apologized for whatever I was doing to upset her, and cried as I literally got down on my knees and begged her to stay. She finally agreed not to leave me, but from that moment on, everything in our relationship changed.

Cheri had always gone out for an occasional after work drink with the girls, but after this fight, she started going out three or four nights a week. I was okay with that; actually, I even encouraged it. I thought her freedom would help mend our rift, but over time her late nights out became a real problem for me. Fortunately, she eventually grew tired of her hectic schedule and cut back to once or twice a week, and sometimes not at all.

And even though she was now exposed to an environment of temptation, I never worried that she'd be unfaithful . . . she made it pretty clear the last thing she wanted in her life was another man, and I absolutely believed her. But the proverbial handwriting was on the wall, and the inevitability of being alone for the first time in my life was more than I could handle, and right or wrong, I turned to other women for emotional survival when I knew the end of my marriage was near. She didn't want anyone else in her life, but it was an absolute necessity for me, and the airport would provide an abundance of choices.

When we moved our airport office from the basement to the mezzanine in 1980, the PPA (Police Protective Association) bought us a small but complete set of weights for our locker room gym, so I no longer had to drive to District Two for my workouts. I'd been working out faithfully for the past two or three years, and was now bench-pressing 400 pounds. At 37-years-old, I was in the best shape of my life, and at 170 pounds with a 32" waist, had the arrogance and conceit of someone twice my size. With my hat on, I looked much taller than I was, and since my uniform always flattered my overall appearance, I was ready for the challenge.

I usually walked eight to ten miles a day while on foot patrol in the terminal and concourses and had already met most of the pretty girls who worked at the airport, so the unintended groundwork had already been laid. I'd always been a flirt, and flirted with just about every woman I met, but if they showed any signs that they wanted to do more, I'd always say, *"That sounds great, but I don't think my wife would appreciate it."* We'd both have a good laugh, and I'd move on to my next stop. Because I **truly** was a happily married man, I always stopped short of any indiscretion.

But things were different now. The same flirtations still worked with most of the same girls, and I soon learned if I didn't mention my wife, my social life got a lot more exciting.

My favorite group of people worked for Continental Airlines. They were probably the friendliest people in the airport, and went out of their way to help their customers in any way they could. It was easy to make friends with happy employees, and I made a point to visit with them as often as I could.

One of my favorite expressions to my lady friends was, *"God Bless You"* (which usually meant bless you for your beauty or reciprocal flirtations), so when they'd see me walking down the concourse, they'd page, *"Rabbi Aumiller (or) Father Aumiller, please come to gate such and such."* It was all in good fun, but if the right girl called me over, it truly was a religious experience.

They partied almost every night after work, and when I knew Cheri was going to be out drinking with her girlfriends, I'd accept their invitations and join them in their drunken debauchery. I didn't limit myself to an exclusive group of people, but most of my affairs were with those wonderful women with Continental Airlines.

CHAPTER 22

"Karen"

While making my rounds during the first week in October 1981, I discovered an incredibly attractive new girl working in the main terminal gift shop between C and D Concourse. I stopped to welcome Karen Nicastle to the airport and was met with the bubbling enthusiasm of a playful child and the seductive smile of an accomplished tease. Just twenty-years-old, she wore a pale blue long sleeved blouse, dark vest, black bolo tie, and dark blue *exquisitely* fitting slacks . . . and at 5'6" and 105 pounds, had a figure all men lusted after and most women would kill for. She had long dark hair and the most beautiful and captivating green eyes I'd ever seen; hypnotic cat eyes that rendered weaker men speechless, including me on occasion. She wasn't wearing a wedding ring, so I assumed she was single, and wasted no time in wooing her with all my best lines. She responded well to my advances and immediately moved to the top of my list of favorites.

The following week, I noticed a diamond ring on her finger. She explained that it had been in the shop for repairs when I met her, but she was, indeed, a married woman, with a one-year-old daughter.

It didn't matter.

I was only interested in the flirtations at that time, and was just thrilled that a woman of such beauty was so anxious to see me when I'd stop by.

But that changed on Friday, October 30th, 1981, when she agreed to go out for coffee with me after work. There were no decent restaurants open near the airport that late at night, so I drove her to Coco's at 6880 East Evans. It was a great first date, and we laughed and carried on like we'd known each other for years. When I drove her back to her husband's muscle "man-toy" pickup in the airport's Taylor Parking Lot, we sat in my Subaru Brat and talked until she had to leave. I leaned over and kissed her goodbye, then asked if she thought she could be interested in someone seventeen years older than her. She said she wasn't sure, but when she got into her truck to drive away, her smile suggested otherwise.

I laid on my best charm for the next four weeks, and on Saturday, November 28th, she told me it was her twenty-first birthday and asked if I could join her for a drink with her friends after work. I met with them at the Metro Inn at 7200 Smith Road, and by the end of the evening, it was pretty clear how we felt about each other.

We carried on for the next several months, and by the summer of 1982, we were ready to take that next big step. Karen left her husband in July and moved into a two-bedroom apartment at 10161 East Girard Avenue, and on Sunday, August 1st, I left Cheri and moved into a one-bedroom apartment at 11100 East Dartmouth Avenue.

I was relieved when it was over, but the move wasn't without its consequences. The constant stress from the friction at home with Cheri quickly faded, but the relatively comfortable life-style I'd known faded even faster. After nearly thirteen years of marriage, I walked away with my three year old Subaru Brat, our new VCR (a big deal in 1982), but no television set . . . an end table, loveseat, lamp, two pictures, two dishes, bowls, cups, glasses, knives, forks and spoons; a sauce pan, frying pan, two bath and wash towels, my clothes, guns and my collection of police bulletins. Thankfully, Mom and Dad gave me a bed so I didn't have to sleep on the floor.

Cheri kept the house, her three-year-old Subaru sedan, and absolutely everything else we owned. (Although, to be fair, when she sold the house nearly four years later, I was given a few thousand dollars as part of our divorce settlement).

I paid $500 each month for child support for the first year and a half we were separated (the norm was $150) and assumed most of the debts we'd incurred, including Kevin's new braces. (My payments were reduced to $400 when we were divorced on Tuesday, January 3rd 1984). With more than half of my net salary from the police department consumed by my child support and other obligations to Cheri, I was forced to find off-duty work five days a week just to survive, a tough situation in any new relationship. But it was important; essential in my mind that my son didn't have to suffer any more than necessary, at least from the lack of money.

On Saturday, September 11th, 1982, Karen and I celebrated our new union with a trip to Disneyland and Universal Studios. We had very little money between the two of us, but she received free airline passes through her employment with Sky Chefs (the parent company of the gift shop), so our only expenses were for lodging and entertainment. It was our first trip alone together and a break we desperately needed.

•

The apartment Karen lived in turned out to be a real pit, and by the end of September, she was ready to move. She'd made friends with the apartment manager's wife Starr, and when Starr and her husband separated, she and Karen moved into a small three-bedroom house at 19541 East Batavia Drive. It was in an area surrounded by miles of open fields in a small rural community just east of Aurora, and two blocks north of East Colfax Avenue. We considered it to be way out in the country. I think my frequent overnight stays wore thin on Starr's patience, and by December, she moved out. Since Karen couldn't afford the rent on her own, I moved in with her on Tuesday, December 14th, 1982.

Christmas was only eleven days away now, and we were more than ready for the festivities. Our Christmas tree was fully adorned and proudly on display in front of our living room window, with the few presents we could afford stacked neatly at its base. The window was trimmed with a string of red, blue and green lights, with fake snow carefully sprayed in the corners of each pane to help give the illusion of the cold and wintry white Christmas we always hoped for.

But by the morning of Christmas Eve, the fake snow was no longer necessary. The infamous Blizzard of '82 began early that Friday morning, and by 1:15 pm, the snow on our street was already five to six inches deep. As I backed out of the driveway to go to work, I shifted into four-wheel drive and confidently drove away. I'd driven through mud and snow on past skiing trips, and often passed Jeeps and four-wheel trucks that couldn't make the grade, so I was certain nothing could stop my little red Brat from getting me to work on time.

I drove west on Colfax Avenue and turned north on Tower Road on my way to Interstate 70. My Brat was skimming effortlessly through the deepening snow, but just a block or two before I reached the highway, my windshield fogged over and I was forced to slow to a snail's pace. I tried to wipe the fog from the window, but soon learned fog wasn't the problem . . . I was driving in a complete whiteout, and couldn't see anything for more than a few feet beyond the hood of my truck. Then without warning, I slammed into a deep snowdrift in the center of the road (that I was too blinded to see), and came to a startling and abrupt stop. I got out to investigate and found I was high-centered in the massive drift, and there was absolutely nothing I could do to get out. We didn't have cell phones in the early 1980s, but fortunately, I had my police radio with me and was able to call our dispatcher for help. Within minutes, Mark Hellenschmidt was on his way to pick me up in one of the airport's two four-wheel drive police units, the only four-wheel drive vehicles in the entire Denver Police Department's fleet.

I waited . . . and waited . . . and waited . . . shivering more with each passing moment as the cold rapidly consumed the warmth of my truck. The minutes slowly ticked away, and after nearly an hour, I heard Mark say he was stuck in another drift on Colfax several miles away and wouldn't be able to help me. With that, Dean Smith, one of my closest friends at the airport, came on the radio and asked how I was doing. I told him I was getting pretty cold, but thought I'd be okay, and just hoped these weren't the famous last words people notoriously say just before their ultimate doom. He told me to hang in there; they were sending a tow, but by three o'clock, I was told the road conditions throughout the city were so bad, even the tow truck couldn't reach me.

The snow and wind were relentless. It was already freezing inside my truck, and with the storm's raging fifty mile-per-hour winds, it was thirty-five below zero outside. With the hood of my truck buried in snow, my heater would only blow cold air (not that it mattered much, anyway, since I'd left home with less than a quarter tank of gas) . . . and because I was only wearing my regular police uniform and short winter jacket, I was seriously concerned for my safety. I'd passed several abandoned cars on my way, but by now, I was the only person still on the road, and just hoped I could survive the bitter cold until someone came to rescue me.

I was stuck on a roadway surrounded by large open fields, and even though I knew there were warehouses somewhere nearby, they were completely obliterated by the driven snow. But no matter what I thought, I wasn't about to leave the relative safety of my truck just to get lost on foot in a foolish attempt to find them. As I sat there contemplating my fate, a man pounded on my window. I cracked my window an inch or two and he told me some stranded motorists had taken refuge in a warehouse just behind me and to my left, and I was graciously invited to join them.

There were a dozen people in the lobby of the warehouse . . . most of them chattering nervously about how bad the storm had become, and clearly apprehensive about being forced to spend the night away from their families in the company of total strangers. We were all grateful to be out of the biting cold, but this was not the place any of us wanted to spend our Christmas Eve.

I called my office to tell them I was safe, then called Karen with the bad news that I'd be stuck here for the rest of the night, and probably through Christmas as well.

Within minutes, two Aurora policemen walked through the door. They'd abandoned their hopelessly stuck cruiser and found their way to the warehouse, but I soon learned they wouldn't be here for long. Their dispatcher was sending volunteer snowmobilers to pick them up, and when they arrived just after dark, one of them offered to take me home. He gave me a ski mask and gloves to help protect me from the bitter cold, and we drove the dark and eerily deserted streets to the entrance of my housing community. The drifts were too deep to take me into my neighborhood, so he dropped me off beneath the orange glow of the desolate corner streetlight at Espana Street and East Colfax Avenue.

I watched as he drove west on Colfax, and as his taillights soon disappeared from view, I turned back to the streetlight . . . and in that brief moment of my turn, I lost all sense of direction. I knew there were homes just two blocks to the north, but they were completely invisible in the raging blizzard and offered no guidance in determining which direction to go. I finally made a decision and started walking.

Unfortunately, I made the wrong choice and headed east on Colfax. There were no cars on the road, or tire ruts in the deep snow to warn me I was on the highway instead of a safe route home, and *everything* around me looked the same. I fought the blinding wind and snow, and after I'd walked for what seemed an eternity, I realized I was heading in the wrong direction. I turned around and retraced the deep imprints of my boots for as long as they lasted, then heard the sound of a pickup approaching from behind. A young farm boy stopped and offered the warmth of his heater for a block, then dropped me off at the base of the street light I'd walked away from. I stood there for several seconds; a clearer vision of direction now, but still confused by the darkness, I started walking again. The snow got deeper with each step, and I suddenly sank to my chest into an abyss of freezing snow. I'd again chosen poorly and had no idea where I was in relation to my home, but knew I was stuck, and in serious trouble. I thought to myself, *"Oh, My God, I'm Going To Die Out Here!"* It was Christmas Eve and all I could think about was that my son was about to lose his father. *What a horrible Christmas present!*

I was finally able to claw my way free from my icy tomb and made my way back toward the faint glimmer of the street light. The wind slowed for just an instant, and in that glorious moment, I saw a small patch of sidewalk exposed by the blowing wind. I knew the sidewalk led north into my neighborhood, so I followed the direction of this miracle until it disappeared from view, and finally got close enough to see the street light at the beginning of my block. Exhausted by my struggle and exposure to the arctic subzero temperatures, I trudged forward through the near waist-deep snow. When I reached Batavia, I could see lights from several homes, and knew my nightmare was over. But when I reached our house, I saw that the snow had drifted to the top of our front door and windows, and knew they'd be nearly impossible to reach. I forged my way through the shallower snow bank on the west side of the house, and when I reached our backyard, I found that portions of the lawn had been swept clean by the violent winds, and the patio door was completely clear. I pounded on the door, and when Karen and her fourteen-year-old sister Bonnie brought me inside, I collapsed to the floor, never more happy to be home.

The snow ended by midmorning on Christmas Day, but left behind nearly four feet of snow, with drifts six to ten feet high. This was the worst snow storm I'd ever seen before (or since), and because of the unusually long cold snap, the grounds and streets were covered with snow for the next forty-eight consecutive days . . . the third longest period in recorded history.

By the 26th, snow removal crews had plowed narrow paths through the four-foot snow mounds that covered most of the major roadways around town, and Karen's father Jerry drove me back to retrieve my Brat. But when we arrived, we found that in their efforts, the plows had nearly buried my truck with snow. I shoveled through the mountain of crusted ice, and when I was able to reach the driver's side door, I discovered someone had broken the window completely out; unlatched the hood from inside the cab, and stole my battery. At first, I was really upset, but when I saw the thief left behind Kevin's new skis and the wrapped Christmas present I had for Cheri (and a gun I had in the glove compartment), I realized he wasn't an ordinary thief, and my battery may have been the only thing that saved his life during the worst part of the storm. It took away the sting of being victimized, but still left me with a situation I could ill afford.

Jerry towed me to the Sears store at the Aurora Mall, where luckily, I still had enough credit left on my account to buy a new battery. But the broken window was another matter altogether. It would take weeks before I could afford to replace it, and until I did, I drove around with a large slab of cardboard duct-taped to the window frame, with a tiny peep-hole cut out at eye level so I could see the traffic to my left. *Oh, the joys of poverty!*

Three people in the metropolitan Denver area died as a result of this storm, including a farmer who lived just north of my home. While I was struggling to get to the warmth and safety of my own home, he left the security of his farmhouse to check on his livestock, and like me, lost all sense of direction. No one knows how long he wandered through the shroud of blinding snow before he succumbed to the cold, but the following day his frozen body was found partially buried in a snow drift just two hundred feet from his house. But for the grace of God and that brief stretch of exposed sidewalk, I surely would have been the fourth victim of the incredibly beautiful but terrifying Blizzard of '82.

●

There were no pretenses with Karen . . . she was raised by a truck driving father and stay-at-home mom in Libertyville, Illinois (a blue collar suburb just north of Chicago), and never acquired a taste or desire for the luxuries of life. She was hypnotic in blue jeans or sweats, and ravishing in miniskirts, shorts, or tight slacks and tops . . . but looked like a little girl playing grown up in dresses and heels. Most times she was pretty . . . sometimes she was cute . . . but she was always incredibly sexy, and just seeing her seductive smile could bring me to my knees.

EVERYONE was drawn to her beauty! Even husbands with their wives stopped to stare when we walked by, and even though I was flattered by the envy I saw in their eyes, I constantly worried that she'd be tempted by the wiles of someone more in her own league and eventually move on. I wasn't comfortable with this fear, but knew if I was going to survive in this relationship, it was something I'd have to learn to live with.

When she left the horde of predators at the airport in March 1983, it helped alleviate some of my anxiety, but her new job as an office clerk at the Pioneer Sand Company at 463 Buckley Road (now Airport Boulevard), just created new problems for me. With an affinity for hard working, beer drinking, shit kicking cowboys, she was definitely in her element here, and it was an element I couldn't control.

Karen had a wonderful sense of humor, and her bubbling personality mesmerized everyone she met . . . and not surprisingly, she was a big hit with every man at work. She'd tell me when they'd flirt with her (which they always did), but assured me I was the only man she wanted, and I had nothing to worry about.

We were invited to a company barbeque/volleyball tournament on Sunday, April 17th, but because I needed to sleep after working the previous midnight shift in the Radio Room, I told Karen to go without me. Sending her alone sounds noble enough, but I had an ulterior motive. This would be my opportunity to see how she behaved with her co-workers away from work while she thought she was alone, and right or wrong, it was something I needed to do.

The barbeque was held at an oversized lot beside the house on the northwest corner of East 2nd Avenue and Buckley Road, so I drove to the school bus parking area a block southeast of the intersection, and parked to watch. Every surveillance requires a good set of binoculars, and this was no exception. I watched as a large group of people played volleyball just south of the house, and saw Karen, in her usual competitive mode, aggressively slamming the ball over the net and berating those who couldn't stop her. Everything looked harmless enough . . . at least until the game was over.

I watched as Karen and one of the boys walked away from the net, and was shocked when they stopped and kissed in full view of everyone at the court. I threw my binoculars to the passenger seat and raced to the home. I pulled into the long dirt driveway, but by the time I reached the court, Karen was gone. I got out of my car; calmly closed the door and walked to the group of men and women and asked, *"Have you seen Karen?"* The men all looked at each other, trying to figure out what they should say, then one of them finally said, *"She went home."*

That was the wrong answer. I'd just seen her seconds before (and her car was still in the driveway), so I frantically searched the grounds and outbuildings for her and her new little friend. As I approached the final shed, the homeowner's son stepped between me and the door and said, *"You can't go in there."*

Certain I'd find them inside, I shoved him away and opened the door.

They weren't there.

I turned and headed for the house . . . the only place left for them to hide. The boy was with me every step of the way, and when I forced my way into the kitchen, he threatened to call the police if I didn't leave. I glared at him for a few seconds, then angrily returned to my car and drove home. This was not something I wanted the police department to know about.

About half an hour later, Karen walked timidly through the door. I was outraged that she'd cheat on me, and as she cowered in fear, I screamed that I was leaving her. She responded exactly as I'd hoped for and held me tightly as she cried and begged me to stay. We talked for hours and hours, and as my bruised ego began to heal, she assured me it would never happen again. And because I was so blinded by love, I believed her.

At my insistence, she quit her job at the gravel company, and as a new Kelly Girl, worked at the Oppenheimer Asset Management Corporation near East Arapahoe Road and South Clinton Street.

In the first week of June 1983, we moved to a townhouse at 15351 East Louisiana Avenue. We'd moved past the indiscretion and for the next three years she'd prove her love and devotion by being the most loving, touching, and caring woman I've ever known. I don't know where she learned her man pleasing skills, but she was a natural in making me feel like I was the biggest, best and smartest man she'd ever been with, and aggressively went out of her way to satisfy my every whim.

And I had a lot of whims.

343

Cheri once complained, *"You don't need a wife, you need a porno queen,"* and she was absolutely right . . . and Karen was absolutely the right woman for the job. But because I believe what a man and woman does in the privacy of their bedroom with a donkey is their own business, I won't say any more.

I transferred to District Four in December 1983, and was finally able to work the coveted 11am-7pm day shift. Being home every night with Karen was a huge change for us, and for the first time in our relationship, we felt just like normal people. We lived from payday to payday, so we really couldn't afford to do much, but entertained ourselves by partying with friends, playing cards with Mom and Dad, or just hanging out at home and cuddling in front of the television until it was time for a full and uninterrupted night's sleep . . . together. What a wonderful concept!

•

On Monday, June 18th, 1984, my eighty-seven-year-old Granddad Aumiller died. He'd been in a nursing home for quite some time now, and had gotten pretty frail over the past two weeks . . . but even though his death really wasn't un-expected, it was a very rough day for all the Aumillers when we lost the true patriarch of our entire Denver family. Following his burial in section T1 0 1080 at the Fort Logan National Cemetery on Friday, June 22nd, the family (including my two sisters), met at Opal's house at 945 Emerson Street for a special tribute to his life.

Granddad wasn't a doting grandfather (at least not to me), and I spent most of my childhood fearful of his imposing stature and the guttural Nick Nolte tone of his voice. But that all changed when I was fourteen-years-old.

In 1958, my Great-Grandmother Aumiller, Uncle Wynn, and Uncle Warren came in from Selden, and Granddad and Opal brought them to our house for a visit. The women settled into the living room, while I sat at the kitchen table with Dad and

344

his elders, listening quietly to every word they said . . . smiling to myself as they got louder and more humorous with each new sip of whiskey . . . slurring their words with more frequency as they happily recalled the good old days when they were still young and rowdy. While Granddad was in the middle of one of his great stories, Dad interrupted with his own memories of the events. Granddad yelled, *"You shut up boy, I'm telling this story."* Stunned that Dad actually stopped talking, I laughed and said, *"Whoa, nobody tells my dad to shut up."* Smiling broadly Granddad declared, *"Well, I can,"* and Dad laughed at the shocked look on my face when I realized his dad had the same authority over him as he had over me. Granddad continued to flex his parental muscles for the rest of the afternoon, and would wink at me every time he'd put his thirty-eight-year-old "kid" in his place, and from that moment on, I understood his gruffness was just a facade . . . that he had a sense of humor I'd never recognized before, and I suddenly appreciated him for the real man that he was.

On Saturday, June 23rd, 1984, the day after Granddad's funeral, my oldest daughter Kim married Wayne Brunmeier in Loveland, Colorado. They'd have three of the sweetest little girls you could ever imagine (no bias here), beginning with Shanna, who was born on Tuesday, December 31st, 1985, followed by Jennifer on Friday, May 8th, 1987, and Ashley on Tuesday, February 19th, 1991. Unfortunately, their marriage turned sour with the passing of years and they were divorced in 1994.

My youngest daughter Cynthia graduated from High School in Loveland that same summer and moved in with her life partner, Todd Wooten. They had two children, Joshua and Brittany (who I've only seen two or three times), and are still together today.

Cynthia was just three-years-old when Sandra and I were divorced, and was raised by her mother and Jim in places too far away for me to have reasonable visitation rights. I couldn't afford to see my girls for the first two years they were gone, and by the time I was finally able to fly them in from Phoenix for the first time, Cynthia didn't even know who I was. I understood she probably considered Jim to be more of a real father to her than I was, and because I accepted that premise as a reality, I wasn't surprised when I rarely heard from her once she turned eighteen and moved in with Todd. We've never had a falling out or had any bad blood between us, and thoroughly enjoy our reunions when we do get together, but we've only seen each other five or six times in the past twenty-five years. It bothered me in the beginning, but when I learned she was almost as reclusive with the rest of the family as she was with me, I stopped taking it quite so personally.

•

Karen and I couldn't have been happier, but on Wednesday, July 4th, 1984, the life I loved was seriously threatened.

I'd just finished covering a routine call on South Sherman Street and stepped back into my cruiser. Suddenly, my heart began to throb. It felt like a huge surge of adrenalin was racing through my chest (which actually felt kind of good), but because there was no reason for it to happen, I knew I was in trouble. There were no chest pains or aching arms to indicate a heart attack, but when I started feeling light headed, I called for an ambulance.

The paramedics put me on a gurney in the back of their ambulance and ran a quick EKG. The test showed something abnormal was happening with my heart, so they rushed me to Denver General Hospital and took me into the Intensive Care Unit. The nurses ran another EKG, checked my blood pressure, drew some blood, then left me alone in the room, still tethered to several monitoring cables. Every five or six minutes an alarm would sound, and a nurse would run into the room to see if I was still alive. My chest didn't feel any different, but when my heart would literally stop for a beat or two, it would set off the alarm. After half a dozen false alarms, they disconnected the machine.

Karen arrived shortly after she was called, and rushed to my side. She was **SO** caring and concerned, and caressed me as she told me how much she loved me. She was everything Sandra was not.

They released me within three or four hours and referred me to a cardiologist for more comprehensive tests.

The cardiologist concluded that I had an irregular heartbeat, and suggested the twenty cups of coffee I drank each day was probably the cause. I cut back to three or four cups of decaf, and the problem eventually went away, but the thought of my heart giving out gave me great cause for concern. At forty, I wasn't exactly old, but knew I was at an age when heart attacks could occur, and in what was probably the most unromantic proposal ever made, I asked Karen to marry me . . . just so she could get my pension if I died.

Eight days later, on Thursday, July 12th, 1984, I married the fourth true love of my life, twenty-three-year-old Karen Sue Nicastle, in Courtroom #10 at the Denver City and County Building. My ten-year-old son was my Best Man.

Neither of us could get time off from work during the summer months, so our honeymoon was delayed for the next fifty-one days. Then on Saturday, September 1st, 1984, we left for our belated ten day honeymoon and flew to London. From there we took a hovercraft across the English Channel from Dover to Oostende, Belgium, then took a cruise on the Rheine River in Cologne, Germany. We toured Heidelberg, Munich and the Dachau Concentration Camp in Germany; continued to Innsbruck and Vienna, Austria; Venice, Italy; Paris, Lisieux and Cherbourg, France, then crossed the English Channel to Portsmouth for our return to London.

I was promoted to lieutenant on November 1st, and we took Kevin and Laura to Disneyworld and the Kennedy Space Center to celebrate. Then on Saturday, January 19th, 1985, we moved to a four-bedroom bi-level rental at 3753 South Quintero Street. It was much larger than the townhouse, and for the first time since my divorce, Kevin had his own bedroom to sleep in on his weekend visits.

•

Karen worked at her new Kelly Girl position with the Xerox Corporation until it was eliminated in April 1986, then found a permanent job with a company in the Denver Tech Center near East Belleview Avenue and Interstate 25.

I had nearly everything I'd ever wanted in life now. My daughters were all grown up and moving on with their lives; my twelve-year-old son was still a straight "A" student who'd adjusted remarkably well to the breakup of his mother and me (he was the only mature person in our family), I had a beautiful and loving wife, and a successful career that was on the fast track to my final goal. It was a wonderful life . . . until it totally collapsed at 9:17 on Wednesday evening, April 23rd, 1986, when I caught Karen parked beside her office building, "engaged" with another new friend.

The following day I temporarily moved in with my parents until I was able to find my own two-bedroom apartment at 16892 East Wyoming Circle. It was a desperate attempt to save face (after all, I left her, she didn't leave me), and allow her enough time to realize what a horrible mistake she'd made. But it had the absolute opposite effect, and instead of wanting me back, she reveled in her new freedom. It was devastating . . . but not because she'd physically been with another man (I could have lived with that), but because of her total indifference toward me and her desire to be with someone she'd secretly been seeing for the past four months. My brain burned with the images of my wife and her lover, and my heart literally ached with grief . . . it felt like someone had reached inside my chest and was squeezing my heart, and nothing could relieve the pain.

I couldn't sleep for more than three or four hours a day, and nearly stopped eating for the next two months. I stopped watching television and reading the newspaper, and when I wasn't at work, I had absolutely no idea what to do with my time. I obsessed over every moment Karen was with her new lover, and knew when they were together, she was loving him . . . touching him . . . and doing all of those wonderful things she'd done with me while we were cheating on our spouses.

I lost thirty pounds in the first thirty days, and privately cried in unbearable pain for forty straight days. Well-intentioned friends told me to turn to God for help, but I thought it would be nothing more than self-serving hypocrisy to ask for His help after blatantly ignoring Him for so many years. I finally couldn't stand the pain anymore, and in a fit of self-pity and rage I cried out to God, *"You only made it rain for forty days and forty nights . . . make it stop."* The crying stopped, but the memories, dreams, and pain lasted for the next thirteen years.

It's sad to say, but it would have been so much easier for me if she'd died. I don't want to belittle the enormous grief people feel when they lose someone very close to them, but their loved one's didn't leave them . . . *they died.* There was no deceit or hatred in their hearts when they died, and there's a great deal of comfort in knowing that up until that final moment, you were loved and cherished by the most important person in your life. But when someone leaves you to share their lives, their souls, and their carnal love with someone else, there's absolutely no comfort. The sanity and normality of life is gone, and all that's left is an incredible sense of insecurity, overwhelming sorrow and inconceivable emotional pain. Anyone who's been through this kind of trauma understands exactly what I'm saying, but for those of you who haven't . . . *count your blessings!*

It had been a short and exciting ride, but when karma finally raised its ugly head, I learned that what goes around, comes around wasn't just a saying . . . it was an absolute truth. I'd cheated on my first two wives and was now *severely* punished for my past sins!

By the time my divorce was final on Thursday, October 23rd, 1986 (exactly six months later), I learned my fellow officers were secretly taking bets on how long it would take before I killed Karen and her lover (or just myself), and to be honest, there were a lot of days and nights when it looked pretty iffy for both her lover Steve and myself. I understood why he was with her (after all, I'd been in his exact same shoes when I first met her, and I certainly couldn't resist her charm), but somehow it always felt like the problem would go away if he just wasn't there anymore. I think the only thing that kept me away from that dark path was the unexpected kindness I received from my ex-wife Cheri, who once again became an important part of my life. She'd justifiably been angry with me for the past four years, but when she saw how much pain I was in, forgave me my indiscretions and offered the comfort of her shoulder to cry on. It wasn't a romantic overture (she was already deeply involved with another man), but an act of kindness, so rich in compassion, that it saved the last tattered fiber of my sanity, and probably my life as well.

But Karen was never at risk . . . I loved her far too much to deliberately hurt her, and I really didn't blame her for what she'd done. I knew I'd driven her away with my obsessive-compulsive need to control her every move, and even though I hated what was happening, I knew it was ultimately my own fault.

By September, I had a new love interest in my life (who would become my next wife), and Cheri and her significant other were quick to welcome us into their home.

You couldn't help but like Bobby Charter. With the cherub-like face of an altar boy and the animated humor of John Belushi, he was the life of every party, and just being in the same room with him brought a smile to your face. The four of us often got together for dinner and cards, golfed together during the summer months and skied during the winter. We celebrated a New Year's Eve together at the Brown Palace Hotel, and Linda and I were honored to share in the joy of their union when they were married on Saturday, August 8th, 1987. Bobby had been just as supportive as Cheri when I was going through my crisis, and the two of them became my most appreciated friends.

CHAPTER 23

"Linda"

On Monday, July 28th, 1986, while working an off-duty security job at the Empire Savings and Loan Branch at #2 Steele Street, I met a stunning young beauty on her very first day on the job. Linda Navaro was as tall as me, had beautiful blond shoulder length hair, white silky skin, gorgeous pale green eyes, and was elegant and refined with a flair for fashion; attributes Karen lacked. She moved gracefully in her high-heel shoes, and her conservative peach colored dress served her well in complimenting her voluptuous Marilyn Monroe figure— *Who Could Want More?* But as striking as she was, the first thing I noticed about her was her *incredibly* precious little girl smile—I just wanted to pinch her cheeks! She looked to be in her early twenty's (my favorite age group), so I wasted no time in welcoming her to the bank.

Over the next few Mondays, I flaunted my new and improved thirty pound lighter made-for-lovin' body, and flirted with her with the zeal of a deranged stalker. When I finally asked how old she was, she coyly pursed her lips; batted her deceptively innocent eyes, then uttered those two little words no forty-two year-old man ever wants to hear . . . *"I'm eighteen."* A cold shudder ran up and down my spine as I groaned and backed away; glancing nervously around the room for that hidden child predator news camera-crew who would expose me for the degenerate that I truly was. Confused by my reaction, she asked, *"Is there something wrong?"* . . . and I laughed and said, *"Oh, sweetie, you're just a little too young . . . even for me."* Without hesitating, she looked me in the eyes and purred, *"But I'm almost nineteen."*

*Nineteen? . . . **Nineteen?*** I thought it over for a couple of seconds, then said to myself, *"What the hell, that's old enough, and at that age, she'll be easier to train."* But even with that great opening, it still took another two or three weeks before I finally asked her out, and only then when she offered to walk on my back in her high-heel shoes. *Now that was an invitation!*

We met for lunch at Rick's Café at 80 South Madison Street on the following Thursday, September 25th. Even though she was still a teenager, she had the elegance and sophistication of a much older woman, and was surprisingly easy to talk with. When we finished lunch, I walked her to her car at the rear of the restaurant and we talked until it was time for her to leave for work. I definitely wanted to see her again, but because she was so much younger than me, I was afraid I'd scare her away if I acted too quickly, and hesitated as we stood there saying our goodbyes. Then, as if to show me everything was alright, she leaned into me . . . and we kissed. It was a wonderful first date!

The following evening, I took her to dinner at the Loading Dock Restaurant at 10660 East Alameda Avenue. The private glass-enclosed intimate little dining rooms were the perfect touch for our romantic candlelit dinner, but as great as our filet mignons were, the only thing either of us could think about was returning to my apartment for an even more intimate evening alone.

I gave her a quick tour of my apartment then offered her a glass of wine. It didn't occur to me at the time (since I wasn't used to dating anyone nearly that young), but it's pretty clear now that I was guilty of contributing to the delinquency of a minor. Thank God there's a statute of limitation for that type of violation!

We sat down to watch a video I'd rented (My Chauffeur), but by the time we finished our first drink, neither of us were interested in watching a movie. I shut the television off . . . we drank a little more wine; made ourselves a lot more comfortable (carelessly spilling my drink in the process), then ended our evening sitting on my couch and talking.

I learned that she was born in Cincinnati on Friday, November 3rd, 1967. Her parents separated in 1972, divorced in 1974, and her father Richard (a respected and successful Prudential Life Insurance salesman), would later marry Jayne (Luti) McKlveen and become the stepfather of her only son, Brad. She lived in a storybook English Tudor at 3919 Eileen Drive, where at just four-years-old, she stood on her front porch and embarrassed her father with a brand new word she'd learned from her brothers Greg and Don. As a little old couple walked hand-in-hand in front of her home, she smiled her biggest smile, waived her tiny little hands and yelled in her sweetest voice, *"Hey, you fuckers."* Richard told me that exact same story twenty-three years later, and said as embarrassed as he was, he still laughs when he remembers the expression on that couple's faces, and how precious his little girl looked.

In 1978, she and her mother and sister Cindy moved to Littleton, where her mother, Mary Navaro, found work as a Licensed Practical Nurse at Denver's Presbyterian/St. Luke's Hospital.

She had six living siblings: Steve, who was born in 1951, Rick, in 1952, Tom, in 1954, Greg, in 1957, Don, in 1958, and Cindy, in 1959. A sixth brother, David, died at just one day old in 1956.

Steve was between marriages when I first met him and would later marry Sue Fine (his longtime significant other) and become the stepfather of her three sons, Jamie, Brian and Bobby. Rick was involved with a longtime girlfriend, but would later marry Lauren Johnson; adopt her son Nathan, and have two daughters, Katherine and Julia. Tom was already married to Kim Lorenz, and they had their first two children, Tim and Claire, and would later have their second daughter, Erin. Greg was a single parent raising his two young daughters, Chrissy and Holly, but he'd later marry Gloria Rossero and become the stepfather of her two sons, Kevin and Brandon. Don was also between marriages, and would later marry Tonia

Cook and have two daughters, Brennan and Tristen. And Cindy (the best looking of her remaining handsome siblings), was married to Russell Burk, and would have two daughters, Alex and Natalie.

Linda was the most responsible young woman I'd ever met. She graduated from Heritage High School in 1985, and now, in addition to working a part-time job at the bank, was attending Metro State College full time. She was making regular monthly payments on her 1979 Datsun, and was paying for her own car insurance without any help from her mother. She kept emergency roadside equipment and a first-aid kit in the trunk of her car, and was completely capable of changing a flat tire if the situation ever arose—not something your typical teenage girl even thinks about, let alone is capable of doing. She was proud to have her very own Sears credit card, and unlike far too many of us, always paid more than the minimum amount she owed, and always before it was due. She was unusually candid with her thoughts and feelings (sharing far more than I would have expected), and I believed when she told me something, I could be assured it was the truth. After the deception I'd just gone through, this kind of honesty was very important to me, and thankfully, it's still a level of honesty I can depend on even today.

We started seeing each other as often as we could, and on Halloween, Friday, October 31st, with her mother's blessing, I took her to San Francisco for a three-day weekend getaway to properly celebrate her upcoming nineteenth birthday.

We took the cable car up Powell Street, where I bought her a bottle of Shalimar perfume at Saks Fifth Avenue (we didn't have one in Denver in those days), then took in all the sights of Fisherman's Wharf, toured the prison island of Alcatraz, walked the streets of China Town, visited the Ghirardelli Chocolate Factory, had lunch at Alioto's and dinner on the wharf, and took a helicopter tour over the city. And on Monday, November 3rd, her actual birthday, I took her to the

Broker Restaurant at 1444 South Havana in Aurora for a very romantic dinner. I like to think I made a good impression on her, because eight days later, on Tuesday, November 11th, she moved in with me.

Linda was a big hit with my parents and was immediately welcomed into the family. Dad liked her because she was a pretty green-eyed young blond, and because he was a dirty old man. And she liked Dad because, well . . . because he was Dad. But Mom liked her because of her sophisticated mannerisms and her incredible energy, but mostly because she'd drawn me out of my deep depression and returned my life back to normal again.

She dropped out of college shortly after we started seeing each other and found a better paying job with the First Denver Mortgage Company on Parker Road near Tamarac Street. We adjusted quickly to our very comfortable and secure relationship, and on Wednesday, July 1st, 1987, we bought a two-bedroom, one and a half bath, two-story townhouse at 2009-C South Hannibal Street.

I transferred back to the midnight shift at the airport in 1986, and by the end of 1987, I was in command of the 6am-2pm day shift. It was easy to forget the harsh realities of the job while working in the relaxed and friendly environment of the airport, but on Tuesday, February 9th, 1988, I was once again drawn back into the real world when a fellow officer was killed in the line of duty.

It all started when Phillip Hutchinson robbed the Rio Grande Credit Union at 4593 Pecos Street. As he fled in his brown Chevy Blazer, he was pursued by several Denver police officers and a Channel 4 News helicopter that had hurried to the scene. As pilot Mike Silva followed the chase from the air, photojournalist Jim Stair video recorded the speeding Blazer as the driver swerved dangerously close to the approaching police cars, narrowly missing them as he sped past. Detective Bob Wallis and his partner set up a partial roadblock at West 48th Avenue and Tennyson Street, and when Bob saw the Blazer racing directly toward their car, he jumped from the driver's seat and tried to run for cover.

He didn't make it.

The suspect swerved away at the last possible second, increased his speed, and deliberately slammed into him as he ran across the street, knocking him a hundred feet through the air, killing him instantly. The pursuing officers stopped to help their fatally wounded comrade as the suspect raced from the scene, and within moments, he crashed into a tree near West 52nd Avenue and Tennyson Street. He jumped from his truck and ran through backyards and streets, firing rounds at the helicopter in an unsuccessful attempt to make it leave. He tried to steal a car from a woman who was parked on the street, but fearful of what he would do to her and her baby, she quickly sped away. He raised his gun and fired at her, then continued running until he found an old man and his autistic daughter standing next to their pickup truck inside a mobile home park. He allowed the woman to stay behind, but forced the man into the truck and had him drive slowly away. As they drove from the park, they passed two or three Denver police cars, but the officers had no way of knowing their suspect was in the truck and let them pass. Horrified that he was getting away, the pilot flew directly over the hijacked truck until the police realized what he was doing. The police followed the helicopter to a parking lot just north of West 52nd Avenue on Sheridan Boulevard, and as they closed in for the showdown, Mike landed his helicopter directly in the path of the truck and blocked it from going any further. And there, in what could only be described as true poetic justice, the final graphic seconds of Phillip Hutchinson's life were video recorded for the five o'clock news as a hail of police bullets ripped through the back window and cab of that old green truck; just moments before the hostage was safely pulled to freedom.

Word of Bob's death spread like wildfire throughout the Department, and within minutes I received a call from the Chief's Office. His new wife Judy was due to leave on a Frontier flight and I was asked to find her and give her the unspeakable news. I'd delivered several death notices to strangers during my career, but this time it was personal. Bob was an old Academy classmate and friend of mine, and I was having a very tough time with his loss.

I checked to see which gate Judy was departing from and raced to D Concourse to meet with her . . . but I dreaded being the one to tell her and secretly hoped she'd already be gone by the time I arrived. There's no good way to tell a policeman's wife her husband's been killed . . . the news is traumatic no matter how it's presented, but I couldn't have done a poorer job if I'd tried.

The closer I got to the boarding gate, the more I thought of how I'd tell her, and finally decided if she was still here, it would be better if I took her to our office to break the news. I rationalized that it would be easier for her to deal with her grief out of the public's eyes, but in reality, I was more afraid that I wouldn't be able to control my own emotions at that moment of truth. It seemed like the right thing at the time, but during the incredibly long and silent seven-minute walk back to the office, I realized I'd made a terrible mistake. Forcing her to wait for the most horrible news of her life was the worst thing I could have possibly done, and I've regretted that decision every day of my life. I can only hope she's forgiven me for my well intended but incredibly inept behavior.

When we reached my office, I closed the door for privacy and told her Bob had been killed, and as delicately as I could, described how it happened. She just stared at me . . . her face grew pale and tears welled in her eyes, and as she started to tremble, I held her in my arms. I didn't know if that was the proper thing to do, but knew it was what I would have needed under the same circumstances.

Telling her was the hardest thing I've ever done on the job, and that moment was the only time in my career that I regretted being a policeman.

•

On Wednesday, September 21st, 1988, Mom and Dad marked their fiftieth year of marriage . . . a full forty-nine years longer than their parents ever expected. Linda volunteered to organize an anniversary party (with Cheri and Bobby's help), and on Saturday, September 17th, nearly a hundred of their dearest and closest friends met at the Elks Club at 1455 Newland Street to celebrate this wonderful moment. With champagne toasts and hugs and kisses, friends and family paid tribute to two of the most loved people I've ever known. It was one of the very few times our family was all together at the same time, and was indeed, a very special day.

•

On Thursday, June 1st, 1989, at the age of forty-five, I married my fourth wife (the fifth true love of my life), twenty-one-year-old Linda Mary Navaro. She's definitely "the one" in my life, and is absolutely my last wife (not to be confused with my last wife).

This wedding couldn't have been more perfect! Thanks to the generosity of Linda's brother Steve and his soon to be wife Sue Fine, we drank champagne in the back of our elegant white Rolls Royce (once owned by the Shah of Iran) as we were chauffeured by Sue's son Jamie through the mountain foothills to the Rockmont Church in Mount Vernon Canyon. Darrell Bolton (now our Division Chief of Patrol) acted as my Best Man, and Linda's sister Cindy was her Maid of Honor. As I stood at the altar, I watched my stunningly beautiful young bride in her angelic white wedding dress as she was escorted down the aisle by her father Richard. When she finally reached my side, tears began to form in her eyes. I smiled to help reassure her, and just hoped they were tears of happiness and not tears of regret, but I really wasn't sure which way she was leaning until she smiled and lovingly said, *"I do."*

After the wedding ceremony, our guests joined us for a dinner celebration at the Chart House Restaurant just south of I-70, and that evening, we finished packing our bags for the fantasy honeymoon I'd always wanted.

This was a wedding of firsts for me. It was the first time I'd ever been married in a church . . . the first time I'd worn a tuxedo at my own wedding, the first time I'd given my bride a diamond ring, and my first actual, honest to goodness honeymoon. *It was my best wedding, ever!*

We got up early the next morning and fought rush hour traffic all the way to the airport. We arrived well before our flight was scheduled to leave, so we checked our bags at the ticket counter and headed for breakfast at the Stapleton Plaza Hotel at 3333 Quebec Street. This was my usual workday breakfast spot, and I was anxious to have my favorite waitress meet the woman I'd been bragging about for so many months.

Sharon Walton always had a quick wit, but it was never more evident than when I introduced her to my new bride. She shook Linda's hand, took a step back; stared at Linda's youthful face and said, *"Why in the world would you marry such an old fart? In ten years he'll be having you bring him his slippers and walker, and you'll be spoon feeding him mashed potatoes!"* Without even flinching, Linda responded, *"What do you mean in ten years? I do all of that today."* It was good to see the girls bond.

When we finished our meal, we returned to the airport and caught our flight to JFK International Airport in New York City. Since we had a full hour to kill before our next flight, we found a cafeteria for a quick cup of coffee. Linda grabbed a table for us while I got in line to be served, and as I stood there waiting, I heard the familiar shrill voice of an FAA agent I knew from Denver as she was telling a dirty joke to someone just ahead of me. I walked up behind her and said, *"Hey, lady. We're getting complaints on a loud party here."* A startled Jill Blackburn turned and looked at me and screamed, *"Bill! What are you doing here?"* When I told her I was on my way to Frankfurt, Germany on my honeymoon, she said, *"That's where I'm going. What flight are you on?"* When I answered, she said, *"Uh-oh, that's the same flight we're on; you need to be careful."*

Well, that didn't sound good.

I took her to our table and introduced her to Linda, and the thrill of our honeymoon immediately ended. Jill told us she was called at the last moment to take this flight because of a terrorist threat at the Frankfurt airport, then added, *"But don't worry, there's no problem on this flight; we're just going there to keep the plane safe until it gets back to the States."* She kept assuring us there was no problem on our flight, but by the time she left, we were absolutely certain there was a serious problem. We finished our coffee, and I walked a very frightened young girl to our departure gate.

Just before it was time to board our plane, the chief FAA agent from Denver came to where we were sitting and offered his congratulations. I introduced him to Linda, and after a short conversation, he asked if he could borrow me for a couple of minutes. We walked several feet away and he reiterated there was no specific threat to our plane, but because Libyan Colonel Muammar Gaddafi had threatened to bomb the Frankfurt airport, he recommended that we get out of there as soon as we could. I thanked him for the heads up and walked back to Linda.

She was in tears!

"Oh, My God!! she cried, *"I'm only twenty-one-years-old and I'm going to die on my honeymoon!"* I tried to assure her that everything would be alright . . . that airports receive threats like this all the time, but her confidence was severely shaken when four plain clothes sky marshals boarded our plane and greeted me as one of their own.

When we finally taxied to our gate in Frankfurt, Linda grabbed my arm and dragged me down the aisle, then we rushed to the baggage claim area and anxiously watched for our bags to come down the belt. Linda's came right away, but mine never arrived. Murphy's Law was alive and well, and by the time I finished filling out the lost bag report, we were the last two people from our flight to leave the airport.

We rushed to the Bahnhof (train station) in the basement of the airport and caught our first class passage to Heidelberg for our first night's stay. My suitcase was delivered to our room just after we returned from dinner.

We toured the famous medieval Heidelberg Castle; continued on to Innsbruck, Austria (the host city for the 1964 Winter Olympics), took in a Tyrolean show in the town square, then went to Berchtesgaden, Germany, where we visited Hitler's Eagles Nest retreat at the peak of the foreboding but beautiful Kehlstein Mountain. Because of my fascination with World War II Germany, this was one of my favorite places. We continued to Hohenschwangau, Germany and toured Mad King Ludwig's Neuschwanstein Castle (the real Disneyland castle), followed by a long trip south through the beautiful Swiss Alps (with a glimpse of the majestic Matterhorn), and ended this leg of our journey in Lugano, Switzerland, where we ate and drank in old-world sidewalk cafés and sipped wine on a sunset cruise across Lake Lugano.

After a two-day visit, we headed for Paris, but our train only took us as far as Bern, Switzerland. We found a restaurant near the railroad station for dinner, then boarded our next train that we thought would take us to all the way to Paris.

Here's the first rule in train travel in Europe: always check the placards outside each railroad car that lists the originating departure city and the final city on its route. If your destination doesn't fall between these two cities, you're on the wrong train.

We didn't check.

There weren't a lot of people on the train, but because it was going to be an all-night trip, we didn't want to share our compartment with anyone else. If we were alone, we could pull the cushions from the opposing seats together to form a bed in the center of the room, so whenever anyone walked by our compartment, we acted like we were having a fight, just to make our room as uninviting as possible. It worked. The train pulled from the station and we were all alone. We quickly made our bed and cuddled in for what we hoped would be a full night's sleep.

Sometime around midnight, our train stopped in Basel, Switzerland. We were sound asleep and didn't realize we were stopped until railroad workers started banging on the outside of our car; yelling something in German we didn't understand. Finally, one of them yelled in English that we had to get off because our connecting train was ready to leave on another track. We jumped up and gathered our bags as quickly as we could, but by the time we got off the train, the Paris bound train was already leaving the station.

We just stood there, bags at our sides, and watched as our train crept out of view. We looked around the silent and ominously dark railroad yard, and saw that we weren't alone. Another hapless young American tourist had also slept through the transition, but he laughed at the absurdity of our situation and thought it was just another great story to tell his friends when he got home. We didn't share his feelings and weren't at all happy with the prospect of spending our night sleeping on hard wooden benches in a railroad depot. The three of us walked back to the station and found that another train would be leaving for Paris within the hour.

Our Eurail passes gave us first class passage, but we decided a sleeping berth would be the best way to continue our trip. I paid the small fee for the supplemental pass and we soon found our bedroom for the remainder of the night. There were two sets of single bunk beds in our compartment, but unfortunately, we had to share the room with another couple. I slept for most of the night, but the noise from the blinds rattling in the windows and Linda's concern about sharing our room with complete strangers kept her awake for the entire trip.

When we arrived, we found a cheap hotel across the street from the Gare Du Nord (the north train station), but it was much too early to check in. We left our bags at the reception desk and headed out to explore the city.

I'd been to Paris before, so I knew how to navigate the Metro subway system. Linda was sullen and quiet during the ride, but I was sure she'd cheer up when we made our first stop. As we walked from the underground stairs to the crowded city sidewalk, we turned, and there it was . . . the Eiffel Tower, in all its splendor! I looked at Linda and asked, *"Well, what do you think?"* She looked at the imposing tower (obviously not impressed), and said, *"I already saw it at King's Island,"* (an amusement park in Cincinnati). I'm sorry, I don't care how tired she was, that was not the reaction I was looking for.

By midafternoon, we returned to our hotel and found that our room was ready. It was a small room, but very clean, and had a large and inviting shower in the bathroom. We shared a hot shower, crawled into bed, and after fourteen hours of uninterrupted sleep, we were ready for our grand tour of Paris.

During our two day stay, we saw the Arc de Triomphe, Champs-Elysees, took a cruise down the River Seine past the legendary Left Bank, toured the Notre Dame Cathedral and the Louvre Art Museum, spent a day at the Palace of Versailles, and finished our Paris adventure with dinner on the Eiffel Tower.

We spent a day and night in Rouen, France (where Joan of Arc was burned at the stake on May 30th, 1431), then took a day trip to Le Havre, France, hoping to find passage to the infamous Omaha Beach (the beachhead depicted in Steven Spielberg's epic movie, Saving Private Ryan). We were within fifty or sixty miles of the battle site, but couldn't find anyone who'd ever heard of Omaha, Utah, Gold, Sword or Juno Beach, even when I collectively referred to them as Normandy Beach. Their refusal to help was either an arrogant response to my American accent, or they had a very clouded memory of their liberation, but in either case, I was deprived of the visit I'd always wanted to make.

We left the depot and walked to the train platform for our ride back to Paris, and in one final gesture of their inhospitality, a loud and rudely French seagull swept over the platform and made a large "deposit" on my head. I was convinced it was specifically trained for American tourists!

•

When we returned from our honeymoon, we quickly resumed our routine of getting together with Mom and Dad three or four nights a month for dinner and cards (and of course, that never empty bowl of popcorn Dad always had on hand).

During one of our regular visits, Mom and Linda were busy fixing dinner in the kitchen, and Dad and I were sitting at the table drinking our usual coffee. The television was on in the living room and suddenly the theme music "Bad Boy, Bad Boy" from the show COPS drifted into the kitchen. Dad sat straight up in his chair and said, *"Come on, kid, you've got to watch this—viewer discrimination advised."* Linda and I laughed at what we thought was an obvious Freudian slip, but when we saw the puzzled expression on his face, we knew he had no idea why we were laughing. Discretion and discrimination probably meant the same thing to him, but in our minds, his disclaimer was far more honest.

An evening of cards with Mom and Dad was a standard for me, no matter who I was married to, but I never had a wife as competitive in cards as Linda. Before she met me, she'd rarely played any type of card games at all, and probably hadn't even heard the term Pinochle before. But she was a quick study . . . actually, a little too quick!!

Dad and I played partners against Mom and Linda, but the competition was entirely between Dad and Linda. They had a special chemistry together and loved to taunt each other over the bid neither of them were willing to give up. The real fun of the game was watching the two of them in their battle of wills, while Mom and I sat back and laughed, perfectly content with our subordinate roles.

One night the bidding war reached epic proportions when they both had potentially great hands. A normal high bid was between forty and forty-five, but this time it reached an astounding sixty points. Linda really thought Dad was pushing his luck, and finally, frustrated by his stubbornness and refusal to give her the bid, said, *"I don't know what you think you have. I've got everything broke."* She reluctantly passed, and he named hearts as his trump suit. It was the worst suit he could have called! I moaned to myself as I passed him two bastard cards I knew couldn't help him, and a jack and ace of hearts, the only hearts in my hand. I watched his face for any reaction as he slowly lifted each card, then without any sign that he'd gotten what he needed, he laid down a thousand aces (100 points, the second highest meld in the game). Linda yelled FUCK! and Dad about fell out of his chair in shock. He turned bright red and busted out laughing, saying, *"I can't believe you just said that"* . . . then in a low and lecherous tone, murmured, *"Say it again."*

We laughed and laughed until tears streamed down our cheeks. It was one of the funniest moments we'd ever had, but was typical of the kind of fun we always had together.

Linda and I soon decided it was time for the pitter-patter of little feet in our house and bought a Lhasa Apso puppy. We took her to Mom and Dad's house for one of our regular get togethers, and even though Puddin' was such a cute little puppy, Dad wasn't at all impressed. When Linda handed her to him and said, *"Go see Grandpa,"* he snapped, *"I'm not any goddamned dog's grandpa"* and turned away. About ten minutes later, we all had a great laugh when he leaned down from his chair and said, *"Come here puppy, come to Grandpa."* And that was that . . . he was hooked.

Dad loved that little dog and insisted that we bring her with us whenever we came over. But we erred one night and left her at home. When Dad met us at the front door, he looked around and asked, *"Where's the dog?" "She's at home,"* we replied and he shut the door and walked back to his chair. Linda and I stood on the front porch, stared at the closed door and laughed, knowing who was more important.

•

Raising a dog without a yard to play or poop in really became a hassle, so in the winter of 1991, we started looking for another house. By now, Linda was working for her brother Steve at his foreclosure acquisition business, and had learned a great deal about the process of buying and selling homes. We looked at twenty or thirty homes before Linda found one she liked, but I was working on the day she previewed it, and didn't get a chance to look at the interior before closing day. But she told me it was a very nice home . . . I believe "crisp" was the term she used, and I trusted her judgment.

Linda sold our townhouse (by herself), and in January or February 1992, we moved into our $102,000, three-bedroom, two bath, two car garage, ranch style home at 5207 East Davies Drive. It was a very good price for a house this size, but once we moved in, we found a lot of problems. In addition to having to repair all the minor damage to the walls and doors, we had to restain all the trim work (including the sunroom and kitchen cabinets), install new carpet, paint the interior and exterior, hang new curtains and drapes, retile the kitchen floor, and replace all the kitchen appliances. And by the following summer we realized the grounds had been just as neglected as the house. The lawn was overrun with weeds, and several of the dormant trees weren't just in hibernation for the winter . . . they were completely dead. We had Swingle Tree and Lawn Care come out and cut down six or seven of our trees, and hired them for their regular weed control and lawn fertilizer service.

Linda loved working in the yard, and with the help of Swingle, nursed our lawn back to life. She mowed the lawn 99.9% of the time, and even though I felt kind of bad that she did most of the work, I didn't feel bad enough to volunteer to help. Instead, I'd sit in the shade of our porch, sip from a tall glass of iced tea, smoke my pipe, and raise my glass to toast her every time she looked my way.

Finishing her last pass in the front yard, she stopped, turned the mower off, dumped the grass clippings into a bag, then walked to the porch for a sip of tea. She wiped the sweat from her brow, turned and looked around and said, *"You know, I wonder just what kind of disability our neighbors think you have?"* I didn't care. The neighborhood women might have thought it was wrong, but the men thought I was a god.

My second wife, Cheri Gruben

My third wife, Karen Nicastle

This is me as a 30-year-old
Denver Police Sergeant

My son, Kevin Edward

FOUR GENERATIONS OF AUMILLERS

Dad, Granddad Aumiller, Kevin and Me

Me, Kevin and Darrell Bolton—I guess he was taller than me

My stunning fourth
wife, Linda Navaro,
being escorted
down the aisle by
her dad, Richard

A Perfect Wedding!

My Childhood Home—1340 W. Alice Place-A

Linda's Childhood Home—3919 Eileen Drive

Who was spoiled?

The Couple of the Hour

Me, Dad, Mom & June
Their 50th anniversary, but June & I still claimed to be in our 30s

50th Wedding Anniversary
June, Dad, Mom, Darlene & Me

June, Me, Mom & Linda

Mom and Dad
Just like the Good Old Days

CHAPTER 24

"Mom and Dad's Retirement Years"

When Dad retired on January 16th, 1973, Mom quit her job at Monaghans, and the two of them settled into the next phase of their lives.

Dad had been the family's unofficial mechanic for as many years as I can remember, and *everyone* came to him when they had car trouble. He considered working on cars to be more of a pleasure than work, and now that he was retired, had much more time to enjoy his one and only hobby. He continued with the painstaking care of his home and yard, but also found time to meet with friends for drinks at Sherry's Lounge, 1910 South Depew Street or his old standard, the Big O at Florida and Federal Boulevard. Mom occasionally joined him for a drink or two, but spent most of her time bowling or playing golf with her friends, and devoted as much time as she could to her beloved grandchildren. But by the following year, all but one of the grandkids were gone, and with only our months old son still around to dote after, Kevin definitely got a lot of her attention.

Now that they were "free, free at last," a whole new world of social activities opened for them, and they started spending a lot more time with their old friends at their favorite neighborhood bar, the Big O.

It was an unappealing no-frills little bar, but was filled with some very friendly people. I know I'm probably forgetting some of them, but the friends I still remember were their neighbors Bob and Judy Leslie, then Chick and Norma Miyoshi (Norma was a childhood friend of Mom's), Milt and Donna Rish, Elmer and Lou Koch, Carl and Dee Huerta, Roger and Mary Jensen, Gene and Mae Van Dyke, Bob and Betty

Buddecke, Ernie Hand, Nancy Knox, and three of my fellow officers, Abe and Amy Alonzo and Don Gillespi.

Mom and Dad were proud owners of season tickets to the Denver Bronco games, and spent many cold and snowy Sunday afternoons with their friends drinking and cheering from the notorious south stands of the old Mile High Stadium. And when the Broncos weren't playing at home, they'd all get together at someone's house to watch the game on television, and win or lose, everyone always had a great time.

This same group of friends would occasionally get together for an entire week of fishing and partying aboard a luxurious houseboat at Lake Powell in southeast Utah, or fly to Las Vegas or Elko, Nevada, for weekends of unbridled gambling. And to help fill the gaps in their spare time, Mom and Dad joined the Flounder Heads bowling league and spent the next several years bowling with our cousins Pudge and Bud Bullock, and Ray and Phillis Stoumbaugh.

They partied a lot, but were never deterred from driving when they'd had too much to drink. Thankfully, they only lived six blocks from the bar, so the short drive home lessened the odds of getting into trouble and they were never stopped by the police. Dad was probably the most honest man I'd ever known and had a tremendous respect for the law, but he never gave a second thought about driving after he'd been drinking. It was something I never understood, and always worried about.

•

Sometime in the late 1950s or early 60s, Grandma Oldson and Aunt Daisy sold their house on Galapago Street and bought a new mobile home. They lived at the Shady Nook mobile home park at 4325 Morrison Road until Aunt Daisy moved to Ogden, Utah to live with her daughter Maxine and her husband Vaughn McKenzie.

Grandma moved to a basement apartment in the 1300 block of South Decatur Street, then after a few months, moved to a senior citizen high-rise condominium at 19th and Larimer Streets in downtown Denver. Shortly after Mom and Dad retired, they invited Grandma to live with them, where she stayed until her death on Thursday, August 28th, 1975. She died of pneumonia at St. Anthony's Hospital, and was buried at Fairmont Cemetery. She was eighty-eight-years-old.

Her sister Daisy was born on October 16th, 1880 in Mount Vernon, Illinois, and was married to Isaac Curtis Smith from Thursday, July 25th, 1912 until his death on Saturday, March 24th, 1945. He was the town marshal in Cawker City, Kansas, but I have no idea how long he held that position. Aunt Daisy died at the age of ninety-seven on Sunday, January 29th, 1978 in the Ogden Nursing Home in Ogden, Utah, and was buried in the Prairie Grove Cemetery in Cawker City, Kansas.

●

For the next several years, Mom and Dad made annual pilgrimages to one of their favorite places: Las Vegas, Nevada. But they weren't there for the shows or buffets . . . they were there for some serious hardcore gambling. Mom spent her days at the two-dollar Blackjack tables, and Dad would belly up to the bar and spend his days playing the 25-cent video poker machines. Mom usually made a little money, but Dad always seemed to be the big winner, and frequently came home with more than a thousand dollars in winnings.

But their favorite trips were to Phoenix to visit with Charlie and Dad's sister Annie. They were the rich ones in the family (owned a dairy) and lived each day like it was a party. Social drinking was elevated to an art form with them, and when Mom and Dad were there, it didn't get any more social. They'd party all night long, then get up early the next morning and start all over again.

Charlie flew cargo and troop planes over Europe and Africa during World War II, and continued to fly as a hobby in civilian life. During Mom and Dad's many trips to Phoenix, he'd fly them in his twin-engine Beechcraft to Hermosillo, San Carlos, Guaymas, and Puerto Vallarta, Mexico for days of partying and deep sea fishing, and even flew them to Acapulco when two of his friends, Claude and Alice Sharpenstein were married. Mom said they had a wonderful time, but I had to laugh when she told me about their trip. I think it's time to admit you're getting old when you invite two other couples along on your honeymoon just to make sure you have something to do in your free time.

But Charlie and Annie's generosity didn't stop with their trips to Mexico. They also took Mom and Dad to New Orleans (a fitting town for their level of partying), and to the beautiful Hawaiian island of Kauai. Kauai is known as the Garden Island, and the exotic location for the movies South Pacific, Blue Hawaii and Jurassic Park.

They stayed at the exquisite Waiohai Resort on Poipu Beach, where Dad spent most of his time watching sports on television in the comfort of his air conditioned hotel room, while the rest of them toured the island then drank Mai Tai's at the pool or beach. We all have our priorities, but I can't help but believe Dad's would have changed if there'd been half-naked hula dancers luring him to this part of heaven.

Before leaving the Hawaiian Islands, they flew to Oahu, where in a more somber moment, they toured the USS Arizona Memorial at Pearl Harbor. It was a heartrending experience to stand over the battleship where 1,177 sailors were still entombed following the Japanese invasion of 1941, and evoked some powerful memories of the tragic death of Uncle Lyle at the hands of Japanese forces so many years before.

●

In the summer of 1978, Charlie and Annie got out of the dairy business and opened a new mobile home park in the Phoenix area. Mom and Dad moved there for a few months to help set it up, and when they returned home, used their earnings to upgrade their kitchen. They replaced the old white metal cabinets with dark wooden cabinets, retiled the floor and counter tops, and turned a dated and plain kitchen into a beautiful and modern showcase.

Dad was meticulous with the maintenance of his house and would regularly paint the interior and exterior himself, but the remodeled kitchen was only the second actual upgrade they'd made to their house. In 1961, several of Dad's firemen friends poured a huge concrete patio at the rear of the house that added a whole new dimension to their home entertainment. The house provided shade in the late afternoons and there was rarely a summer day that wasn't spent with company in the cool comfort of the outdoors. These same firemen offered to cover the patio and build an attached garage on the south side of the house, and like the patio, they'd do it all for the cost of materials. It couldn't get any cheaper than that, but Dad turned it down. He just couldn't bring himself to add anything to his house that would increase his property taxes, and in the end, it always came down to the money.

Early in 1982, Charlie and Annie asked Mom and Dad if they'd be interested in returning to manage their mobile home park for a few months. They thought it was a great idea, and this time, made a one-year commitment. They rented their house to my cousin Marci (Ray and Phillis Stombaugh's daughter) and her husband Jug; packed whatever clothes they needed, and moved to Phoenix. They lived in one of Charlie's furnished double-wide mobile homes in the park, and for the next full year, worked and partied hard with two of their all-time favorite people.

By the time they moved back to Denver in the summer of 1983, things had dramatically changed. Cheri and I'd separated on August 1st, 1982, and I was now living with my future wife Karen and her three-year-old daughter Laura. My divorce from Cheri would be final on Tuesday, January 3rd, 1984.

It was great to have Mom and Dad back in town again, and a feeling of normality began when my new family was welcomed into their home. I had custody of Kevin on weekends, and on those days, we were frequent guests at Mom and Dad's house for two of my favorite things: dinner and cards.

Mom & Dad - A typical night out

Also typical

385

Friends from the Big O at Lake Powell —
Dad must have been taking the picture

A good day in Las Vegas
after a $1,000 win

A better day —
$1,500.00 jackpot

Dad, Mom, Claude & Alice
In front of Charlie's plane in Acapulco

The Good Life

Having a really good time in Mexico
(Just how drunk do you think Dad was?)

Dad & Charlie
Having a gay time

Dad
In one of his favorite settings

Dad fishing in Mexico

Mom with a pretty good catch

Dad, Annie, Mom, Alice, Claude & Charlie in Acapulco —
on Claude & Alice's Honeymoon

The French Quarter in New Orleans

Mom & Dad in Kauai, Hawaii

Dad, Mom, Charlie & Annie on tour in Kauai

CHAPTER 25

"The Good, the Bad . . . and the Ugly"

1992 was a year of doom and gloom. Johnny Carson left the Tonight Show, Prince Charles and Princess Diana separated, Bill Clinton was elected President . . . and Darlene turned fifty. *Oh, the agony!!*

Darlene *really* wasn't looking forward to her upcoming birthday, so Mom and Dad drove to Washington to stay with her for a week or two, just to help cheer her up. That sounded like a good idea, so Linda and I decided to drive out on our own, and Mom and Dad agreed that it would probably be more fun if we just surprised her by showing up unannounced a day or two before her birthday. We had a beautiful new custom cobalt blue and white GMC van, complete with four plush oversized reclining captain chairs, accent and overhead reading lights and individually controlled air/heat vents (just like on an airplane, but with far more seat and leg room) . . . a VCR and nine inch color television set, big full-view side windows to enjoy the scenery, and a rear bench seat that folded into a queen size bed with the simple flip of a switch . . . the perfect mode of transportation for such a long and exhausting road trip.

We stopped in Grand Junction on our way and picked up June and her son Tommy, but our motive for this journey wasn't nearly as virtuous or selfless as Mom and Dad's. They'd gone to offer Darlene their love and support in her time of need—we were making the thousand-mile trip just to make fun of her in person. That's what brothers and sisters do.

We arrived in Kalama on Sunday afternoon, June 21st. It was a pretty little town . . . not really a lot of streets to choose from, but the few winding hillside roads were just confusing enough to get us lost at the very first fork in the road. Linda called the house for directions, and luckily, Dad answered the phone. He didn't want to spoil the surprise of our visit, so in a game of twenty questions, he'd only answer yes or no until she was able to deduce the route to their home. We should have just gone to a gas station for directions.

Dad was waiting by the side of the road when we drove up to their driveway, and snuck us into the house through the front door. Darlene was busy peeling potatoes at the kitchen sink when we crept in behind her, and to our delight, was completely surprised to see us. That was the good news, the bad that she had four unexpected guests in her home; all hungry and whining for dinner. But that was okay . . . she'd learned well from Mom's past social experiences and "just threw another potato in the pot," and magically had enough to feed us all. We spent the rest of the evening sitting out on their deck; drinking and smoking and having a great time . . . the women talking about recipes, kids and their work, while the men lamented over the demise of everything good at the hands of the left-wing establishment.

The next day, Mom and Dad stayed home with Darlene, while Bob took the rest of us, including his grandson Jessie on an afternoon tour of the Columbia River. The six of us rode comfortably as Bob raced up and down the river in his new and powerful boat, and the only thing that kept me from getting hopelessly sick was the constant bouncing across the waves instead of the gentle bobbing of an idle boat. Bob did well!

On Tuesday, Bob stayed at home to work, Tommy went to Portland with Robbie, and the rest of us loaded up in my van and Darlene guided us on a tour of northern Oregon. We visited the quaint little town of Astoria, the reconstructed Lewis and Clark Village, the concrete seawall bunkers at the World War II military compound at Fort Stevens, and ended our tour searching for crabs on our walk along the beach in Long Beach, Washington. Dad had been having problems with his hip for the past two or three years, so he didn't get out of the van to do any of the sightseeing with us. Instead, he opted to sit in the comfort of one of the "lieutenant" chairs in the back of our van, and napped and smoked the entire time we were gone . . . it was like he'd never left his living room. With nightfall rapidly approaching, we returned home to continue with the family's traditional favorite pastime: playing cards.

On Wednesday, June 24th, we took Darlene shopping at her favorite little boutique in Kalama, then celebrated her birthday that evening with a store-bought cake and plenty of presents. And despite of our snide and vicious remarks about her age, we had a truly great time! Fortunately, I videotaped most of our visit, because this turned out to be the last time we'd all be together.

•

By that fall, Linda and Mom began their second year of league bowling on Tuesday nights, and while they were out raising hell with all their friends, Dad and I stayed at home . . . all alone . . . in the dark . . . cold and hungry . . . and forced to fix our own meals. It's a wonder we didn't starve to death.

When spring came, the bowling season ended and they made plans for their big banquet on Tuesday, May 4th, 1993. Dad asked me to take the night off from work so he and I could go drinking at the American Legion Hall at 5110 Morrison Road, but because most of my experience with bars involved breaking up fights or handling shootings and cuttings, my first reaction was to decline. I had nothing against drinking, and certainly never held back at private parties, but bars never seemed to me to be good places to go for entertainment. After thinking about it for awhile, though, it occurred to me this was probably Dad's favorite thing to do (and something I never did with him), so I finally said, *"Yeah, let's do it."*

I drove Linda to Mom and Dad's house, and when she and Mom left for their evening out with the girls, Dad drove me to the Hall. The place was almost empty when we got there, and I was happy to see that the few people who were in the bar didn't look like the kind of people I'd have to worry about fighting. We sat at the bar, ordered a couple of beers and began to talk.

It was always easy to talk with Dad. He really was my best friend, and we had years of experiences and common interests to share with each other. When we had our second beer, Dad got a little more talkative, but beer really wasn't my kind of drink, and definitely wasn't strong enough to get me to that special place I wanted to be. When it was time for my next round, I switched to my favorite drink, Jack Daniels and Coke, and in no time at all, I started feeling *"pretty darn good."*

The bar was getting busier and a lot noisier by now, and Dad introduced me to some of the people he knew. We started having the kind of fun I think you're supposed to have in a bar, and every time the barmaid came by to offer another drink, we'd flirt with her with all the enticement two drunk old geezers could offer, then sat back and watched as she rolled her eyes; shook her head, and walked away muttering to herself, *"Why me?"* Who says booze doesn't make you more attractive to women?

Dad talked about his life in the army; the great times he'd had on the fire department, and about all the jobs he'd had in his life. He talked about his childhood in Selden, then told me about how mad he got when his dad married Opal. Dad and Opal had always gotten along well with each other for all the years I could remember, but I knew there'd been a lot of animosity between them when they were young, and thought he'd fill me in on all the sordid details now that we were both so drunk. He didn't tell me about any of their early fights, but told me the reason he got so mad at his dad was because he wanted Opal for himself. **WOW!** I really didn't see that one coming and was really shocked! But I promised I wouldn't tell Mom if he bought me some potato chips . . . and this time, I kept my word.

The following Sunday, May 9th, was Mother's Day, and we had Mom and Dad to our house on Davies for dinner and a few games of Pinochle. It was another great night with the two of them . . . full of love and a lot of laughter, but it turned out to be the last time I'd see Dad alive.

Just four days later, on Thursday, May 13th, 1993, Dad started the last day of his life just like he'd done ten thousand times before. Mom fixed their usual fried eggs, potatoes and bacon for breakfast, then puttered around the house with her cleaning chores while Dad sat at the kitchen table and read the Denver Post; smoked a cigarette or two, and sipped from his heavily creamed and sweetened cup of coffee. When he finished with the paper, he settled into his easy chair to watch TV, and Mom poured herself a cup of tea and sat down at the table to work her crossword puzzles.

When they finished lunch early that afternoon, they played a couple of games of Spite and Malice, and within minutes after getting his butt severely kicked, Dad started having chest pains he tragically misjudged as just another case of indigestion. He nursed himself with all the remedies that usually worked for him, but today none of them seemed to help. The pain got steadily worse as the day progressed, and by that evening it was so bad, Mom told him she was going to take him to the hospital. He scoffed at the mere thought of her doing that and snapped, *"I don't want to die in some goddamn hospital. I'll be alright here."* But by 11pm, he couldn't stand the pain any longer and had Mom call for an ambulance.

Mom tried to call me from Swedish Hospital, but I was already en route to work, and since I didn't have a cell phone in those days, I wouldn't hear about Dad's condition until I arrived at the airport. When I got off the elevator on the third floor of the Core Building in the main parking structure, I was met by Phil Gotlin (one of my sergeants and a very good friend) who greeted me with the news. He said he was told it wasn't serious, but Mom still wanted me to meet with her as soon as I could.

There was no sense of urgency as I drove to the hospital, and when I arrived at the Emergency Room, one of the nurses told me Dad was being attended to in one of the treatment rooms and asked if I wanted to see him first, or go to the waiting room with Mom and Linda. I chose poorly.

I just sat down with Mom and Linda after pouring myself a cup of coffee, when I heard *"Core Zero, Room Such and Such"* blare from the P.A. system. I knew what that meant and half whispered, *"Uh-oh! Someone's having a heart attack."* Visibly shaken, Mom jumped from her chair and yelled, **"That's Kennedy's Room!"** We raced to find his room and were met by his doctor just outside the door. He told us Dad had suffered a massive heart attack and they'd already tried several times to revive him, but he was gone. He died at 1:20 am on Friday, May 14th, 1993, at the age of seventy-three.

He looked like he'd just gone to sleep and there was no evidence of the pain and trauma he'd just been through. He was at peace now, but seeing his lifeless body and knowing I'd never be able to talk with him again was the second most painful thing I'd ever experienced, and it was an ***incredibly*** difficult moment for me.

After I finally managed to compose myself, I called my sister Darlene. I thought I was okay by then, but when she answered the phone, I couldn't even speak. My throat was completely paralyzed, and the only sound I could make was a simple gasp as she kept saying, *"Hello . . . Hello."* I was so afraid she'd think it was a prank call and hang up on me, and the only thing I could think to do was hand the phone to Linda. It shouldn't have fallen on her shoulders, but she was the one who had to deliver the horrible news of Dad's death, and I'm eternally grateful to her for how well she handled it! I don't remember for sure now, but I think Darlene made the call to June.

Mom called Aunt Rainie, and she and Uncle Bill arrived while we were still in the room with Dad. After about an hour, Mom asked the hospital Chaplain to say a prayer for Dad, and as we were leaving the room, Uncle Bill stood beside Dad; gently touched his arm and said, *"Goodbye old buddy."* It had been a great friendship!

While I was driving Mom home, she broke into tears and said, *"I'm not ready for this!"* I tried to comfort her as best I could, but the truth is I wasn't ready for it either. ***None Of Us Were!*** Dad had been sedentary for quite some time now, and looked and acted much older than he was, but none of us expected him to die this soon.

Dad's half-brother Truman and his precious wife Bonnie were waiting at the curb when we arrived and tearfully consoled us as the reality of Dad's death set in. By noon, the house was filled with friends and family, and for the first time in her marriage, Mom was the center of attention. With each new visitor, she'd describe her last day with Dad, and seemed to get stronger with each new telling. Talking with all that company definitely made it easier for her to deal with her loss.

Around 3pm, Linda and I went home for a nap, and when we returned later that evening, we brought Puddin' with us. While the rest of us sat at the kitchen table, Puddin' sat mournfully on the living room floor, whimpering as she stared at Dad's empty easy chair . . . knowing instinctively that he was no longer alive. *It was a very rough night!*

We said our final goodbyes to Dad at his viewing on the cold and drizzly afternoon of Tuesday, May 18th, and on the much warmer following day, Wednesday, May 19th, 1993 at 2pm, the entire family and dozens of friends gathered to pay their final respects at his funeral service at Fort Logan National Cemetery. He's buried on Denver Drive, in Section 4, Grave 2772.

Dad and I never actually said the words, but there was never a doubt in either of our minds about the love we felt for each other, and even though he wasn't a touchy kind of man, he always greeted me with a smile and firm handshake . . . and those handshakes were all the hugs I ever needed!

And I was so thankful for that special night Dad and I spent drinking together just fifteen days earlier!! I can't remember another time in my life that just the two of us had that much fun, and in some small way, I think it helped make up for my missing his retirement party some twenty years before.

I rarely saw Opal or my aunts before Dad died, but from that day on, Opal, Rochella, Roberta, Mona and Roxie became a huge part of my family. They were there for Mom from the very beginning, and over the next thirteen years, treated her like their sister and included her in nearly every one of their family activities.

Mom missed the love and constant companionship of their fifty-four year marriage, but was torn between her enormous grief and unfamiliar new freedom. She was alone now, but for the first time in her life, she could do whatever she wanted, whenever she wanted. This was a freedom she'd never experienced before and made her loss much easier to deal with.

Dad didn't believe in life insurance, so there were no cash bonuses when he died, but money wasn't a problem. Mom had more than $30,000 in cash and stocks, and a widow's pension equal to two-thirds of Dad's original pension. They paid off their house when Dad retired in 1973, so the only monthly bills she had were for her car and the peripherals of normal home ownership (utilities, water and telephone), and between her new pension and Social Security checks, she was able to live quite comfortably for the remainder of her years.

The week after Dad was buried, she spread her newfound wings and went on an unrestricted and guilt-free shopping spree. She bought as many new clothes as she wanted, and even bought a new electric typewriter. It was something she'd always wanted but could never have, because Dad thought it was a frivolous waste of money. She used it to write thank you notes for all the generous cash gifts she'd received to help offset the funeral expenses, but as it turned out, writing wasn't nearly as much fun as she'd imagined, and she never typed again. In the end, Dad just may have been right.

For the next few years, Mom stayed as active as she could. She bowled in leagues three days a week, went on gambling junkets to Black Hawk, Central City and Cripple Creek with Aunt Rainie, Opal, and our cousin Juanita Small, and she and Opal spent a lot of their afternoons and evenings donating their money to the neighborhood Bingo parlor. She took a few trips to Las Vegas with the Aumiller girls, and even took a cruise around Nova Scotia with one of her lady friends. And for the next several years, the "girls" would get together at Mom's house for some lively games of cards.

On weekends during the summer months, Linda and I would meet with Mom at the John F. Kennedy or Harvard Gulch Golf Courses for some very non-competitive rounds of par-three golf. We all golfed with the same handicap . . . no talent . . . but that didn't stop us from having a great time! And we always ended our day with lunch at one of our favorite restaurants.

•

In the beginning, Crystal, Pam and Becky (my sister June's girls), would come to Mom's house to offer their support and help in any way they could, but eventually Mom's home became a safe haven for them whenever they needed shelter or a helping hand.

Pam lived with Mom for several months while she was going through a rough patch in her life, and when her ex-husband Bret died of a drug overdose, Mom opened her heart and home to Pam's teenage daughter Alisha. Alisha lived with Mom for a year or two, then left when she finished high school.

Sometime around 1996, when Pam's new marriage ended, she brought her two-year-old son Zephaniah (Zeffie) to live with Mom, and while Pam was "indisposed" for the next two years, Mom raised Zeffie as her own. Then on Sunday, December, 13th, 1998, at just thirty-nine-years-old, Pam also died, and within weeks, the courts awarded custody of Zeffie to his paternal grandparents.

By now Alisha was living on her own and had a job with the U.S. Bank. In August 1999, she asked Mom to co-sign for a $10,000 line of credit, and promised she'd take care of her obligations *("Oh, Grandma, don't worry . . . I'd never make you pay for any of this.")* Mom willingly signed, and for the next four years, everything seemed to go along smoothly.

We were all proud of how well Alisha was doing, especially since she'd lost both parents while she was so young. She found a new job selling cars at Emich Oldsmobile just off East Colfax near Quebec Street, and soon bought a new Oldsmobile Allero and a condominium in Aurora . . . and even took a trip to Hawaii. By all outward appearances, she was very successful. (We'll revisit this story in Chapter 26).

●

In May 1994, after working for four years as her brother Steve's assistant in the foreclosure market, Linda quit her job and went to work for Dann Degan (one of our neighbors) as his assistant at Re/Max Masters. She had no desire to sell real estate, but earned her real estate license in order to better understand what was expected of her, and to help Dann with his showings whenever he wasn't available.

In 1997, Dann helped sell our house on Davies and brokered the purchase of our first new home at 9228 South Foxfire Drive. We moved in on Saturday, June 21st, 1997.

It was a beautiful four-bedroom, two and a half bath, two-story house, with a formal dining and living room, three fireplaces, a recreation room and office, and three-car garage. At $254,000, it was by far the best home I'd ever had, and even though people with real money might laugh at how inexpensive it was, owning it was an incredible achievement for a man of my background.

In October 1997, after three and a half years with Dann, Linda quit her job, and on Saturday, November 8th, went to work for Jim Wanzeck (the co-owner of Re/Max Masters) at nearly double her previous pay. If I'd known she was going to make that much money, I'd have bought a bigger house.

•

On Thursday, December 25th, 1997, we took Mom with us to Ft. Collins for what should have been another wonderful Christmas celebration with my daughter Kim and her three precious little girls. When we walked through their door with our arms filled with presents, everyone was thrilled to see us... except for my six-year-old granddaughter Ashley, who'd been sick since early that morning. By the time we arrived, she could barely move from the couch, and remained there during our entire visit. Every now and again she'd struggle to raise her head from her pillow to watch the girls open their presents (too weak to open her own), then after a few brief moments, she'd meekly settle back down to rest, trying her best not to spoil the party for everyone else. It broke our hearts to see her like this.

Kim took her to the hospital as soon as we left, and within hours discovered the horrible news . . . Ashley had Type One Diabetes (children's diabetes), and would require daily insulin shots for the rest of her life. It was a life-altering event for such a fragile little girl (and her mother), but one they both handled with extraordinary ease. She bravely learned how to test her own blood/sugar levels and administer her shots by herself, but when she started high school several years later, she was stricken with fibro myalgia (an aggravated condition of fibrous tissue and acute muscle pain); scoliosis (curvature of the spine), and severe bouts of vomiting and depression even a parade of doctors couldn't control. Yes, life isn't always fair, and this is a perfect example of just how unfair it can be. She's always been such a shy and sweet little girl, and is much, much too good to suffer like this . . . we can only pray that she can find relief with the passing of time.

•

On January 28th, 2001, I finally retired. I'd spent the past thirty-six years doing something I absolutely loved, and between the inherent dangers of police work and the diversity of four different wives, I'd experienced more excitement, more pleasure and far more grief than any one man could possibly deserve. Every fantasy or desire I'd ever had was fulfilled, and the only things left on my bucket list were the names of the very few places I still wanted to see.

Traveling has always been my way of proving to myself that I wasn't poor (like Dad's affinity for new cars), and is something I enjoy more than anything else. And with the freedom Linda and I've enjoyed during our (now) twenty-five years together, we've been able to take some incredible trips. If I died tomorrow, I'd still be a happy man . . . I've done everything I'd ever wanted . . . *it's been a wonderful life!*

Reading about our trips is a stroll down Memory Lane for Linda and me, but if you get bored and want to skip ahead, I'd completely understand. However, if you're still interested, I'll keep it as brief as I can.

Our travel adventures began with Linda's nineteenth birthday celebration in San Francisco, and continued with our first trip to Puerto Vallarta in 1987, where we sunned ourselves on the sandy beaches, parasailed over the Banderas Bay, rode horse-back in the nearby mountains, then flew to Disneyland for Linda's very first visit.

In 1988, we took my son Kevin to Disneyworld and the Epcot Center to celebrate his fourteenth and my forty-fourth birthday; Linda and I drove through the Black Hills of South Dakota and stood in awe at the base of Mount Rushmore, then flew to Las Vegas on her twenty-first birthday, where she sat at a Black-Jack table; drank her very first legal drink... took a long draw on her filtered cigarette and smugly said, *"Hit me."* Then in 1989, seven months later, we left for the storybook European honeymoon I'd always wanted.

In November 1990, we drove to San Antonio for Don and Tonia's wedding (Don is Linda's brother), visited The Alamo and cruised the canals at the River Walk, then in 1991, we took Kevin with us on a road trip to the Grand Canyon in Arizona.

We drove to Kalama, Washington in 1992 to visit Darlene and Bob (for Darlene's fiftieth birthday), then flew to the eclectic city of Vancouver, Canada; toured the old Gastown section, then took a spectacularly beautiful ferry ride to the simple quaintness of Victoria, British Columbia. We stayed at the elegant old Empress Hotel, where we ate tiny little scones and sipped High Tea (at fifty dollars a cup), took an intimate dinner cruise around the bay, visited the amazing Butchart Gardens, and toured the historic graystone Craigdarroch Castle.

We flew to Cincinnati to visit the Navaro family in 1993, and returned the following year for Tom's surprise fortieth birthday party. That same year, we flew back to Kalama with Mom, and fished for salmon on the Columbia River, witnessed the still vivid destruction of the 1980 Mount St. Helen's eruption, then in 1995, we drove to Carlsbad Caverns, White Sands, and Santa Fe, New Mexico.

In 1996, we flew to Boston for an autumn tour of New England; found our sea legs aboard the USS Constitution, visited the Bull and Finch Pub (where the exterior shots of Cheers were filmed) and had lunch and a beer upstairs in the restaurant we all know as Melville's. We took a guided city tour, then basked in the beauty of the Boston Commons . . . ending our day with dinner and a show at one of the city's comedy clubs.

We continued to Salem to visit The House of Seven Gables (from Nathaniel Hawthorne's famous novel), and toured the Witch Museum and Cemetery where the tortured witches were buried. We drove to the site of Plymouth Rock and stood at the very spot where the pilgrims landed in 1620, then toured a replica of the Mayflower that brought them all to America. We drove the entire stretch of old Cape Cod, ending our trip in the super festive (gay) town of Provincetown, then took a ferry (the floating kind) to Martha's Vineyard and toured most of the island by Jeep.

We stayed at the Maine Stay Bed and Breakfast Inn in the quaint little town of Kennebunkport, Maine (seeing the Bush Compound in the bay and old-world lighthouses along the coastline), then drove down rural country roads and across picturesque hundred-year-old covered bridges in New Hampshire and Vermont; enraptured by the full autumn foliage that make them such inviting places to visit. We stopped to see the Great Stone Face of the Old Man of the Mountain, then stayed at the exquisite Mill Fall Inn overlooking Lake Winnipeaukee in Meredith, New Hampshire. We ended our vacation in Woodstock, Vermont, and stayed at the Lincoln Inn, a quaint little bed and breakfast that was originally owned by Abraham Lincoln when I was just a boy.

In 1997, we took my daughter Kim and her girls to Disneyland and Universal Studios for an incredible summer vacation; drove Mom to Albuquerque in 1998 for the hot air balloon festival on her seventy-sixth birthday, then celebrated our tenth wedding anniversary in 1999 on a Caribbean Cruise that began in San Juan, Puerto Rica. We drank non-stop for the next seven days while we toured the islands of St. Thomas, Guadeloupe, St. Lucia and Grenada, then bought Cuban cigars at our last stop at Santo Domingo in the Dominican Republic.

In 2000, we snorkeled in the clear turquoise waters of the Caribbean Sea and tanned ourselves on the pure white beach at the Fiesta Americana Cozumel Dive Resort . . . returned to Cincinnati for a family reunion, lost our shirts one more time in Las Vegas, then enjoyed Sunday brunch at the famous Hotel Del Coronado on a weekend flight to San Diego.

Three weeks after I retired in 2001, we flew to Maui for my fifty-seventh birthday and stayed at the Marriott Hotel in Kaanapali; took a helicopter tour over the entire island . . . went on a whale watching excursion, sailed on a submarine to see the variety of local fish, and went to an incredible luau on the hotel strip.

We spent an entire day winding our way around more than six-hundred mountainous curves, and crossed fifty-four single car bridges on the *excruciatingly long* fifty mile drive to Hana . . . but the serenity of the gentle waves breaking against the coastal rocks and the bounty of lush tropical flora and cascading hill-side waterfalls made the trip more than worth the effort.

We flew to Oahu for a one-day visit and toured the USS Arizona Memorial at Pearl Harbor; the USS Bowfin (a World War II submarine), and the awe-inspiring USS Missouri (the Mighty Mo); the battleship the Japanese formally surrendered on while anchored in Tokyo Bay on Sunday, September 2nd, 1945, ending World War II.

Two months after the horror of 9/11, we penned our Last Will and Testament and took a second Caribbean cruise with our friends Steve and Diane McCray; this time adding the islands of Martinique, Curacao and Aruba to our list of exotic ports of call.

But not all of our trips were for pleasure. Shortly after I retired, we flew to Cincinnati to visit with Linda's father (who was suffering from the debilitating effects of Alzheimer's disease), and returned a second time following his premature death on Monday, December 17th, 2001. It was an especially horrible day for his wife Jayne (who Linda and I both adore), but it brought all of his children together for one of the very few times since I became a member of their family, and I was privileged to hear them reminisce about their childhood years with their father.

We flew back to Maui in 2002 with two of our best friends for my fifty-eighth birthday and stayed in a high-rise condominium just two or three miles north of the Marriott Hotel. We drove to the very top of the island's Haleakala Volcano and saw a landscape so barren, we could have been on the moon. We had a horrible cheeseburger at the inviting Cheeseburger in Paradise Restaurant (who would have thought), then enjoyed Warren and Annabelle's magic show in the festive town of Lahaina. We had a great day snorkeling off the Molokini Island, then nearly lost my policeman friend to the riptide on a boogie board incident in the Maalaea Bay. We celebrated his survival on an evening dinner cruise along the island's beaut- iful coastline.

In 2003, we took a spectacular trip to Pre-Hurricane Katrina New Orleans, then celebrated our fourteenth wedding anni- versary at the rustic Old Faithful Inn in Yellowstone National Park; ending our trip at the Grand Teton Mountains and Jackson Hole, Wyoming. We ended the year with a trip to Tucson for Holly and Jeremy's wedding (Holly's Linda's brother Greg's daughter).

We returned to Europe in 2004 for an early celebration of our fifteenth wedding anniversary, and drove the Romantic Road through the ancient towns of Frankfurt, Wurzburg, Bad Mergentheim, Rothenberg and Garmisch . . . continued on to Berchtesgaden, and Munich, Germany (with a somber tour of the Dachau Concentration Camp), then stayed in Bolzano, Italy, where we saw the frozen remains of the Ice Man, Otzi, who died on the Schul Valley glacier in the northern Alps of Italy 5,300 years ago. We ended our trip in the enchanting city of Venice, where we took a romantic gondola ride under the Bridge of Sighs and listened to the dueling orchestras in St. Mark's Square while we sipped Italian wine in the briskness of the evening's crisp Adriatic air.

We flew back to Puerto Vallarta for more fun in the sun on Linda's thirty-seventh birthday, saw Elton John and the Broadway show Mamma Mia on a trip to Las Vegas in 2005 for my sixty-first birthday, then flew to Mazatlán with two of our best friends for an early celebration of our sixteenth wedding anniversary. We climbed to the peak of the El Faro Lighthouse (the second highest natural lighthouse in the world); got **"LOST"** in the coconut groves of the nearby Stone Island, then I watched in amazement as Linda talked our way out of a ticket by telling a city policeman my erratic driving friend was a "Retardo Policeman," when she really meant he was retired.

We ended 2005 with a flight to Houston with my mother-in-law Mary for the first of three consecutive Thanksgiving holiday visits with Linda's sister Cindy, Russell and their two girls.

We flew to London in 2006 for an early celebration of my sixty-second birthday, and spent four nights at the luxurious Chesterfield Mayfair Hotel. We toured Buckingham Palace, Westminster Abbey, St. Paul's Cathedral, Piccadilly Circus, Trafalgar Square, and chatted with English bobbies just outside the Prime Minister's residence at #10 Downing Street. We cruised the Thames River to the Tower Bridge and the infamous Tower of London, where we saw the impressive collection of the Queen's famous Crown Jewels, then took an evening ride on the London Eye, and ended our tour at

Madame Tussaud's Wax Museum. (My heart still pounds when I think about standing next to that three-dimensional, *"Oh, My God!!"* amazingly beautiful wax figure of Marilyn Monroe).

We took day trips to the Cathedral in Salisbury, the mysterious formations at Stonehenge, and the ancient Roman spas in Bath, then left for our three week photo safari in Africa, where we'd see every wild animal you could imagine . . . up close and very personal.

We started in Nairobi, Kenya, and were driven by our first guide Peter to the Amboseli National Reserve (across the savanna from Mount Kilimanjaro) for an exciting two-day hunt. We were escorted through a primitive village of cow dung homes by Ipatec, one of the village chief's sons, where Masai warriors clad in bright red tunics chanted and danced for us, then invited us to trade goods with them in their open-air marketplace. They offered clothing and war masks, carved animal figures and handmade jewelry, and all in exchange for small rectangular sheets of American green paper . . . and they preferred the sheets with large numbers on them.

Our next and favorite guide, Richard the lion hearted man, drove us to our two day game drive at the Ngorongoro Crater in Tanzania, then to the Serengeti for another two day safari. We took a puddle jumper shuttle flight to Lake Manyara for a one day game drive, then drove to Arusha and took another shuttle flight for our two day hunt at the Masai Mara in Kenya. We took a shuttle flight back to Nairobi, grabbed a jet to Johannesburg, South Africa, then flew to Livingstone in Zambia. We toured Victoria Falls and the Mukuni Village, then took a sunset cruise on the Zambezi River. We ended our trip with a personal guided tour through the beautiful and modern city of Cape Town on the southern tip of the continent.

This was the most expensive trip we'd ever taken ($32,000 if you're counting) but it certainly wasn't our last.

We flew to the island of Kauai that same year for Linda's thirty-ninth birthday, saw the beautiful mountains of Bali Hai, and the spectacular scenery of the Waimea Canyon (the Grand Canyon of the Hawaiian Islands). When we finished touring most of the remainder of the island in our open convertible, we returned to the Grand Hyatt Kauai Resort on the southern coast of Poipu, and sunned ourselves in the luxury of private cabanas on the white sandy beaches of paradise.

We drove across the Florida Keys in 2007 for my sixty-third birthday, took a sunset catamaran cruise along Key West's coastline, toured the home of Ernest Hemingway, drank margaritas in a gay filled bar of old Hemingway wannabe's, and ended our trip on the notorious Girl's Gone Wild beaches of Ft. Lauderdale. *If only they'd been there!!*

We rode the Maid of the Mist at Niagara Falls with the same two friends we flew to Maui and Mazatlán with, and ended our trip touring the picturesque town of Niagara-on-the-Lake and Buffalo, New York.

A week later, my son Kevin and his wife Erin joined us for an amazing trip to San Francisco. We stayed at the Whitcomb Hotel (just down the street from the historic Orpheum Theater), and rode old 1940s and 50s era streetcars to mingle with the crowds at Fisherman's Wharf. We stopped in every store (I think), then toured the USS Pampanito submarine. We took a champagne cruise around the harbor aboard the California Hornblower; saw the picturesque row of Victorian homes from the Alamo Square, then drove down the winding red brick road of Lombard Street. We walked the streets of China Town, had dessert at the Ghirardelli Chocolate Factory, and spent hard-time in the confines of the Alcatraz Prison. We marveled at the beauty of the Golden Gate Bridge, then drove through the Presidio Army Base on our way to the magnificent Palace of Fine Arts. When we were finished, we drove to the beautiful vineyards of Napa Valley.

We spent the night at the Montview Hotel in Calistoga, then soared over the valley in a hot air balloon before crashing into the rear parking lot of the Judd's Hill winery. We had our first wine tasting at the Monticello Cellars, then left for our over-night stay at the Old World Inn Bed and Breakfast in the quaint little town of Napa. We ended our vacation with a wine tasting tour through the caverns of the Frazier Winery (Erin's fav-orite).

In 2008, we celebrated our nineteenth anniversary drinking ourselves senseless on the beaches of Cancun, Mexico, then flew to Savannah, Georgia for Linda's forty-first birthday. We took a midnight guided Halloween tour in what is purported to be the most haunted city in America, where for the second time in my life I saw the horror of ghosts again . . . and pirates and witches and zombies, and maybe a hooker or two.

We enjoyed the magic of Disneyworld in Orlando again in 2009 on my sixty-fifth birthday; watched crazy men wrestle alligators at the world famous Gatorland compound, searched for alligators and snakes on an airboat excursion through the Everglades; toured the Kennedy Space Center, and ended our trip with dinner at a great little restaurant on the Cocoa Beach Pier.

We returned to Maui for our twentieth wedding anniversary and stayed at the Royal Lahaina Resort. We'd already seen most everything there was to see on the island, so this time we spent our time sunning ourselves on the beach and drinking and eating great food in the old town of Lahaina or in the res-taurants at the Whaler's Village. We were entertained by hula dancers at the Old Lahaina Luau, and danced to the sounds of romantic music (for only the second or third time of our marriage) . . . then ended our trip with a private guided tour of the plantation island of Lanai.

We flew to Tucson in August and toured the historic town of Tombstone with Linda's brother Greg; his wife Gloria and my mother-in-law Mary. We walked through the legendary Boot Hill Cemetery then stood at the very site where the infamous October 26th, 1881 Gunfight at the O.K. Corral took place. This gunfight between Wyatt Earp, his brothers Morgan and Virgil; Doctor John Henry "Doc" Holliday, and the Clanton and McLaury brothers was one of the Old West's most written about gunfights, and was played out in pretty graphic detail by Kurt Russell and Val Kilmer in their 1993 blockbuster hit, Tombstone.

On our last trip (so far) in 2010, we celebrated our twenty-first and Kevin and Erin's eighth wedding anniversaries at the Marriott Pointe Hotel in Palm Beach, Florida, where Alex and Skyler kept us entertained with their antics at the pool and beach, then thrilled us even more when they swam with the dolphins at the Seaquarium in Miami, and parasailed off the coast of Singer Island. *It was a wonderful week's vacation.*

●

With the obvious exception of Richard's tragic death, 2001 was a very good year for me. After incessantly whining to Linda about having to work for the past nine years, I was finally able to retire. I had more money in the bank than I ever dreamed possible, and immediately started spending it on anything that would make me happy. I'd bragged to my friends that I always paid cash for all my new cars (each and every month), but when I bought our new Toyota Highlander on Monday, March 5th, this time it wasn't a joke. I bought a new Sony TRV900, 3CCD digital video camcorder and a Pinnacle Studio 7 editing program for my new high-octane XPS Dell computer, and when Linda and I returned from our first trip to Hawaii, I spent most of my spare time totally engrossed with my new video editing hobby.

Yes, it was a very good year for me . . . until that wall of security we all call America was shattered on September 11th, 2001. I think everyone remembers where they were and what they were doing when the towers fell on that Tuesday morning

(I know I remember), and to help me deal with my enormous grief, I committed my thoughts to writing:

December 7th, 1941 . . . A Date Which Will Live in Infamy!

The sneak attack at Pearl Harbor that cost the lives of over 2,400 innocent and honorable American men was a day so horrible that even as a child I was stunned by the incredible carnage I saw in newsreels and magazines. I was six or seven years old when I first became aware of that infamous day in our history, and in each of the fifty-plus years of my life since that first awareness, I still get a chill whenever I see the images of that attack. How could any human being commit such an unspeakable and unprovoked act of inhumanity? There was nothing moral or ethical about this outrageous attack. We were not at war . . . we had no enemy. And even at that age of long lost naïveté, I knew that it just wasn't fair!

It was the innocence of the victims that bothered me the most.

After I retired, Linda and I went to Maui for a ten-day celebration. We devoted one of those days to fly to the island of Oahu and toured the USS Arizona Memorial at Pearl Harbor. It was the first time I'd been at a place where I could actually feel the horror and death of such a monumental day in American history, even though it occurred nearly sixty years ago. It was chilling . . . it was frightening . . . it was nearly overwhelming!!

But it was no September 11th, 2001.

I woke up that morning and found a voicemail from Linda, who'd called from her office at Re/Max Masters. She was crying and telling me that the two towers at the World Trade Center were gone! Completely gone!!! I turned on the television and watched as one, then another commercial jet airliner crashed into the towers. I watched as they crumbled to *the ground . . . and I wept. Oh My God, **Oh My God!!** How could any human being do this to another?*

*The videos of this cowardly and incomprehensible attack against humanity will be played for many generations to come, just as the attack on Pearl Harbor has been. And I'm sure that most Americans feel the same as I do . . . that this was an evil so profound and unconscionable that clearly no human being could be capable of committing such an act!! **Only a SUB-SPECIES of the lowest form could be capable of such a horrendous and barbaric attack!!***

I'm not anxious for war, but I believe there are far too many countries who've been waiting for any opportunity to do battle (the nuclear threats between Pakistan and India; the volatile and continual skirmishes of several countries in the Middle East), and I have a real fear that this, like Pearl Harbor, could thrust us into a conflict that reaches global proportions. I worry about my son, and the sons of most of my friends. Nearly all of them are at risk of being called into the military and being killed in a war that none of us have asked for. But something has to be done. Justice or retribution . . . you pick your term. It really doesn't matter.

It was the innocence of the victims that bothered me the most.

•

On Friday, August 1st, 2003, we sold our house on Foxfire and moved into the Summerfield Suites at South Clinton Street and East Costilla Avenue while we waited for our new home to be built. Then on Friday, November 21st, exactly sixteen weeks later, we moved into our beautiful $328,000, two-story, two bedroom, two and a half bath, two-car garage townhouse at 670 Sherman Street in Castle Pines North.

That's a far cry from the $15,200 I paid for my first home in 1965, and shows just how far out of control inflation has become. But it's always fun to look back in time and compare the changes from one generation to the next, and years from now my great-great-grandchildren will probably be just as amused by the low cost of housing in the 1990s and 2000s as I am when I look back to the 1940s and 50s.

During one of Kevin and Erin's first visits to our new home, we migrated to the kitchen for our traditional games of Pinochle and Garbage, while Skyler and Alex went upstairs to watch TV. Kevin and I played partners against my card savvy wife and spunky little Irish daughter-in-law, but in spite of our superior playing, Linda and Erin were kicking our butts. I was happy to take a short break to lick my wounds when the girls' movie ended, and as I searched through our collection of DVDs, Alex, my eight-year-old granddaughter asked, *"So why did you and Linda move out of your mansion?"* I chuckled and said, *"Well, we didn't need all that room, and we wanted a home we could just walk away from when we took our trips. Here we don't have to mow the lawn or shovel the snow, because someone else does that for us . . . we don't have to do anything ourselves."* She thought it over for a second or two and said, *"Oh, so this is a nursing home."* Roars of laughter rang up from the kitchen as I tried to explain to this precious little angel that Linda and I weren't nearly as old as we looked.

Both girls inherited their mother's pretty features and crystal blue eyes, but Skyler had her own special look. When she was nine-years-old I told her I thought she'd grow up to look like Shawnee Smith (the attractive and slender girl who played the scatterbrained assistant Linda on the Becker television series). She had no idea who I was talking about, so I pulled up an episode I'd already recorded and fast-forwarded to a scene with Linda standing next to Margaret (the portly black middle aged nurse), and said, *"Now, that's who I think you'll look like."* She stared at the set for a few seconds, then said, *"Which one?"*

Television set:	$2,500
Monthly cable service:	$80
Granddaughter's innocence:	Priceless

•

Kevin and Erin live in a quiet little neighborhood about three miles north of downtown Firestone, so the seventy-mile drive from our home negates any impromptu visits we might think about, and limits our trips to see each other to only once every two or three months. But special occasions supplement our little get-togethers, which began when they moved in together and he became a family man.

On Christmas 2000 (a year and a half before they were married), they started a tradition of hosting annual Christmas brunches at their home (in Arvada at that time), where we enjoyed the true spirit of the holiday season in the company of my mom, Bobby and Cheri, Erin's wonderful parents Mike and Peggy McCarty, her younger sister Megan (the best story teller I've ever known) . . . Peggy's bubbly sister Kathy, and in later years, Megan's impish man-child husband Matt, his fun loving parents Bud and Alice McDonald, and, of course, his youngest sister Kate.

Erin would spoil us with a lavish spread of gourmet dishes (my favorite was her French toast casserole), and Cheri would treat us with her famous Dippity-Chippity dessert bars. The families would split into two equally competitive teams and play the latest games Linda and I'd given to Megan for Christmas, while most everyone drank Erin's perfectly blended Bloody Mary's, sipped her fine wines, or chugged down enough Jack Daniels and Coke to render us incapable of knowing (or caring) if we were winning or not. It was such a wonderful time, but the things I loved more than anything else were the bright eyes and excited laughter of Alex and Skyler when we gathered around their perfectly trimmed Christmas tree and opened our presents. It reminded me of all those cherished holidays we'd spent with my daughter Kim and her beautiful little girls when they were still very young. I loved those innocent days!!

417

But this was just the first of our annual traditions. On or near Alex's October 11th (1995) and Skyler's April 3rd (1997) birthdays, the families get together at Cinzetti's Italian Restaurant at 281 West 104th Avenue, where Kevin and Erin treat us to a celebration dinner for their special day . . . and in the summer months, we reclaimed a tradition that Kevin and I enjoyed from the time he was five years old until his mid-teens. Linda and I bought a new Coleman pop-up camper the year after I retired (I still loved to camp, but couldn't handle sleeping on the ground anymore), and on Friday, August 13th, 2004, Kevin, Erin and the girls met with us at the Stillwater Campground at Grand Lake, where we began the first of many family camping trips together.

I loved sitting around the campfire at night with the kids . . . poking the crackling logs with sticks we'd found in the brush; laughing and joking while we cuddled close to the flames for warmth and roasted our hot dogs and s'mores . . . but in 2008, when I got tired of having to get up so many times in the middle of the night to go outside and water the nearest tree, we sold the camper and began a new tradition of summer getaways at our Grand Timber Lodge timeshare in the ski resort town of Breckenridge.

•

In April 2004, Linda quit her job with Jim Wanzeck and joined me in retirement. I thought it was wonderful, but after seven short months (even though she denies it), being home with me 24-hours a day was just a little more than she could handle. When she returned from grocery shopping one day, she told me King Soopers was looking for new employees and thought she'd apply for one of their part-time positions. I argued that it would interfere with our freedom to travel, but her argument was much stronger than mine. The pay wasn't that great, but the company provided health insurance, and since we were paying over a thousand dollars a month for the policy I had, her plan sounded like a pretty good idea. I finally gave in and she started her new job in their bakery at the end of November . . .

and now, plagued by a lifetime addiction to Long Johns (a cream filled éclair), I had my very own private drug dealer. And just when I thought life couldn't get any better!

June, Tommy, Dad, Me, Mom, Darlene & Jessie
Playing a hot game of Garbage in Kalama, Washington

A boy and his mother

Darlene puckering up for her 50th birthday kiss

My brother-in-law, Bob
Always happy to be there

Kevin and Erin—Their Wedding Day

Their daughters—Alex (L) and Skyler (R)

Kim's girls—Jennifer (L), Shanna (R) Ashley (B)

CHAPTER 26

"A Very Rough Year"

On Saturday, January 5th, 2002, Mom took her car to Luby Chevrolet at 2033 South Wadsworth Boulevard for a routine maintenance appointment, and while climbing into the shuttle van, slipped and scraped her right shin on the blunt edge of the running board. It wasn't a big deal . . . just two little cuts, but by the end of February, the wounds had tripled in size and Mom was in a lot of pain.

Fortunately, I'd retired the year before, so I had all the time I needed to dedicate to Mom's plight. I took her to her doctor's office, but the treatment Dr. Victor Doyle recommended didn't help at all. Within a month's time, the two sores merged into one large ulcerated wound and her pain radically increased. Dr. Doyle referred her to a podiatrist and Dr. Eric Weinstein (an incredible vascular surgeon), but their consensus of opinion was that the circulation in her lower extremities was just too poor to facilitate the healing.

As the months rolled by, things only got worse. She no longer left her house except to go to doctor's appointments, and even missed Kevin's wedding on Saturday, June 1st, 2002 (Linda's and my thirteenth wedding anniversary) when he married his adorable wife Erin McCarty and became the stepfather to her precious little girls, Alexandra and Skyler.

By now Dr. Weinstein told her she had only two viable options: to have her leg amputated or have the artery in her leg replaced. Mom didn't even consider the first suggestion, so when the doctor felt she was strong enough to survive the surgery, I took her to Porter's Hospital at 2525 South Downing Street for an arterial bypass.

Even though she'd been weakened by nearly six months of debilitating pain, our diminutive but tough seventy-nine-year-old mother breezed through the operation.

She spent the next few days in the hospital, then was sent to a nursing home for rehabilitation. Following a relatively mild therapy session, the artery ruptured, and when they applied pressure to keep her from bleeding to death, the new artery collapsed. Dr. Weinstein was afraid the bypass had been destroyed, but by the grace of God, blood still managed to reach her lower leg.

When she was finally sent back home, a visiting nurse came to her house every other day to clean and dress her wound, and on the off days, I'd do the same. Mom continued to manage her pain with heavy doses of Percocet, and even though the medication made her pretty lethargic, she was able to cook, wash her dishes and do her own laundry without help. The only thing she couldn't handle was her house cleaning. She hired a lady to come in every other week to clean (someone Linda recommended), but Linda Weaver was much more than just a housekeeper. She soon became a friend who'd stop by for routine visits, and always brought some kind of dessert to nibble on while they enjoyed each other's company.

The wound wasn't getting any worse, but it wasn't getting any better, either. It looked just like a long slab of raw bacon, and Mom still suffered from an incredible amount of pain. By September, Dr. Weinstein put her in a Unaboot (a self contained medicated boot), and the healing finally began.

In October 2002, Darlene flew in from Washington, and June and her one-year-old granddaughter Cheyenne drove in from Grand Junction. And on Saturday, October 12th, Uncle Bill Oldson; Red (his ex-son-in-law), and Red's daughter Valerie joined us for a laugh filled evening as we celebrated Mom's eightieth birthday at her home. It was a wonderful party, especially since Mom was finally feeling so much better.

By the end of December, the wound had completely healed and the nightmare was over. It had been a very tough year for Mom . . . in and out of the hospital nine different times and in three nursing homes for rehabilitation, but she was finally able to live on her own without the assistance from her visiting nurse or the constant care from me.

But in April 2003, a new problem developed. Mom received a call from the U.S. Bank and was told Alisha had stopped making payments on her loan, and Mom was now responsible for the new $20,000 debt . . . double the amount she'd originally co-signed for. Mom told them she'd never been notified of the increase, but the bank wasn't at all sympathetic. They weren't required to advise her of any increases, and if Alisha failed to mention it, that was her fault.

Alisha quit or lost her job; let her condominium go into foreclosure and moved to Washington State to live with another of her grandmothers . . . and Mom was forced to make Alisha's outrageous $500 per month payments for the remaining three years of her life. I guess that was Alicia's way of thanking Mom for all her generous and loving care. *What a gal . . . she must have been very proud!!*

For the next three years, Mom lived in relatively good health. She had a short bout with anemia, and another with a bleeding ulcer, but they were easily corrected with the treatment from Dr. Doyle. Late in 2005, she passed out and broke her collarbone when she fell to her kitchen floor, but she healed fast and had very little pain.

She rarely left her house, but was perfectly comfortable with her lifestyle. She kept busy with the slow process of taking care of her household chores, and spent most of her evenings sipping tea and working crossword puzzles. She never lost her mental faculties and remained alert and uncommonly wise until the very last few days of her life.

My sisters and I called Mom every night, and if we couldn't get an answer, her good friends Judy Leslie or Kathy Barnes from across the street would graciously check to make sure she was okay.

June and Darlene came to visit as often as they could, and I'd come over twice a week to bring her groceries and stay for a few games of two-handed Pinochle or Rummy Cube. Crystal came by often and would spend her day cleaning when Mom's housekeeper was off. Mom really appreciated her company and marveled at her energy. No one could clean a house like Crystal . . . except maybe, my wife, Linda.

Linda never missed an opportunity to help out. She pretty much took over Dad's maintenance duties when he died, and over the years, kept the house in order. She painted the exterior trim and siding, put together a new storage shed for the backyard, scrubbed Mom's cigarette smoke stained kitchen walls, washed her windows on a regular basis, cleaned her curtains, replaced faulty electrical plugs and even hung a new ceiling fan in her kitchen. And Mom never once had to ask for help. When Linda saw something that needed to be done, she just did it. It's no wonder Mom held her in such high esteem!

Happy 80th Birthday

This took all the wind she had

Feeling great for her birthday

Darlene, Mom, June & Me—Always a happy family

CHAPTER 27

"The Final Chapter"

On Wednesday, April 12th, 2006, I brought Mom her weekly supply of groceries and we sat down for our usual games of Pinochle. She said she'd had trouble sleeping the night before because of a sharp pain in her back, but by now it was just an annoying ache. I gave her a couple of Motrin, and by the time I left, the pain was gone. She beat me three games in a row, so it felt like a pretty good day to me.

Mom called at 2:20 the following morning and told me she had really bad stomach and back pain and asked me to take her to the hospital. I lived about thirty-five minutes from her house, so I told her to call 911 if the pain got worse before I could get there.

When I turned onto Bryant Street, I saw emergency lights flashing from an ambulance and fire truck parked in front of her house. When I walked through the front door, the para-medics were checking her blood pressure, and after a cursory examination, took her to Porter's Hospital where they immed-iately gave her something for the pain. They didn't have any idea what was wrong with her and the doctor told me they'd keep her at least overnight while they ran some tests.

They ran tests all day Thursday, and by early Friday afternoon, the doctor told me he thought Mom had cancer, but wouldn't know for sure until the pathology tests were completed on Monday.

By Saturday, Mom was feeling better, but her medicine made her sleep most of the time. She did manage to eat a little today, but her appetite was definitely waning.

When I arrived at the hospital on Sunday, April 16th, I met Bob Brown's sister Tish as she was walking out of Mom's room. She told me something was wrong with Mom and she was on her way to get a nurse. I raced into the room and saw Mom sitting in the chair beside her bed with her head tilted back and her eyes and mouth wide open. I touched her shoulder and asked, *"Mom, are you all right? Mom, can you hear me?* She was still breathing, but I couldn't get her to respond. Tish and a couple of nurses rushed into the room behind me and one of the nurses started shaking Mom and calling her name. Mom tilted her head back down, closed her mouth and slowly looked around the room. When she finally showed signs that she was conscious, the nurse jokingly said, *"We were getting a little worried there . . . I was just about to go get that young good looking doctor for some help"* . . . and Mom just smiled. She was better now, and within two or three minutes, was completely lucid.

But it was pretty scary and a definite sign to me that there was something seriously and urgently wrong. I took Tish aside and asked her to call Darlene and tell her it was time to come to Denver.

On Monday, April 17th, the doctor took me to look at Mom's x-rays and PET scans. He showed me the cancer in her liver, lungs, spine and twelve other spots throughout her entire body and told me she probably only had three to six more weeks to live.

Mom already knew she probably had cancer, but today she learned it for sure. The doctor asked if she wanted to undergo treatment, but she told him she'd had far too many friends and family who'd chosen chemotherapy and it seemed to her the cure was worse than the disease. The only thing she asked for was something to manage her pain.

Mom and I'd talked about our mortality for some time now, and were comfortable with the knowledge that we'd die someday . . . ***But This Was Now And This Was Real!*** In the privacy of her hospital room we had an impassioned and tearful conversation that left no doubts about how either of us felt. It was the talk I wished I'd had with Dad before he died, and it really helped a lot!

On Tuesday, April 18th, I took Mom from the hospital and drove her to the Johnson Hospice Center at 5020 East Arapahoe Road. She got sick on the ride over and passed out when I pulled into the complex. Two of the nurses wheeled Mom to her room, and she soon regained consciousness then settled into her bed for a nap. While I sat with Mom, Linda drove from our home to Denver International Airport and picked up Darlene.

Darlene was here for the duration. She and Bob agreed she should stay as long as she was needed, and after spending the next two days with Mom at the hospice center, knew she could give her the same kind of care at home.

On Thursday, April 20th, Darlene talked with the hospice staff and made arrangements to have a hospital bed delivered to Mom's house, then had an ambulance crew take her home. Mom was so excited to leave the center and even happier to be back home. By the time June and Cheyenne arrived that afternoon, Mom had accepted the inevitable and seemed content with the knowledge that her life was drawing to an end, and was happy that all her children were with her. She was home now . . . exactly where she wanted to be . . . and I thank God my sisters were there to take care of her!!

On Friday, April 21st, several friends and relatives came by to see Mom, but by now she'd stopped eating and drinking, and was so weak she could hardly stay awake. Later that day, in the last full conversation Mom had with anyone, she talked with Bob on the phone and told him she just didn't want to linger on like this . . . she was ready to die.

On Saturday, April 22nd, 2006, just five days after Mom learned she had cancer and eleven days since her first pain, Darlene called and said she thought I should come over. The thirty-five minute drive seemed much longer today, and when I walked into the living room, I saw my sisters sitting beside Mom's bed while she laid sleeping, laboring for each gasping breath. It was pretty clear she didn't have much longer to live and I broke into tears. *It was so hard to see her like that!* Pudge and Bud were there to pay their respects and waited in the kitchen while the three of us gathered around the bed. Mom's eyes suddenly opened and she stared directly into Darlene's eyes. We all touched her hands and told her we were there, that we loved her, but she never looked away from her precious daughter; the child she believed would miss her most. June told Mom it was okay now; the angels were there for her . . . and after another ten or fifteen deep breaths, the hushed drone of her oxygen machine stopped as she took her very last breath. We all looked at each other as if to ask, *"Is it really over?"* and after a few short seconds, we were sure. She was so peaceful now, and the years of solitude and suffering were over. This was a good and just woman who never put herself before her loved ones, and deserved far more in life than she ever received. She was always so cheerful, and rarely uttered a bad word about anyone, no matter how much they deserved it. She taught us if we didn't have something good to say about someone, we shouldn't say anything at all, and even though I've always had a little trouble with that premise, she actually followed her own advice. *She was a saint!*

It was heartbreaking to witness the end of her life, but we all took comfort in knowing she was now in the company of the Lord, and would surely be blessed for the goodness of her soul.

We called the hospice center and they sent a nurse to help with the arrangements, and when she arrived, listed Mom's time of death as 4:20 pm. It's probably only important to me, but when Mom took her last breath at eighty-three years of age, it was exactly 2pm.

On Thursday, April 27th, we had a family viewing at the Bear Valley Christian Church at 6800 West Hampden Avenue, and on Monday, May 1st at 2pm, we had a brief service at the Fort Logan Cemetery. Mom would have been thrilled to see the number of people there to honor her, and would have been proud of the amazing job June did in presiding over her funeral!!

When the service ended, the family met at the Denver First Seventh-Day Adventist Church at 6200 West Hampden Avenue, where Rochella and her daughters Denise and Nancy, and her sisters Mona and Roxie made all the arrangements for the reception . . . and once again, the Aumiller girls were there for my family.

When the reception was over, my sisters and Linda and I returned to the cemetery. It was a beautiful sunny day, with just a whisper of a breeze blowing through the nearby trees. A sea of white military headstones lined the carefully manicured lawn, and the silence of hallowed ground respectfully welcomed Mom to her final resting place. As I stared at the freshly turned sod in front of Dad's headstone, I was filled with a sense of calmness and relief . . . Mom was with Dad now, and serenaded by angels, they were eternally together . . . forever as one.

Made in the USA
Las Vegas, NV
06 October 2021